Evaluation in Text

Evaluation in Text

Authorial Stance and the Construction of Discourse

Edited by
SUSAN HUNSTON and
GEOFF THOMPSON

OXFORD
UNIVERSITY PRESS

OXFORD

UNIVERSITY PRESS

Great Clarendon Street, Oxford OX2 6DP

Oxford University Press is a department of the University of Oxford.
It furthers the University's objective of excellence in research, scholarship,
and education by publishing worldwide in

Oxford New York

Athens Auckland Bangkok Bogotá Buenos Aires Calcutta
Cape Town Chennai Dar es Salaam Delhi Florence Hong Kong Istanbul
Karachi Kuala Lumpur Madrid Melbourne Mexico City Mumbai
Nairobi Paris São Paulo Shanghai Singapore Taipei Tokyo Toronto Warsaw

and associated companies in Berlin Ibadan

Published in the United States
by Oxford University Press Inc., New York

First published 2000
New as Paperback 2001

British Library Cataloguing in Publication Data

Data available

Library of Congress Cataloging in Publication Data

Data applied for
ISBN 0–19–823854–1 (hbk.)
ISBN 0–19–829986–9 (pbk.)

1 3 5 7 9 10 8 6 4 2

Typeset in Minion
by Hope Services (Abingdon) Ltd.
Printed in Great Britain
on acid-free paper by
Biddles Ltd, www.biddles.co.uk

Preface

For some years, both of us have felt the need for a single volume which would collect together a variety of approaches to the notion of evaluation (under its various names of *stance, affect, modality,* and so on), and which would be available both to make the case for the centrality of the concept in the description of language and text and to serve as an introduction for students wishing to pursue research in this area. This volume is an attempt to fill this need.

Our aim in selecting papers was to represent as wide a range of approaches as possible, while allowing our writers the luxury of comparatively long contributions. We wanted to present a multiform view of language: as grammar, as lexis, and as text, and we wanted to highlight the role of language in reflecting and constructing ideas and opinions. We have chosen papers that variously represent a particular language theory (systemic functional linguistics), a particular discourse type (narrative), a particular methodology (corpus linguistics), and a particular view of the relation between language, knowledge, and the world (the study of language and ideology).

One paper is sadly missing from this collection. Eugene Gatt Winter, whose pioneering work on evaluation inspired many of the writers included here, was unable to finish his contribution before his death in 1996. We feel that his influence none the less informs much of this book.

We hope that the reader will come away from this book with an increased understanding of the importance of evaluation to how language works, and an enthusiasm for following one of the many avenues of research opened by the writers in this collection.

Acknowledgements

Permission to reproduce material has been obtained from Methuen for extracts from *Educating Rita* (Chapter 8) and from the *Guardian* for 'We Need Sects Education' (Chapter 9).

Michael Hoey's paper 'Persuasive Rhetoric in Linguistics: A Stylistic Study of Some Features of the Language of Noam Chomsky' (Chapter 2) was originally published in *Forum Linguisticum* 8/1 (1984).

Contents

List of Contributors

DOUGLAS BIBER is Professor in the Applied Linguistics Program of the English Department, Northern Arizona University. His research interests focus on grammatical and register correlates of linguistic variation. His previous publications include *Variation Across Speech and Writing* (1988, Cambridge University Press), *Sociolinguistic Perspectives on Register* (1994, Oxford University Press, edited with E. Finegan), and *Dimensions of Register Variation* (1995, Cambridge University Press).

JOANNA CHANNELL runs a consultancy and research business specializing in language and communication. Her interest in lexis began in 1981 as a joint author of *The Words You Need* (1981, Macmillan, with B. Rudska, P. Ostyn, and Y. Putseys) and continued through her involvement with Collins COBUILD and its dictionaries, on which her contribution to this volume is based. Her recent reseach work has mainly been with government and public sector organizations, leading to a special interest in the concept of 'plain language' and effective, reader-friendly writing. Her published work includes EFL materials, articles on language teaching and descriptive linguistics, HMSO publications of research reports, and *Vague Language* (1994, Oxford University Press).

SUSAN CONRAD is Assistant Professor in the Department of English and Program in Linguistics at Iowa State University. Her research interests include variation in academic prose across disciplines and audiences, the acquisition of disciplinary writing skills by students, and corpus-based grammatical analyses. Her work has appeared previously in *Applied Linguistics, Linguistics and Education*, and *TESOL Quarterly*.

MARTIN CORTAZZI is Senior Lecturer in Linguistics and Education at the University of Leicester, where he has been training teachers and supervising international research students since 1978. He has taught in Iran, China, Turkey, and Lebanon. He is Visiting Professor at the Universities of Nankai (Tianjin), Renmin (Beijing), and Hubei (Wuhan). His research interests and publications are in narrative analysis, discourse, teaching methodology, and intercultural communication.

MICHAEL HOEY is Baines Professor of English Language and Director of the Applied English Language Studies Unit at the University of Liverpool. His major publications are *Signalling in Discourse* (1979, University of Birmingham), *On the Surface of Discourse* (1983, Allen & Unwin, reissued 1991), *Patterns of Lexis in Text* (1991, Oxford University Press), which was awarded the Duke of Edinburgh English Speaking Union Prize for the best book on Applied Linguistics in 1991, and the edited collection, *Data, Description, Discourse* (1993, HarperCollins).

SUSAN HUNSTON is Senior Lecturer in English Language at the University of Birmingham. Her research interests include evaluation in text, discourse analysis, and corpus linguistics. She is co-author (with Gill Francis and Elizabeth Manning) of the Collins COBUILD Grammar Patterns series. Her work has appeared in *Applied Linguistics, Functions of Language, Language Awareness,* and other journals. She has taught applied linguistics at the National University of Singapore and the University of Surrey.

LIXIAN JIN is Senior Lecturer in Linguistics at De Montfort University where she teaches general linguistics, sociolinguistics, syntax, and clinical linguistics. She has taught TESOL and linguistics courses and trained teachers since 1982 at universities in China, Turkey, and Britain. She is Visiting Professor at Renmin (Beijing) and Hubei (Wuhan) Universities. She has published in the areas of her research interests, namely intercultural communication, academic cultures, cultures of learning, second language acquisition, and narrative analysis.

J. R. MARTIN is Associate Professor of Linguistics at the University of Sydney. His research interests include systemic theory, functional grammar, discourse semantics, register, genre, multimodality, and critical discourse analysis, focusing on English and Tagalog—with special reference to the transdisciplinary fields of educational linguistics and social semiotics. He is the author of many publications, including: *English Text: System and Structure* (1992, Benjamins), *Writing Science: Literacy and Discursive Power* (with M. A. K. Halliday, 1993, Falmer), and *Working with Functional Grammar* (with C. Mathiessen and C. Painter, 1997, Arnold). He is editor of *Genre and Institutions: Social Processes in the Workplace and School* (with F. Christie, 1997, Cassell) and *Reading Science: Critical and Functional Perspectives on Discourses of Science* (with R. Veel, 1998, Routledge).

JOHN SINCLAIR is Professor of Modern English Language at the University of Birmingham and Director of the Tuscan Word Centre, Italy. He is widely known for his pioneering work in discourse analysis and in corpus linguistics. He is joint author of *Towards an Analysis of Discourse: The English used by Teachers and Pupils* (1975, Oxford University Press, with Malcolm Coulthard), author of *Corpus Concordance Collocation* (1991, Oxford University Press), and editor of *Looking Up: An Account of the COBUILD Project in Lexical Computing* (1987, HarperCollins).

GEOFF THOMPSON is Lecturer in English Language at the University of Liverpool. His research interests include systemic-functional grammar and interaction in written discourse, and he has taught courses on these topics in Brazil, Venezuela, Colombia, and Austria. He is author of *Introducing Functional Grammar* (1996, Arnold) and *Guide to Reporting* (1994, HarperCollins). Other work has appeared in *Applied Linguistics, Text,* and other journals.

JIANGLIN ZHOU is Associate Professor of English at the Huazhong University of Science and Technology in the People's Republic of China. He has published a number of textbooks on vocabulary, and is co-ordinator of the University's English Corpus Research Team. The paper in this book is a development of research that he initially carried out at the University of Liverpool for his MA dissertation.

1

Evaluation: An Introduction

Geoff Thompson and Susan Hunston

What do we Mean by Evaluation?

(1.1)

In most holiday destinations, high summer naturally means high season, but around the capital cities of Europe the streets are often practically deserted. This makes July and August the perfect time to catch up on your culture so whilst the Parisians flock to Corsica or the Cote d'Azur, you can enjoy Paris without the traffic jams and experience the city's many open spaces at their best. Barcelona is perfect for a summer break, and you can be both culture vulture and beach bum depending on your mood.

In this extract from a leaflet for a holiday package company (*Simply Travel*), one of the writer's central purposes is clearly to express his positive or negative opinion of the locations being described, and there are a number of expressions whose function is at least partly to carry out this purpose. *Perfect* (twice) and *at their best* are the most salient examples, in that they express positive opinion almost exclusively: they have more or less unlimited potential to be used to opine about any state of affairs (a world may be *perfect*, a tin opener may be modern design *at its best*, and so on). Other expressions have more referential 'content', but include in their meaning an element of opinion that may be greater or smaller and more or less an inherent feature of the expression: in oversimple terms *jams* can be decomposed into 'a lot of traffic' + 'bad'; while—in this context at least—*practically deserted* can be decomposed into 'with very few people' + 'good'[1] (compare the effect of describing an underground car park in an unfamiliar city at night as *practically deserted*). This last example highlights the potential role of context in bringing out the opinion element. An even clearer example of this is *high season*. This can be used as a 'neutral' technical label for periods when most holiday travelling is done. In this extract, however, the *but* signals a contrast being set up with *practically deserted* streets; the latter are then said to make this a *perfect* time, so by inference the writer's opinion of *high season is* negative—in decomposed terms, 'period when most holiday travelling is done' + 'bad' (on the role of conjunction in constructing viewpoint, see 'Maintaining Relations' below).

---

[1] To be more precise, *practically* is almost exclusively associated with the expression of opinion and therefore signals that there is an opinion here; the context makes it clear that the opinion is positive.

The extract has been chosen to illustrate the fact that the expression of the writer's or speaker's opinion is an important feature of language;[2] that it needs to be accounted for in a full description of the meanings of texts; and that this is not always a straightforward matter. The analysis above is, of course, far from complete: there are other expressions such as *can enjoy* and *culture vulture and beach bum* whose opinion-related meanings would need to be explored. However, these would take us into more complex areas which are best reserved for the following chapters (particularly those by Martin, Hunston, and Channell). At this stage we have a preliminary issue to deal with that is in some ways simpler but in other ways deceptively tricky: what terminology do we use to talk about the phenomenon?

There is a wide range of terms in use, some of which are in effect synonymous, while others cover slightly different overlapping areas. Some of the well-established terms used in talking about language expressing opinion are *connotation* (see e.g. Lyons 1977), *affect* (see e.g. Besnier 1993), and *attitude* (see e.g. Halliday 1994; see also e.g. Tench 1996, for its use in intonation studies). The first of these focuses on the language items (it is words which 'have' connotations), while the second and third take the perspective of the language user (it is people who 'have' attitudes). This difference in perspective perhaps underlies the distinction that Leech (1974: 15–18) makes between *connotative meaning* (which relates to 'the "real-world" experience one associates with an expression') and *affective meaning* (which relates to 'the personal feelings of the speaker'—see also Cruse 1986). It is no accident that contributors in the present volume all share the language user perspective, since all take a broadly functional approach to the description of language in use. However, even within this one book different contributors use different terms: Martin talks of *appraisal,* while Conrad and Biber talk of *stance,* and our title attempts to hedge our bets by talking of *evaluation* and *stance* (we could have tried to fit in *appraisal,* but that would probably be a hedge too far).

So far, so confusing. However, we have to go one more step before the mists may start clearing. The examples that we discussed from the extract above were all clearly related to the writer's judgement of the good (and bad) aspects of the holiday destinations. In the following extract from a newspaper financial report, we have more expressions which are equally clearly related to the writer's opinion but which do not fit easily into a category of 'judgement of the good (and bad) aspects':

(1.2)
Meanwhile the Bank *will no doubt* be getting nervous about the implications for wages of the continuing rise in the headline rate of inflation, which is often used as a benchmark by pay bargainers.
This, indeed, is a worry. If wage deals continue to ratchet upwards, the economy *could* get caught in a vicious pay spiral. But, the City and boardroom aside, *there is little*

[2] In this introduction, unless we are referring to particular examples, we use 'writer' and 'speaker' (and 'reader' and 'listener') interchangeably. We do not wish to imply differences between written and spoken language, unless specifically stated.

evidence to suggest that pay deals are heading into the stratosphere. (*The Guardian*, 17.6.98, p. 21)

The italicized expressions in this extract relate to the writer's opinion concerning the likelihood of the various events. The traditional term for this is, of course, *modality* (see e.g. Halliday 1994; Perkins 1983), though it is worth noting that there is a good deal of overlap with the concept of *evidentiality* (see e.g. Chafe and Nichols 1986), which relates to 'the kinds of evidence a person has for making factual claims' (Anderson 1986: 273). An oversimple tabulation of some of the opinions in the two extracts brings out both similarities and differences (see Table 1.1):

TABLE 1.1. *Writers' opinions in Examples 1.1 and 1.2*

Thing/event	Writer's opinion
high summer	*high season*
July and August	*perfect*
the streets	*practically deserted*
Barcelona	*perfect*
the Bank [is] *getting nervous*	pretty certain—*will no doubt*
the economy get[s] *caught in a vicious pay spiral*	possible—*could*
pay deals are heading into the stratosphere	unlikely to be true—*little evidence to suggest*

In both cases, we can separate out something that is written about and the writer's opinion of that something; and in both cases the opinion can be seen essentially in terms of positive and negative (good/bad, certain/uncertain). One potentially significant difference is that, in these examples at least, the first type of opinion relates to entities (expressed by nominal groups) whereas the second relates to propositions (expressed by clauses). Another is that, again in these examples at least, the second type of opinion needs to be paraphrased to make it fit in the table: the wordings in the extract do not fit into the *Y* slot in an '*X* is [seen by the writer as] *Y*' pattern. This reflects the fact that the second type appears to be more grammaticalized than the first. That is, it is more integrated into the structure of the clause, with its own dedicated structures (e.g. modal verbs), whereas the first is chiefly expressed through linguistic elements such as adjectives that also serve non-opinion-expressing functions.

However, these differences are to some extent misleading, in that both types of expressions of opinion do share certain structural possibilities. One of the most notable of these is illustrated in the following examples from elsewhere in the texts from which the two extracts above are taken:

*It is **gratifying** to receive recognition from our travel industry partners.*
*It is **fairly certain** that you would take those odds seriously.*

The first expresses an opinion of goodness/desirability, and the second of certainty. But the something in the second part of the sentence of which the writer gives his opinion in the first part is a proposition in both cases; and the expression of the writer's opinion of likelihood in the second sentence can be fitted into the *Y* slot in an '*X* is [seen by the writer as] *Y*' pattern. This suggests that there is a fair degree of common ground (for discussion of another shared structure, see the chapter in this volume by Thompson and Zhou on disjuncts; and see also 'Parameters of Evaluation' below).

Nevertheless, the common ground is by no means complete. It is noteworthy, for example, that opinions of likelihood, unlike those of goodness, seem generally, if not always, to be restricted to propositions and do not apply to entities. Further, another sentence from the second extract is a reminder that the two types of opinion can easily occur together in the same stretch of language and are fairly clearly performing different functions:

> *This, indeed, is a worry.*

The double expression of opinion here can be as shown in Table 1.2.

TABLE 1.2. *Writer's opinions: entities and propositions*

Entity/proposition	Writer's opinion
this [pay bargainers using the rising rate of inflation as a benchmark]	*a worry*
this is a worry	true—*indeed*

Intimately bound up with the issue of terminology mentioned above is the question of how the relationship between these two types of opinion is viewed. There are two basic options: one emphasizes the differences, gives each type a separate label, and analyses them in the main as separate phenomena; the other emphasizes the similarities, includes both under a single label (though usually with a label for each at the next step down in delicacy), and analyses them at least partly, if not chiefly, as aspects of the same phenomenon.

Halliday (1994) can be taken as a representative of a 'separating' approach: he deals with modality separately from attitudinal meaning. He explores modality at much greater length, establishing two main sub-categories: *modalization* (relating to probability and usuality) and *modulation* (relating to obligation and inclination). He places both modality and attitudinal meanings in the category of interpersonal meanings, but that category also includes other areas such as mood, and he has no superordinate term which covers only those two areas. Martin (this volume; see also e.g. Eggins and Slade 1997) follows this separating approach, but expands the account of attitudinal meaning greatly, using the term *appraisal* and establishing three sub-categories: *affect*, *judgement*, and *appreciation*. Many other linguists, including, for example, the contributors to Bybee and Fleischman (1995), distinguish between modality, with the two main sub-categories of *epistemic* (probability) and *deontic* (obligation) modality, and *evaluation* which relates to the speaker/writer's view of something as desirable or undesirable.

Within the 'combining' approach, there are a number of different superordinate terms. Conrad and Biber (this volume; see also e.g. Biber and Finegan 1989) use the term *stance* to cover *epistemic stance* (roughly modalization in Halliday's terms) and *attitudinal stance* (roughly appraisal in Martin's terms); and they also include *style stance*, which relates to the speaker or writer's comment on the way in which the information in a clause is presented—for example, the disjunct *frankly* expresses style stance. Stubbs (1996) focuses on modality, which he talks about in terms of the speaker/writer's 'commitment and detachment to propositional information'. This formulation brings it close to Halliday's concept of modalization, but in fact Stubbs covers a much wider range of phenomena, including vague language, and certain kinds of lexical features (such as the *-y/-ie* morpheme in words like *auntie*) which are very close to the expression of attitudinal stance. Within the more specialized area of literary stylistics, the investigation of *point of view* involves a number of linguistic features which indicate the source responsible for the text or segment (either a narrator or a character, or a blend of both); and the fact that both modality and appraisal must have a source—the person whose viewpoint is being expressed—makes them central to the investigation (see e.g. Simpson 1993; Stuart 1996).

For reasons which should become clear in the rest of this volume, we take a combining approach, and therefore need a superordinate term. Up to this point, we have deliberately brought in our preferred term only incidentally, but from now on we will use it consistently and unapologetically: *evaluation*. For us (and see also e.g. Georgakopoulou and Goutsos 1997), evaluation is the broad cover term for the expression of the speaker or writer's attitude or stance towards, viewpoint on, or feelings about the entities or propositions that he or she is talking about. That attitude may relate to certainty or obligation or desirability or any of a number of other sets of values. When appropriate, we refer specifically to modality as a sub-category of evaluation. The term *evaluation* is, admittedly, as slippery as any of the others in this field: there is a well-established tradition in discourse analysis of using it to refer to elements of textual patterns (see e.g. Labov 1972; Hoey 1983), and it is also sometimes used in a more restricted sense in analysing lexical expressions of the speaker or writer's emotional attitude (see e.g. Carter 1987)—that is, more or less equivalent to Martin's appraisal or Conrad and Biber's attitudinal stance. While recognizing this potential for confusion, we feel that it applies no more to this term than to any of the others available. A strong practical reason for preferring the term is its syntactic and morphological flexibility: not only does it express a user-orientation in terms of the two perspectives mentioned earlier (it is the user who evaluates), but it also allows us to talk about the *values* ascribed to the entities and propositions which are *evaluated*. Given that we, in common with all the other contributors to this volume, are primarily interested in evaluation in action—why, when, how, and what speakers and writers evaluate—this flexibility of use matches the flexibility of focus on which our approach relies.

Why is Evaluation Important?

So far we have simply assumed that evaluation is a topic worthy of study. It is now time to argue for its importance. Briefly, there are three functions that evaluation is used to perform, and each of these make it an object of interest to the linguist. These functions are:

(1) to express the speaker's or writer's opinion, and in doing so to reflect the value system of that person and their community;

(2) to construct and maintain relations between the speaker or writer and hearer or reader;

(3) to organize the discourse.

The functions are not exclusive, that is, a single instance of evaluation may well perform two or three of the functions simultaneously. We shall now look at each of these functions in turn.

EXPRESSING OPINION

The most obvious function of evaluation—the one we focused on in the opening section of this introduction—is to tell the reader what the writer thinks or feels about something. Identifying 'what the writer thinks' tells us about more than just one person's ideas, however. Every act of evaluation expresses a communal value-system, and every act of evaluation goes towards building up that value-system. This value-system in turn is a component of the ideology which lies behind every text. Thus, identifying what the writer thinks reveals the ideology of the society that has produced the text. For example, here is a letter printed on the 'problem page' of a popular British women's magazine (*Woman's Own*, summer 1998: 32). The sentences have been numbered for ease of reference, and the most obvious indications of what the writer thinks have been italicized.

(1.3)

[1] My husband runs his own business and is a *workaholic*. [2] Last year he *kept putting off* our plans for a break and *I got so fed up* I went away with four friends. [3] *We had a great time, even though I missed him*. [4] I want a holiday for just us this year but he *keeps saying* I'd probably have a better time if I went with them. [5] How can I get him to see *I'd rather go with him*?

Adding these evaluations together, the writer's feelings are clearly that she disapproves of her husband's reluctance to take a holiday. She enjoys holidays and prefers to spend them with her husband. Although these opinions belong to the writer as an individual, several ideological assumptions are at work here, including: that taking holidays is normal behaviour, whereas continuous work is not; that couples are expected to take holidays together, other arrangements being acceptable only under extreme circumstances (*I got so fed up*); that arrangements for how a couple spend their time should take account of the wishes of both partners (*he kept putting off our plans*). Sentence 3 reflects an issue of less certainty. The happiness of women who love their husbands is not dependent on the presence of the husband, but a woman having a good time in the absence of her husband needs to reassure us that this is remarkable and that she would be happier if he were there (*even though I missed him*). These assumptions reflect (and reinforce) an ideology based on a particular economic system (work is done out of economic necessity and is separate from other parts of life; work may be enjoyed, but not as much as holidays), and on a particular system of family life, in which husband and wife behave as a discrete unit, but not exclusively so. The fact that the husband–wife unit is currently under tension in British society is reflected in the contradiction in sentence 3: the woman should be independent of her husband emotionally and/but husband and wife should find their greatest joy in being together.

The ideology reflected and reinforced by a text may belong to a sub-group, rather than to a whole society. The next example is the beginning of an academic paper by members of a particular discourse community (Swales 1990) who might be characterized by the term 'applied linguists'. The constituency of the discourse community is determined not by gender or nationality or even native language (though English must be one of the languages that they operate comfortably in), but precisely by the fact that its members write and read papers like this.

(1.4)
[1] Nonnative speaker (NNS)–native speaker (NS) interaction is *of interest* for theoretical and empirical research into the nature of (mis)-communication (9 references cited). [2] The *importance* of this research increases as the focus moves out of experimental settings and into contexts where the interactions have immediate social and physical consequences, as in settings involving the delivery of health services. [3] In medical contexts, miscommunication is common and may emerge from many sources [11 references cited]. [4] Despite the many ways communication may go wrong, research in medical anthropology/sociology and interactional studies of medical contexts appears to converge on the general finding that interaction between patients and medical professionals *is best understood* as a case of complicated, fitful, and asymmetrical cross-cultural communication. (*Applied Linguistics*, 18/4: 415)

As well as certain general assumptions about communication (that communication can either succeed or fail; that failure of communication in medical settings is a serious problem), there are assumptions about the nature of research, peculiar to this speech community, that also underlie this extract. First, research may be theoretical (sentence 1) or applied (sentence 2): both types of research are valid, but applied research is more significant (the title of the journal is **Applied Linguistics**). Secondly, the aim of the researcher is to understand a phenomenon, by relating it to a model or theory (sentence 4): the understanding is not intuitive or personal but verbalized and shared. Thirdly, a consensus among researchers probably means that their understanding is correct (in sentence 4, *despite* a problem of diversity, there is a solution which is convergence of interpretation). As well as this evaluation *in* the text, evidence is provided for evaluation *of* the text, by the reader (the distinction is Cortazzi and Jin's, this volume). In keeping with Swales's observations about the move 'Claiming centrality' found in introductions, the writers demonstrate that the topic they have chosen is interesting (sentence 1), important (sentence 2), and the subject of investigation by many other researchers (the numerous references cited in sentences 1 and 3). In this way they also lay claim to their own academic credibility.

Ideologies do not exist in silence, but neither are they usually expressed overtly. They are built up and transmitted through texts, and it is in texts that their nature is revealed. It has become commonplace to examine texts in order to lay bare the ideologies that have inspired them (e.g. Fowler 1990; Fairclough 1989; 1992; Hodge and Kress 1993; Meinhof and Richardson 1994; Stubbs 1996; Caldas-Coulthard and Coulthard 1996). Because ideologies are essentially sets of values—what counts as good or bad, what should or should not happen, what counts as true or untrue—evaluation is a key linguistic concept in their study.

MAINTAINING RELATIONS

The second function of evaluation is to build and maintain relations between writer and reader. This has been studied in relation to three main areas: manipulation, hedging, and politeness. In each of these areas, the writer can be said to be exploiting the resources of evaluation to build a particular kind of relationship with the reader.

First, evaluation can be used to manipulate the reader, to persuade him or her to see things in a particular way (see, e.g. Carter and Nash 1990). Hoey points out (1983: 95), for example, that evaluation of an aspect of a situation as a problem is driven by a particular view-point. He says, 'A Problem can only be a Problem for someone . . . Consequently if there are two participants, there are potentially not one but two Problems possible . . . ' Expressing something as a problem, however, makes it difficult for the reader not to accept it as such. For example, the 'workaholic husband' example above (Example 1.3) is told from the woman's point of view—the problem as perceived by her husband may be something quite different ('I loathe holidays but my wife keeps insisting that we go on one')—but it takes a conscious effort of detachment for the reader not to identify with the writer's point of view, or the ideology that underlies it.

As Hoey's chapter (this volume) points out, evaluation is particularly difficult to challenge, and therefore is particularly effective as manipulation, when it is not the main point of the clause. One way that this may be the case is when information that is 'given' in a clause is expressed evaluatively. In the following example, *solemnity, pomposity, frivolity,* and *triviality* are all treated as given, not new, information. The reader is not positioned to make a decision as to whether or not to agree with these evaluations; instead, the reader's acceptance of the evaluation is simply assumed.

(1.5)

In retrospect, the solemnity—and, to modern eyes and ears, pomposity—of the politics and media of the past may be seen as in part a reflection of the current or very recent reasons to be serious: the daily expectation of invasion or death.
Similarly, the frivolity and triviality of much modern discourse . . . is a product of a decade in which nothing seemed to matter very much . . . (The *Guardian*, 30.5.98, p. 23)

Francis (1986; 1994) points out that certain nouns ('discourse labels') have an important role in summarizing previous text. These discourse labels may simply summarize (*these words, this question*), or they may evaluate (*this claim, this nonsense*). Because these words typically occur as given information, the reader is unlikely to question their validity. Here is an example from a letter to a newspaper:

(1.6)

[1] You quote President Clinton as saying after the Pakistani nuclear tests that he could not believe that the Indian subcontinent was 'about to repeat the worst mistakes of the 20th century when we know it is not necessary to peace, to security, to prosperity . . . '.
[2] *This admission*, by the leader of the country with the largest stockpile of nuclear weapons, *that they are not necessary for a country's security*, destroys all the rhetoric of the last half century. (The *Guardian*, 30.5.98, p. 22)

The noun group at the beginning of sentence 2 evaluates President Clinton's comments as an *admission*, that is, an acknowledgment of the truth of something damaging to the speaker. The placing of the noun makes it likely that the reader will accept it as a valid evaluation, and once that is accepted, the subsequent argument, that Clinton's speech *destroys all the rhetoric of the last half century*, is more likely to be accepted also.

Thus, the less obtrusively the evaluation is placed in the clause, the more likely it is to successfully manipulate the reader. Perhaps the most extreme example of this is the use of a conjunct or subordinator to imply evaluation. Conjuncts such as *and* and *but* and subordinators such as *because* and *although* assume a common ground between reader and writer in terms of what is expected or unexpected at any given point in the discourse (Winter in Huddleston *et al.* 1968: 570). The reader is led into supplying information which substantiates this common ground. The following example is taken from a newspaper report of a young woman who committed suicide by walking into the middle of a busy road. She died after being struck by a coach.

(1.7)

In a statement read to the inquest, the coach driver . . . said he had seen something in the middle lane directly in front of him *but* could not do anything *because* he had a coach full of passengers. (The *Guardian*, 30.5.98, p. 11)

Anyone unfortunate enough to have witnessed this incident would no doubt have felt extreme sympathy for the coach driver and would have reacted with approval to the decision he took. The way that the incident is reported here engenders the same degree of fellow-feeling. The reader interprets *but* to mean 'against expectation' and supplies the information 'the natural expectation is that someone seeing something in the road will try to avoid it'. The subordinator *because* indicates natural cause, and the reader supplies 'a good reason for failing to avoid something in the road is to avoid harming a large number of passengers' (see Thompson and Zhou's chapter, this volume, for further examples of dialogue between writer and reader implied through conjunctive elements). Thus the coach driver is construed as a reasonable person, who has the same values as the reader (wishing to avoid harm to someone in the road; and wishing to avoid harm to passengers), values which in this case conflict.

Secondly, the role of evaluation in adjusting the truth-value or certainty attached to a statement has been extensively studied under the heading of 'hedging' (e.g. Lakoff 1972; Prince *et al.* 1982; Holmes 1984). This is particularly common in academic writing, so much so that it is an important aspect of any academic reading or writing course and has been extensively studied in the context of English for Specific Purposes (e.g. Hyland 1994; 1998; Banks 1994; Crompton 1997) and the social construction of knowledge (Myers 1989; 1990). Myers (1990) notes that a biologist he studied introduced or strengthened hedging in his writing at the behest of reviewers and editors. This might be interpreted to mean that the degree of certainty attached to particular knowledge claims is the subject of negotiation, and that the final version must be very precisely modified as a result. There are, however, indications that hedging might not always have the purpose of moderating the certainty of knowledge claims as such. Simpson (1990), for example, notes that some writers in literature use modality in an unexpected way, leaving their most contentious claims unmodified. Studies by Butler (1990) and Rizomilioti (in preparation) suggest that disciplines vary widely in their use of modality. Myers argues that in science, hedging may be used as a purely rhetorical device: 'toning down, not one's claims for one's research, but one's language' (1990: 48). He suggests, in fact, that one purpose of hedging is to mark a knowledge claim as unacknowledged by the discourse community, not as uncertain (1989: 12). In other words, the hedging is a politeness device, a strategy in the maintenance of relations between writer and reader.

ORGANIZING THE DISCOURSE

We have discussed above how evaluation can be used to build a relationship between writer and reader, in particular by assuming shared attitudes, values, and reactions which it can be difficult for the reader, as the subordinate in this relationship, to dispute. This relationship does not exist only in terms of the information in the text, however, but in terms of the text itself. In other words, the writer does not only tell the reader 'this happened, and this is my opinion about it', but also tells the reader 'this is the beginning of our text, this is how the argument fits together, and this is the end of our interaction'. To take a simple example, if a mother writes a letter to her daughter, an interaction will take place between them as mother and daughter reacting to events in the world, but in addition an interaction will take place between them as writer and reader keeping track of the progression or organization of the text. In short, the letter-writer and letter-reader have two relationships: as mother and daughter and as discourse-producer and discourse-recipient.

Sinclair (1987) argues that evaluation, in writing as in speech, tends to occur at boundary points in a discourse, thereby providing a clue to ('monitoring') its organization. In dialogue, this monitoring function is fairly clear: both the teacher's *Yes, That's right*, or *Good* after a student's contribution, and the less overt *Mm mm, Sure*, or *Yeah* in a casual conversation indicate that the discourse is on track and that what has been said is not being challenged. In monologue, especially in written monologue, evaluation at the end of each unit (for example, at the end of a paragraph) marks that a point has been made and that the reader's acceptance of that point is assumed. It is as if the writer kept up a constant commentary on the progress of the discourse itself: 'The discourse has started, and it is going to be divided into three parts. Here is the first part, here is the end of the first part *and this is why it is interesting*. Assuming you are with me so far, now we move on to the second part . . . ' (evaluation in italics).

To see how this works in practice, here is a paragraph taken from an article arguing that capitalism has become a religion (D. Loy, 'The Religion of the Market', *Journal of the American Academy of Religion*, 65: 275–90). The writer has just suggested that people in capitalist systems live by two principles (or propositions): that market forces 'are right and just', and that 'value can be adequately signaled by prices'. He continues:

(1.8)

[1] The basic assumption of both propositions is that such a system is 'natural'. [2] If market capitalism does operate according to economic laws as natural as those of physics or chemistry—if economics were a genuine science—its consequences seem unavoidable, despite the fact that they have led to extreme social inequity and are leading to environmental catastrophe. [3] Yet there is nothing inevitable about our economic relationships. [4] That misunderstanding is precisely what needs to be addressed—and this is also where religion comes in, since with the increasing prostitution of universities and the media to these same market forces there seems to be no other moral perspective left from which to challenge them. [5] Fortunately, the alternative worldviews that religions offer can still help us realize that the global victory of market capitalism is something other than the simple attainment of economic freedom: rather, it is the ascendancy of one particular way of understanding and valuing the world that need not be taken for granted. [6] Far from being inevitable, this economic system is one historically-conditioned way of organizing/reorganizing the world; [7] it is a worldview, with ontology and ethics, in competition with other understandings of what the world is and how we should live in it.

We might investigate this paragraph first of all from the point of view of clause relations (Winter 1977; 1982; 1994 and Hoey 1979; 1983; 1994). It begins (sentence 1) with what Winter (1994: 62–5) calls a 'hypothetical' statement, that is, one which the writer is clearly not committed to (an *assumption* is often cited in order to be criticized). A 'hypothetical' statement leads the reader to expect (prospects) a 'real' statement, that is, one to which the writer is committed (ibid.). This appears in sentence 3. In other words, sentence 3 evaluates what has been said in sentences 1 and 2 as untrue. Sentence 4 begins with an anaphoric noun group (Francis 1986; 1994), *That misunderstanding*, which summarizes sentences 1 and 2 in the light of sentence 3 and again evaluates them as untrue. It also serves the function of re-interpreting sentences 1–3 as a problem (again using Winter and Hoey's terms): people misunderstand the nature of the marketplace. Sentence 4 offers us a response to the problem—understanding the market in religious terms—and sentences 5–7 evaluate the response as likely to be successful. In addition, in sentences 6 and 7 we return to the 'real' element in the 'hypothetical-real' sequence, which evaluates the assumption in sentence 1 again as untrue.

If we now look at the paragraph in terms of divisions within it, we can argue that sentence 3 marks the end of the first part of the paragraph. What follows (*That misunderstanding* in sentence 4) treats sentences 1–3 as a unit capable of being summarized in a single noun group. Sentences 5–7 constitute the final part of the paragraph. We therefore might suggest a three-part structure for the paragraph (and note that Sinclair 1987 proposes the three-part structure as a basis for organization in written discourse) consisting of sentences 1–3; sentence 4; sentences 5–7. Evaluation does play an important role in these divisions. Sentence 3 evaluates 1–2, and the evaluative anaphoric noun in sentence 4 also identifies 1–3 as a unit. Sentences 5–7 evaluate the response to the problem, thus, in a sense, 'ending' the discussion, while sentences 6–7 also return to the evaluation of 1–2, mirroring sentence 3 as they do so.

While this commentary does not amount to 'proof' of Sinclair's proposals regarding the role of evaluation, it does at least illustrate his approach. The evaluation in the paragraph organizes, and does so interactively. As the relationship between writer and reader is built up, part of that relationship is a mutual awareness of the boundaries in the discourse and the nature of the connection between its various parts.

Evaluation which both organizes the discourse and indicates its significance, might be said to tell the reader the 'point' of the discourse. 'Point' is the term used by Labov in discussing the role of evaluation in narrative. His description of the stories told by adolescent boys in New York (Labov 1972; and see Cortazzi and Jin's chapter, this volume) contains perhaps the earliest recognition of the importance of evaluation to discourse. Labov identifies what he calls 'the basic narrative clause', without which a story cannot exist, but then adds that evaluation is 'perhaps the most important element in addition to the basic narrative clause' (Labov 1972: 366). The worst fate that can befall a story-teller, according to Labov, is if, after the story is finished, the hearer asks 'So what?'. In this case, the story-teller has failed to put across the point of the story: why the events narrated are worth relating and paying attention to. Evaluation indicates that the events in the story are funny, amazing, terrifying, and so on. Thus evaluation pre-empts the 'So what?' question by indicating the point of the story and how the hearer is expected to react. Although evaluation occurs throughout the narrative (forming a 'secondary structure' alongside the narrative one) it tends to cluster at various points, notably in the Abstract, at the beginning of the narrative, in the Coda, at the end of the narrative, and just before the narrative's denouement, suspending the action. Essentially, it is evaluation that enables monologic narrative to be interactive and to fulfil a communicative function.

How do we Recognize Evaluation?

Most readers of any text agree about what counts as evaluation in it. For example, here is a short text from an information bulletin about CD-ROMs in a university library. The text is organized around a problem and its solution. The most obvious evaluation is italicized.

(1.9)

[1] As well as a number of networked CD-ROM databases, Information Services also holds many other CD-ROM databases which have not been networked because of cost, technical reasons or lack of demand. [2] Hitherto these have mainly been issued from Library Enquiry desks and used on dedicated CD-ROM PCs, meaning that *the CD-ROMs were only available during desk opening times* in exchange for the user's library card number.

[3] With the growing numbers of databases available this way, *this procedure is becoming unwieldy*, particularly in the Main Library. [4] Therefore a CD-ROM autochanger was installed on trial six months ago in Zone GC. [5] Making standalone CD-ROM databases available in this way means that *they no longer have to be issued by the Information Desk staff* and thus *are available whenever the Library is open, not just when the desk is staffed*.

[6] *The trial was successful*, and it is now planned to install CD-ROM autochangers in most of the Main Library subject areas, in order to place databases nearer the most relevant bookstock.

In this text, the current system is evaluated negatively for being inconvenient to users (*only available during desk opening times*) and to staff (*unwieldy*). The new system is convenient (*[databases] no longer have to be issued by the Information Desk staff; are available whenever the Library is open*) and *successful*. How, though, do we recognize this information as evaluative?

There have been both conceptual and linguistic answers to this question. Conceptually, evaluation has been noted to be comparative, subjective, and value-laden. Identifying evaluation, then, is a question of identifying signals of comparison, subjectivity, and social value. Labov (1972) emphasizes the comparative nature of evaluation. That is, evaluation consists of anything which is compared to or contrasts with the norm. One example of this is the use of a negative, which compares what is not with what might be. Thus, *they no longer have to be issued by the Information Desk staff* (sentence 5) is evaluative. Another example of a comparator is *only* in sentence 2 (*CD-ROMs were only available during desk opening times*), which draws attention to the relative unavailability of the CD-ROMs.

The subjective nature of evaluation is not illustrated in Example 1.7, but we may find many examples in Example 1.3 above (the workaholic husband example): *I got so fed up*; *I missed him*; *I'd rather go with him*. The first two of these are similar to Labov's category of Internal Evaluation, in which someone's (subjective) reaction to an event is reported. (The third example cannot be compared with Labov's analysis of narrative.)

An attempt to account for the value-laden nature of evaluation is found in Hunston (1985; 1989). Hunston suggests that 'what is good' and 'what is bad' can be defined in terms of goal-achievement. Something that is good helps to achieve a goal, while something that is bad prevents or hinders the achievement of a goal. If we assume that library managers and users share the goal of having information obtainable at all times and using very simple procedures, this explains how *only available during desk opening times* and *unwieldy* evaluate negatively, whereas *available whenever the Library is open* evaluates positively.

The advantage of looking at evaluation conceptually is that it does not restrict what can be counted as evaluation. For example, if goal-achievement is taken as the basis of evaluation, then lexical repetition can, in context, be interpreted as evaluation. If a goal is established as *Our aim was to isolate the enzyme* and if at a subsequent point the text reads . . . *this led to isolation of the enzyme*, the second clause can be taken as evaluation, even though there is no evaluative language in it, because of the repetition of *isolate the enzyme* . . . *isolation of the enzyme*. The disadvantage of looking at evaluation in this way is that the argument for what constitutes evaluation becomes circular. Returning to the library CD-ROM example, we say that *CD-ROMs were only available during desk opening times* is evaluative because of the goal of making resources available at all times, but we would also have to say that we know about that goal because of the evaluation that refers to it. It would be more accurate to say that the lexical item *only* gives us an indication that evaluation of some kind is going on, and we then use interpretative procedures to establish what that evaluation is and how it relates to the goals of library management.

Turning to the linguistic identification of evaluation, then, we can identify three aspects which we will deal with here under the headings *lexis, grammar*, and *text*.

LEXIS

Some lexical items are very clearly evaluative, in the sense that evaluation is their chief function and meaning. These include:

adjectives: splendid, terrible, surprising, obvious, important, possible, untrue
adverbs: happily, unfortunately, plainly, interestingly, possibly, necessarily
nouns: success, failure, tragedy, triumph, likelihood
verbs: succeed, fail, win, lose, doubt

Although there is a considerable degree of consensus concerning the evaluative meaning of words such as this, it is by no means easy to establish criteria for distinguishing evaluative from non-evaluative items. If we take two clauses, for example, *Jane is a genius* and *Jane is a student*, we might agree that the first is evaluative (*genius* is a comparative term, the assessment of genius-ness is highly subjective, and to be a genius is socially valued). The second clause, however, might be open to disagreement. We might argue that *student* represents an objective category of people, clearly distinguished from others. However, although some people would take *student* to be a value-free, purely descriptive label, others would argue that it had a positive connotation (associated, perhaps, with a reforming, courageous intelligentsia) or a negative one (associated with laziness, unkempt appearance, and heavy drinking habits!).

In recent years, many aspects of language use that in former times were accessible only through intuition have become available for study using large, machine-stored corpora. The intuition of a language user regarding a particular lexical item is the product of tens, hundreds, or thousands of experiences of that item, scattered across years of heterogeneous language experience. In representing the discourse of a community, a very large corpus can mimic, though not of course replicate, that experience.

Instead of appealing to concepts of 'genius' and 'student', therefore, we can obtain thousands of instances of each word, occurring in a naturally occurring discourse yet arranged together so that the cumulative effect of each word is made accessible to explicit observation. Here are 20 randomly selected lines from the Bank of English corpus (held at COBUILD) for *a genius* and *a student*.

a genius (total lines 446)

```
1 e football theme. [Shouts] The boy's  a genius # <ZZ1>normal voice<ZZ0> It
2 A> I think he was very near to being  a genius. <T>We realized almost
3 ered that the child was something of  a genius at mathematics. He whipped
4 of the fundaments, 'you know there's  a genius at work. <LTH> Harry Burns
5 believe that Terence Trent D'Arby is  a genius, Bobby Davro is great
6 y on Nov 26, 1986. Malcolm McLean is  a genius. But the other side of geni
7 phasised the status of the artist as  a genius. For Mr Watson, this change
8 he was convinced that he possessed  a 'genius gene'. And what to do
9 d outside the court: 'My barrister's  a genius. I'm laughing. It is a soft
10  been so ready to abuse Bentham as  'a genius in the way of bourgeois
11 , in my place, should be, at least,  a genius. It's a dreadful insult
12  without conceit, he was considered  a genius. Knew, too, that such gifts
13 e to the West in parts, who is also  a genius. Making sense of all this h
14  OK person, quite good looking, not  a genius perhaps but I have lots of
15 ant to stop where he is. The son of  a genius remains the son of a genius
16 r nothing is Michael Stipe known as  a genius round these parts. Our spie
17 um, Santiago attacks # I may not be  a genius # she told reporters during
18  for equality, her partnership with  a genius such as John had inevitably
19 to talk to Brundle. It did not take  a genius to work out that his season
20  uring </h> <dt>12 August 1992</dt>  A genius who saved millions of lives
```

a student (total lines 1977)

```
1   ust a patron of Buddhism. He became a student and then a teacher, writin
2   e time. I left home my first year as a student and an aunt paid for me to
3   early rehearsal of a play when I was a student. As I rehearsed, I felt li
4   kirk competing in trials while still a student at Dublin University.
5   f a mall. My brother was run over as a student at Florida State. In both
6   economics graduate, and Eileen, 18, a student at Princeton. For them it
7   prompted to do so by a question from a student during one of his lectures
8   larger, Klanac recruited Igor Copo, a student from the political science
9   nly better than those in Tibet. Once a student has survived the Chinese
10  1, Bountiful, Utah): I knew Dion as a student. I got to know him probabl
11  ontroversy surrounding the death of a student in police custody three
12  next step, said Markiyan Ivanyshyn, a student leader. Today's decision
13  ersity lecturer (Mr Ray Ruffon) and a student (Mr Sabelo Dlamini), had
14  bed-sitting room in Earls Court. As a student of politics. My name is Ra
15  t as the source of knowledge. It is a student-oriented-curriculum in the
16  </h? <Dt?29 February 1992 </dt> <t>A student stranded in California aft
17  truth about his visit to Moscow as a student, then he will accept that
18  nk the French Department when I was a student was much more open and fre
19  cy exemption for a dependent who is a student who has attained 24 years
20  creditable 'performance': to guide a student with ten A-grade GCSEs to
```

The lines for *a genius*, taken together, indicate evaluative meaning. Evidence for this includes: the lexis of judgement and subjectivity, such as *believe* (line 5), *consider* (line 12), *know as* (line 16); the lexis of comparison and achievement (lines 2, 3, 19); other positively evaluative lexis (*I'm laughing*, line 9; *gifts*, line 12; *saved millions of lives*, line 20); and the occurrence of *genius* in concession clauses (lines 14 and 17). One line (10) indicates that *genius* is not always positive, but the overwhelming evidence is of positive evaluation. The lines for *a student* show no such evaluative meaning, though there is some evidence that students tend to be associated with vulnerable situations (lines 5, 9, 11, and 16). The difference between the two noun groups may be illustrated by comparing 'know someone as a genius' (line 16) and 'know someone as a student' (line 10). The first is para-phrasable as 'People around here judge Michael Stipe to be a genius' whereas the second is paraphrasable as 'I knew Dion when he was a student'. Only the first is evaluative. Evidence such as this, which examines the typical context of a word such as *genius*, can be used to argue for the word *genius* having an inherently evaluative meaning. In turn, then, it can be argued that even in a bald statement such as *Jane is a genius* the evaluative meaning of *genius* remains and renders the whole clause evaluative.

This does not mean, of course, that it is impossible for a speaker or writer ever to use the word *student* evaluatively. In the following (genuine) exchange, for example, speaker *B* clearly evaluates *student* negatively. This evaluation is not sig-nalled by *student*, though, but by the comparator *just*.

(1.10)
A: Who is he?
B: He's just a student at the University Shakespeare Institute.

The examples of *genius* and *student* are relatively clearcut. In many cases, however, a lexical item gives information in addition to the evaluation, and as a result, its status as evaluation may be more debatable. This is particularly true in the case of verbs and nouns. For example, the following verbs all have a meaning of 'being involved in something or taking part in an activity' (Francis *et al.* 1996: 198) when they are followed by the preposition *in*:

assist	engage	join
collaborate	help	meddle
collude	interfere	participate

They have different evaluative values, however. *Assist* and *help* evaluate the involvement positively, from the point of view of the other people involved in the activity. To assist in a bank robbery, for example, is a positive act from the point of view of the other robbers, though not from the point of view of the bank staff. *Interfere* and *meddle* are evaluatively the 'opposite' of *assist* and *help*, as they evaluate the involvement itself negatively, again from the point of view of the other people involved in the activity. *Collude* is different in that it evaluates the activity negatively as well as the involvement: if someone is described as colluding in a scheme, this evaluates the scheme as criminal or reprehensible. *Collaborate, engage, join,* and *participate* do not evaluate the participation: whether the involvement is considered to be good or bad would depend on the nature of the activity.

To take another example, *abstain, forbear,* and *refrain* (from doing something) all typically indicate a positive attitude towards the absence of action, whereas *flinch, retreat,* and *shirk* indicate a negative attitude.

Many nouns and adjectives are used to describe people, things, or situations in a way which implies approval or disapproval as well as giving other information about them. In the following example (taken from the *Collins COBUILD English Dictionary* (CCED) 1995: 453), the adjectives *dewy-eyed* and *sentimental* both indicate an attitude towards the past, but they also indicate that the speaker dislikes that attitude:

I can never understand why people become dewy-eyed and sentimental about the past.

Similarly, in this example (CCED 1995: 639), the noun *flag-waving* indicates that the speaker disapproves of the type or degree of patriotism being shown:

The real costs of the war have been ignored in the flag-waving of recent months.

Often, there are two words which indicate the same information, but suggest a different attitude towards it. For example, *rebels* and *malcontents* both dislike the current system, but choosing the word *malcontent* signals disapproval of this attitude. Someone's behaviour may be described as *formal* or *mannered*: the latter word indicates disapproval. To take a better-known example: *execution, assassination killing, murder,* and *slaughter* may all be used to describe the same incident, but the sense of moral outrage increases with each successive noun.

As these examples (and others in Channell's chapter in this volume) illustrate, the evaluation associated with particular lexical items can be quite complex and, as Channell and others have argued, may not even be accessible to intuition (Sinclair 1991; Louw 1993; Stubbs 1996). Here again, a corpus can give very useful information, allowing intuitions about the evaluative force of particular lexical items to be investigated, and new discoveries made. For example, Stubbs (1996) has pointed out that the verb *cause* collocates with words indicating undesirable things, such as illnesses and natural or economic disasters. Following Sinclair, and Louw (1993), he describes this as the 'semantic prosody' of the verb *cause,* and suggests that a true definition of the word should not be 'make something happen' but 'make something bad happen'.

GRAMMAR

The relationship of grammar and evaluation will be discussed in detail in the next section. Here we will simply note that several writers have associated certain aspects of grammar with evaluation. Some of the most notable of these are listed below.

Labov (1972)

Labov asserts that 'departures from the basic narrative syntax have a marked evaluative force' (1972: 378), and lists these departures as:

(1) intensifiers, such as gestures, expressive phonology, quantifiers (e.g. *all*), repetition, and ritual utterances (e.g. *And there it was*);

(2) comparators, listed by Labov as negatives, futures, modals, quasimodals, questions, imperatives, or-clauses, superlatives, and comparatives (387);

(3) correlatives, including progressives, appended particles (non-finite '-ing' clauses), double appositives, and attributives (e.g. *a knife, a long one, a dagger; a great big guy*);

(4) explicatives, that is, clauses introduced by subordinators such as *while, though, since,* or *because* and other connections between clauses.

Stubbs (1986)

Stubbs argues for an investigation into language which 'is used . . . to express personal beliefs and adopt positions, to express agreement and disagreement with others, to make personal and social allegiances, contracts, and commitments, or alternatively to disassociate the speaker from points of view, and to remain vague or uncommitted' (1986: 1). He summarizes this concern as a 'modal grammar' or as 'point of view'; we might also summarize it as aspects of evaluation. He links his study with speech act theory, though arguing that this theory is inadequate, and explores the interaction of lexis, grammar, and pragmatic meaning. Some of the topics which Stubbs mentions as belonging to this area are:

(1) expressions of the source of propositions (cf. Chafe 1986);
(2) phrases which limit commitment, such as *all being well, if I can, whatever that means*;
(3) ways of being explicit, for example, through performatives, or being vague (cf. Channell 1994);
(4) choice of simple or progressive aspect of verbs of cognition;
(5) the modal meaning of 'private' verbs;
(6) logical connectors, for example, *and, but, or, if, because*;
(7) past tense indicating remoteness, as in *I did wonder if I might ask you a favour*;
(8) references to future time;
(9) tag questions.

Biber and Finegan (1989)

Biber and Finegan give a list of twelve 'stance markers', defined as 'the lexical and grammatical expression of attitudes, feelings, judgements, or commitment concerning the propositional content of a message' (1989: 93). These markers comprise lexical items selected from particular word classes, as well as some other categories, namely:

(1) adverbs indicating affect, certainty, and doubt;
(2) adjectives indicating affect, certainty, and doubt;
(3) verbs indicating affect, certainty, and doubt;
(4) hedges (vague language e.g. *about, sort of*);
(5) emphatics (e.g. *for sure, really*);
(6) modals indicating possibility, necessity, and prediction.

TEXT

It is clear—and all studies of evaluation have said so—that evaluation tends to be found throughout a text rather than being confined to one particular part of it. This is true to such an extent that in the examples quoted by Winter as Situation–Evaluation pairs, there is evaluative language in the Situation element as well as in the Evaluation element (see e.g. Winter 1982: 191, but see also above the argument that evaluation tends to occur at discourse boundaries).

It is also true, however, that evaluation is identified in some cases because of its position in a text and the role that it plays because of that position. For example, in the text famously used by Hoey to illustrate the text pattern Situation–Problem–Response–Evaluation (Hoey 1983: 68), the final paragraph functions to evaluate a new system of dropping freight from helicopters. Here is a shortened version of the text, annotated with Hoey's analysis of it, and with the final paragraph (sentences 9–11) quoted in full:

(1.11)
SITUATION [1] Helicopters are very convenient for dropping freight by parachute,
PROBLEM but this system has its problems. [2] Somehow the landing impact has to be cushioned to give a soft landing . . .

RESPONSE [5] . . . Bertin . . . has come up with an air-cushion system which assures a safe and soft landing . . .

EVALUATION [9] Trials have been carried out with freight-dropping at rates from 19 feet to 42 feet per second. [10] The charge weighed about one and half tons, but the system can handle up to eight tons. [11] At low altitudes freight can be dropped without a parachute.

There are some signals of evaluation in sentences 9–11, notably the modal *can*, but the role of the paragraph as evaluation depends on its position relative to the Response, and on the fact that it indicates how the product was tested. In other words, describing the paragraph as evaluation indicates that the function of the clauses is to evaluate, rather than that the meaning of the clauses is evaluative.

Evaluation, Grammar, and Lexis

In this section we consider where evaluation is located in terms of a linguist's view of language, in particular in relation to the traditional distinction between grammar and lexis (though see Sinclair 1991 and Hunston and Sinclair, this volume, for arguments that lexis and grammar are not truly distinct).

As mentioned in the opening section of this introduction, of the two main types of evaluation that we have so far focused on one—modality—is far more recognizably grammaticalized than the other. That is, modality is more obviously realized by features of language which are traditionally thought of as belonging to 'grammar' than affect is. As a reflection of this, modality is usually discussed under the heading of grammar, centred around the functionally dedicated class of modal verbs, whereas affect/appraisal is usually treated under the heading of lexis, centred around the functionally promiscuous classes of adjectives and nouns. This is perhaps because, as has already been noted, modal evaluation tends to be exercised on propositions and affective evaluation on entities. Our evaluation of certainty, as construed in the language system, is an essential part of any proposition: a proposition without modality is simply one where the inherent option of signalling intermediate degrees of commitment has not been taken up. Our evaluation of goodness or desirability, on the other hand, is construed as an accidental quality of the entity that need not be expressed in referring to it: the use of an overtly evaluative label (e.g. *fleabag* as opposed to *cat*) is felt to be a marked choice that adds an optional overlay of emotion to the basic referential meaning.

Starting from this prototypical picture, the grammar of modality has been very fully explored (see e.g. Halliday 1994; Palmer 1986; Bybee and Fleischman 1995). The grammar of affective evaluation, on the other hand, has been far less investigated (though see Hunston and Sinclair, and Conrad and Biber, this volume). Lists of signals of evaluation like those of Labov (see 'How do we Recognize Evaluation?' above) point to grammatical areas such as comparatives and superlatives whose links with the expression of opinion are intuitively clear but as yet relatively little described. Such lists can appear to be fairly random collections of grammatical structures, and thus discourage attempts to produce a systematic account. It is significant that one central area of evaluative language, swearing, has attracted only cautious—not to say pussy-footing—attention from linguists; and when the area is examined it is rare that a grammatical approach is taken even though the syntactic patterns are in certain respects startlingly distinctive (see Zwicky *et al.* 1971/1992).

However, within modality studies—for example, through the work of Perkins (1983), Stubbs (1996), and Halliday (1994)—there has been an extension of coverage to include an equally varied range of structural possibilities. For example, Perkins (1983) highlights the role of modal lexical verbs such as *suggest*, Stubbs (1996) mentions the difference in degrees of commitment expressed by simple or progressive aspects of verbs of cognition, and Halliday (1994) explores metaphorical expressions of modality such as *I think* and *there is no doubt that*. These wider possibilities overlap in interesting and revealing ways with affective evaluation: for example, the shared pattern beginning with *it* has already been mentioned, while Winter (1982) discusses the link between interpolation and evaluation of both kinds. This suggests that a structural account of affective evaluation is equally attainable, and that the most productive approach may be to examine both major types of evaluation together as far as possible.

There is still a great deal to do in this field, but as noted above it seems possible to group the linguistic features that have been identified as signalling evaluation into three, each of which prioritizes a different inherent characteristic of evaluation (see also 'How do we Recognize Evaluation?' above):

(1) Evaluation involves comparison of the object of evaluation against a yardstick of some kind: the comparators. These include: comparative adjectives and adverbs; adverbs of degree; comparator adverbs such as *just, only, at least*; expressions of negativity (morphological, such as *un-* and other affixes; grammatical, such as *not, never, hardly*; and lexical, such as *fail, lack*).
(2) Evaluation is subjective: the markers of subjectivity. This is a very large group including: modals and other markers of (un)certainty; non-identifying adjectives; certain adverbs, nouns, and verbs; sentence adverbs and conjunctions; report and attribution structures; marked clause structures, including patterns beginning with *it* and *there*, and 'Special Operations Clauses' (Winter 1982) such as pseudo-clefts.
(3) Evaluation is value-laden: the markers of value. These may be divided into two groups: lexical items whose typical use is in an evaluative environment (the circularity of this definition seems unavoidable); and indications of the existence of goals and their (non-)achievement ('what is good' may be glossed as 'what achieves our goals' and 'what is bad' may be glossed as 'what impedes the achievement of our goals').

Of these three groups, the third seems inherently more lexical in nature; but the first and second are primarily grammatical. Even from a sketchy outline like this, certain areas begin to emerge as candidates for sustained investigation in terms of their contribution to evaluation: not only the obvious area of modality, but also, for example, negation (see e.g. Jordan 1998), and what might be termed the 'packaging' of propositions in *that* clauses and *wh-* clauses in a way that makes them available to be commented on (see Halliday 1994 on 'facts', Thompson 1996*b*).

Stubbs (1986) calls for 'prolonged fieldwork' to establish a modal grammar of English. If we widen the scope of enquiry to include not only the linguistic aspects that he refers to but all the aspects mentioned in the list above, the fieldwork will clearly be even more prolonged. However, as Stubbs argues, it seems essential to view grammar from the evaluative perspective and to build up a coherent overall picture from that angle to complement the 'propositional' or 'content' perspective that has traditionally dominated grammatical approaches. Such a picture will show many grammatical features in a relatively unfamiliar light, and bring out connections between apparently unrelated phenomena.

Parameters of Evaluation

One of the reasons why there are so many different terminologies in the area of evaluation is that the act of evaluating something can be done along several different parameters (here we reprise some of the discussion in 'What do we Mean by Evaluation?' above). The one that usually comes to mind is the good–bad, or positive–negative parameter. In the following extract, the sport of ice-diving is evaluated positively (*not ridiculous, solitude and beauty, make . . . worthwhile*), while possible negative evaluations of it (*might not sound the most appetizing sport in the world*) are rejected:

(1.12)
Plunging into a frozen-over lake on a blustery winter's day might not sound the most appetizing sport in the world. But in this small French resort ice-diving has become something of a craze. And it's not as ridiculous as it sounds: the solitude and beauty of the under-lake world beneath the sheets of ice makes all the preparation worthwhile.

The noun *craze* is another evaluation, but an ambiguous one. Something that is a craze is very popular, but possibly only for a short time. This writer, by choosing *and* as the conjunct in sentence 3 selects the positive evaluation; choosing *but* would select, and then negate, the negative evaluation.

As we said above, evaluations of good and bad are dependent on the value-system underlying the text. In this case, it is assumed that becoming cold and wet is normally undesirable (*plunging into a frozen-over lake on a blustery winter's day*), and that doing something that takes a lot of effort (*all the preparation*) is undesirable unless there is sufficient compensation. It is also assumed that an experience of beauty is a positive and valuable one, and in this text solitude, which can be either positive or negative, is linked positively with beauty (*the solitude and beauty*

. . . makes all the preparation worthwhile). In short, when evaluating leisure activities, aesthetic experience outweighs physical discomfort.

Not all evaluation is of good and bad, however. The following example (from the magazine *New Scientist*) discusses the reliability of clinical drug-trials:

(1.13)

[1] Suppose two hospitals are conducting separate trials of the drug, in which patients are allocated at random to receive either surgery and tamoxifen, or surgery alone. [2] Each hospital will have a different group of patients, surgeons at the two sites will operate differently, each medical team will give slightly different courses of tamoxifen, and so on. [3] How can the two trials be compared? [4] Clearly, the results from the two hospitals are unlikely to be the same: there will probably be a difference in the size of the benefit conferred by tamoxifen on the two groups. [5] When the data consist of just two trials, it is possible that one will show no benefit from tamoxifen at all, because of chance factors. [6] In 100 trials, however, the play of chance is most unlikely to obscure the overall trend.

The most obvious signals of evaluation in this extract relate not to how desirable or undesirable the writer thinks the information is, but how certain the writer is of each piece of information. The level of certainty is indicated by modal auxiliaries and other signals of modal meaning such as *unlikely* and *probably*. In sentence 2 the modal *will* is used to indicate a hypothetical situation that the writer has set up in sentence 1. In sentences 4 and 5 the certainty attached to the statements *the results from the two hospitals are not the same, there will be a difference in the size of the benefit . . . , one [trial] will show no benefit from tamoxifen at all* and *the play of chance will not obscure the overall trend* is modified by *are unlikely to, probably, it is possible that,* and *is most unlikely to*. In the terms used by Hyland and others, the paragraph is 'hedged' to a considerable extent: the writer is exhibiting caution in describing the hypothetical situation.

Another signal of evaluation in this extract is the adverb *Clearly* (sentence 4). This indicates not only how certain the writer is of what is to follow, but how obvious it is to the reader, or expected by the reader. Thus, in the 'tamoxifen trials' example, there are two parameters of evaluation that are signalled: certainty and expectedness. Note that in the case of *Clearly*, it is the discourse itself that is being evaluated as obvious or expected, as well as the information in the discourse.

It is important to recognize, however, that even though good–bad evaluation is not strongly signalled in this example, it is there. The paragraph contains evidence for positive–negative evaluation which the reader can share. If we assume, in accordance with the ideology of scientific research, that sameness in trials is both desirable and important, and that results should be clearly ascribable to control factors rather than chance, then all references to 'difference' (sentences 2 and 4) and 'chance' (sentence 5) are evidence for negative evaluation, and the assurance that chance will not influence the results too much (sentence 6) is evidence for positive evaluation. Furthermore, the moderated certainty that is signalled in the example is evidence for further evaluation in terms of good and bad, in that the reader is positioned to evaluate positively a judicious and cautious assessment of likely events.

A fourth parameter of evaluation is importance or relevance. Evidence for the importance of an issue may be given, as in this example (the *Guardian*, 10.6.98, p. 17), in which the writer is arguing that employees in England should be given time off to watch the World Cup (football) because the England team's participation in the contest is an important event:

(1.14)
Remember, it is eight years since England last played in a World Cup. Over 24 million people watched England play Cameroon in the 1990 quarter final and football fever has grown even more intense since then.

Typically, though, as with the 'obviousness' parameter, it is part of the discourse itself that is evaluated as important, directing the reader towards the main point of the text. This is typically signalled through adjectives and adverbs such as *important* and *significantly*, as in the following example:

(1.15)
Morris's notes and proposals for the book offer insight into his ideas on the necessity for artists to challenge the institutions of art through social and cultural activism. *More importantly*, these notes indicate Morris's antipathy toward art world institutions and his frustrations with artists who tended to distance themselves from efforts to change the system.

There is some evidence that the different parameters of evaluation can have specific roles to play in a discourse. Certain genres prioritize either evaluations of certainty or evaluations of good–bad. In genres which build knowledge claims, for example, the central function of evaluation is to assess the degree of certainty that can be attached to each part of the knowledge claim. In academic research articles, therefore, evaluation along the certainty parameter is particularly important. In genres whose central function is to assess the worth of something, such as restaurant reviews or character references, evaluation along the good–bad parameter is more significant. Evaluations of certainty and goodness therefore seem to be primarily 'real-world-oriented': they express the writer/speaker's view of the status of propositions and entities (in Halliday's terms they are experientially oriented). Evaluations of importance and expectedness, on the other hand, have an added 'text-oriented' function: they can serve to guide readers or listeners towards the intended coherence of what they are reading or hearing. Evaluation along the importance parameter appears to play a key role in the organization of texts, as indications of the importance or relevance of information are found especially at the beginning and end of paragraphs or discourse sections. Swales (1990), for example, notes that introductions to academic research articles often begin with a claim that the topic of the article is central, or important, to the field. Evaluations along the expectedness parameter seem frequently to function at a point-to-point level in textual terms. It can serve to link together steps in an argument, to signal how a proposition fits in with the speaker's views and his/her assumptions about the listener's views, of what constitutes 'normalness' in relation to the topic that has been previously introduced (see Thompson and Zhou, this volume).

We have, then, identified four parameters of evaluation: good–bad, certainty, expectedness, and importance. We would wish to argue, however, that evaluation is essentially one phenomenon rather than several, and that the most basic parameter, the one to which the others can be seen to relate, is the good–bad parameter. In particular, as we have suggested above in our discussion of the 'tamoxifen trials' text (Example 1.13), evaluations of certainty and uncertainty are not neutral with respect to cultural value. In a culture that pursues understanding and control of its physical environment, knowledge is good and lack of knowledge is bad. It is this that enables researchers to 'create a research space', in Swales's terminology, by indicating a gap in knowledge. The association between 'certainty' and the 'good' end of the good–bad parameter may be illustrated by the following extract from an article (*New Scientist*, 30.10.93) discussing new evidence for the value of the Hubble constant (H):

1.16

[1] Michael Jones of the Mullard Radio Astronomy Observatory in Cambridge revealed the latest figures based on the Sunyaev-Zel'dovich effect in a galaxy cluster (*New Scientist*, *Science*, 9 October). [2] These indicate that H lies in the range from 24 to 54, with a 'best' value of 38. [3] The figure is based on observations of just one galaxy cluster, but the team expects to observe five or six more galaxy clusters within two years.

In this paragraph, a knowledge claim is put forward ('H lies in the range from 24 to 54'), in such a way that the certainty level of the claim is also assessed (*latest figures . . . indicate that*). The status of the claim is established as something that is 'indicated' (but not 'shown' or 'demonstrated') by certain calculations based on other observations or interpretations. Then the knowledge claim is assessed in terms of how 'good' it is, in this case, in terms of how good the evidence for it is. The items *just* and *but* in sentence 3 suggest that the evidence is not particularly good at the moment (*just one galaxy cluster*), but may be expected to improve.

In short, evaluation along the certainty parameter is given first, as the knowledge claim is being stated, and evaluation along the good–bad parameter follows. On the other hand, it is also true that all the evaluation in the paragraph contributes both to how certain and to how good the knowledge claim is. A certain knowledge claim is a good knowledge claim: this claim is only partially certain and therefore only partially good.

In much the same way, evaluations of the discourse itself, in terms of importance or expectedness, can be shown to be related to the good–bad parameter. Essentially, these evaluations indicate that a text is either coherent (the parts relate to each other in a way that is expected, or obvious, or relevant) or significant (what is said is interesting, surprising, or important). Both coherence and significance are 'good' qualities in a text. However, whereas a speaker or writer may evaluate aspects of his/her discourse as 'bad' or 'uncertain' as well as 'good' or 'certain', it is less common to find a discourse evaluated as 'irrelevant' (though phrases which mark partial relevance, such as *to digress* and *by the way*, are of course used) or 'uninteresting'.

About this Book

This collection begins with two chapters which investigate the role of evaluation in the construal of ideology in texts. Hoey's chapter, *Persuasive Rhetoric in Linguistics*, investigates the placement of evaluative elements in the clause structure in the writings of Noam Chomsky. Hoey argues that the less overt the evaluation, the more difficult it is to recognize and assess, and that skilful use of evaluation has played an important role in the acceptance of Chomsky's theories by the linguistic world in general. The importance of evaluation as the 'hidden persuader' in the construction of academic theories, and, by extension, of any aspect of knowledge, is demonstrated by this chapter.

Channell's chapter, *Corpus-Based Analysis of Evaluative Lexis*, extends the scope of study from the individual text to a large collection of (written and spoken) texts electronically stored as a corpus of English. This corpus can act as an indicator of the ideological stance of a whole society. Channell demonstrates how words take on a particular social value, what would traditionally be termed 'connotation', through repeated use in different circumstances but in similar linguistic environments. She shows how certain items can be used to insinuate meaning by virtue of their typical use.

Channell's chapter is the first of three that use corpora as a research tool, though in very different ways. Conrad and Biber's chapter, *Adverbial Marking of Stance in Speech and Writing*, uses quantitative data to demonstrate the differences between various kinds of spoken and written discourse in terms of evaluation (or 'stance' in Conrad and Biber's terminology). Conrad and Biber classify the adverbials in their corpus according to their form (mainly adverb, prepositional phrase, and subordinate clause) and according to whether they express certainty, attitude, or style. They then correlate form and meaning with type of discourse, drawing conclusions about the preferred expression of stance in each genre.

Hunston and Sinclair's chapter, *A Local Grammar of Evaluation*, argues that there are particular grammatical patterns that select and therefore identify evaluative lexical items, and lists the patterns that identify evaluative adjectives. Further, Hunston and Sinclair demonstrate how the participating roles in evaluation—the evaluator, the thing evaluated, the category of evaluation, and so on—can be mapped on to these patterns. This work reflects Sinclair's contention that lexis and grammar constitute a single phenomenon, not two separate systems, and his concern to develop ways of parsing text automatically.

With Cortazzi and Jin's chapter we return to a more text-oriented approach. This chapter develops Labov's notion of evaluation as a crucial element in narrative. They argue, however, that the act of evaluation is not only a component of narrative, but also a way of reacting to narrative, and that the story-teller as well as the story is open to evaluation by readers or listeners.

Thompson and Zhou's chapter, *Evaluation and Organization in Text*, discusses the role that evaluative adjuncts, such as *fortunately* or *surprisingly*, play in structuring discourse, especially in signalling clause relations. They demonstrate that these adjuncts do not only indicate opinion, as part of the interpersonal metafunction of language, but play a major role in indicating discourse organization, thus taking part in the textual metafunction of language as well. They show that evaluation is not something 'added on' to the information structure of a text, but something central to the essential coherence of the text.

Martin's chapter, *Beyond Exchange:* APPRAISAL *Systems in English*, examines the role of evaluation (termed *appraisal* by Martin) in systemic-functional linguistics. Martin details the systemic networks needed to account for a wide variety of evaluative meanings, and applies these networks to a scene from the play *Educating Rita*. This chapter goes a long way in exploring the complexity that lies behind evaluation and in dealing with that complexity in a replicable way.

Another chapter which takes as its starting-point the complexity of evaluation is Hunston's *Evaluation and the Planes of Discourse*, which proposes a sub-division of evaluation into status and value and relates these to Sinclair's (1981) concept of planes of discourse. The model is applied to a range of texts, mainly persuasive articles from newspapers.

Our aim in presenting a diverse range of papers is to indicate some of the ways that the topic of evaluation has been tackled, and the place it occupies—under different names—in divergent approaches to the study of language. We hope that this collection will whet the reader's appetite for further investigations in this area.

2

Persuasive Rhetoric in Linguistics: A Stylistic Study of Some Features of the Language of Noam Chomsky

Michael Hoey

EDITORS' INTRODUCTION

* * *

Hoey's chapter is a detailed examination of selected passages from Chomsky's writing, focusing on Chomsky's use of evaluative words and phrases. Hoey's argument is that Chomsky pre-empts criticism of his ideas through a clever use of evaluation, in particular by evaluating negatively any reader whose assumptions about language and about the discipline of linguistics differ from Chomsky's own. Moreover, Hoey argues, Chomsky's evaluations are so embedded in the structure of the clause and of the discourse that they are difficult to challenge.

Central to Hoey's argument in this chapter is the notion of clause relations (see also Thompson and Zhou, this volume). Clause relations are the logical connections that readers perceive between clauses and which give texts their coherence. One such relation is that of Situation–Evaluation, described by Winter (1982: 190–1) as one of the 'basic' and most significant clause relations, which can organize whole texts. According to Winter, the Situation clause (or clauses) tells us what is known, and the Evaluation clause (or clauses) tells us what the writer thinks about the situation. Thus, in terms of clause relations, evaluation is a function of a clause and is clearly separated from 'description of situation'. An Evaluation clause can enter into other relations, most significantly for Hoey's chapter that of Evaluation–Basis (Winter 1982: 71–2), in which a writer first tells us what he or she thinks about something and then offers a rationale for that opinion. Obviously, a triple clause relation can be formed of Situation–Evaluation–Basis. Such a sequence sets out the writer's thinking very clearly—here is a fact, this is what I think about it, and this is why I think that—and as a result the writer's evaluation is open to challenge by a reader holding different opinions. Hoey argues that Chomsky's avoidance of such patterns of organization make it more difficult for the reader to challenge his point of view.

Winter (1982) and Hoey (this chapter; 1983) both make considerable use of question criteria in identifying clause relations. Given two clauses, the analyst interposes between them the question that the second clause best seems to answer. This question reveals the relation between the clauses. In the following invented example taken from Hoey (1983: 55), the question shows the relation between the first clause and the second to be 'Situation–Evaluation':

First clause   *I saw the enemy approaching.*
Analyst's question   **How did you evaluate this?** or **What did you feel about this?**
Second clause   *This was a problem.*

In this chapter, Hoey uses questions to demonstrate that evaluation in Chomsky's writing tends to be embedded in other information, because, although there is a good deal of evaluation, few if any clauses answer a question such as 'What do you feel about this?'

The reader may be puzzled as to why the references in Hoey's chapter appear somewhat dated. This is because it was originally written and published two decades ago. The chapter, with its numerous references to still earlier work by Winter and Hoey, demonstrates that interest in evaluation far predates its current, somewhat belated, entry into the mainstream of linguistic description. For these two scholars, evaluation was an essential concept in describing how naturally occurring discourse worked. Winter (1982: 4) commented that any clause gives 'two kinds of fundamental information': what is known and what is felt, and took this insight as his starting-point for grammatical description. It has taken the rest of the world of grammar a long time to catch up.

*   *   *

Chomsky as Rhetorician

There can be little doubt that the most influential movement in post-war linguistics has been that associated with Noam Chomsky and largely initiated by him in his work *Syntactic Structures* (1957). Until relatively recently it has been difficult to offer new ideas without using transformational-generative grammar as bearings; anyone who has tried to do so has been in danger of being dismissed as hopelessly out of the mainstream of linguistic thought.

Why has this been the case? A number of answers are possible to this question, and the likelihood is that more than one of them is in part correct. First, Chomsky claimed that a grammar should explain the creativity of language, not simply analyse a limited set of sentences. This claim has had the effect of diverting the energies of many linguists from corpus-bound studies to studies of a more speculative theoretical nature, by making the latter seem the more purposeful alternative.

Secondly, Chomsky ascribed to linguistics a more significant role in the world of knowledge. Whereas previously linguists had given attention to the essentially unexciting accumulation of information of a non-general kind about individual languages, Chomsky drew attention to the possibility of finding a system of formal and/or substantive universals underlying the apparent heterogeneity of languages and to the mentalistic implications for psychology and philosophy of such a possibility.

Such, I believe, in general terms would be Chomsky's answer to the question: why has his work exercised so great an influence? He might also acknowledge a third answer, though he would undoubtedly give it much less emphasis. His grammar, as proposed in *Syntactic Structures* and developed in *Aspects of the Theory of Syntax* (1965) and elsewhere, offered a theoretically elegant combination of old and new. The phrase structure component was a familiar idea to Chomsky's readers in an unfamiliar form. Likewise, transformations had been discussed by Zellig Harris as early as 1952; the way they were presented however in *Syntactic Structures* was novel. This meant that readers were not challenged on two fronts at once. They could take as read the set of structural descriptions that Chomsky employed and could therefore concentrate most of their attention on the strikingly original mathematically orientated way of arriving at such descriptions. In short, Chomsky filled his revolutionary new bottles with old wine.

A fourth answer is however possible which Chomsky would be less likely to acknowledge; in this chapter I seek to demonstrate that Chomsky is a skilled rhetorician whose chief rhetorical device is to make it difficult for a reader to support an alternative or opposing view to Chomsky's own without looking foolish, a claim first made in outline form by Botha (1973). Botha argues that the means whereby the transformationalists' arguments acquire persuasive power are to be found in eight strategies of persuasion used 'for purposes of persuading dissenting or neutral scholars to adopt or reject the point of view expressed by [the writer's] hypotheses'. Two of these strategies are:

(1) 'Inflate the apparent merit of your own arguments by emphatically calling them "striking", "powerful", "strong", "forceful", "convincing", and so on. Deflate your opponent's arguments by means of the corresponding antonyms.'

(2) 'Warn your opponent that if he did not accept your theoretical viewpoint, your data, or your arguments,
   (i)   then he would be guilty of irrationality and/or
   (ii) then your common field, as a field of research, would be destroyed.'

He notes that 'the nature and properties of these considerations, as they may be encountered in the field of transformational grammar constitute, however, the subject for a full-fledged separate study'. The present chapter represents a first step in that direction. I leave aside the falsity or veracity of Chomsky's views as such; it will be apparent that I feel he has at times cheated in his presentation of his arguments, but cheating in presentation of arguments is not a priori evidence that the arguments are faulty. My paper will have served its purpose if it encourages a more critical approach to Chomsky's discourses.

Evaluating Claims

I shall examine in some detail two passages from Chomsky's writings. The first of these is an extract from 'Formal discussion: the development of grammar in child language' in U. Bellugi and R. Brown (1964); the second is a passage from *Aspects of the Theory of Syntax* (1965). It is not maintained that these two passages are entirely typical; they appear to me to contain slightly more examples of the phenomena under consideration than is usual in his work. Nevertheless they are certainly not aberrations. A careful reading of any but his earliest writings will reveal many additional instances; examples will in fact be drawn from elsewhere in this discussion.

The first of the two passages, from Chomsky (1964*a*), is the following (the sentences are numbered to facilitate discussion):

(2.1)

[1] It seems clear that the description which is of greatest psychological relevance is the account of competence, not that of performance, both in the case of arithmetic and the case of language. [2] The deeper question concerns the kinds of structures the person has succeeded in mastering and internalizing, whether or not he utilizes them, in practice, without interference from the many other factors that play a role in actual behaviour. [3] For anyone concerned with intellectual processes, or any question that goes beyond mere data arranging, it is the question of competence that is fundamental. [4] Obviously one can find out about competence only by studying performance, but this study must be carried out in devious and clever ways, if any serious result is to be obtained.

[5] These rather obvious comments apply directly to study of language, child or adult. [6] Thus it is absurd to attempt to construct a grammar that describes observed linguistic behaviour directly. [7] The tape-recordings of this conference give a totally false picture of the conceptions of linguistic structure of the various speakers. [8] Nor is this in the least bit surprising. [9] The speaker has represented in his brain a grammar that gives an ideal account of the structure of the sentences of his language, but, when actually faced with the task of speaking or 'understanding', many other factors act upon his underlying linguistic competence to produce actual performance. [10] He may be confused or have several things in mind, change his plans in midstream, etc. [11] Since this is obviously the condition of most actual linguistic performance, a direct record—an actual corpus—is almost useless as it stands, for linguistic analysis of any but the most superficial kind.

[12] Similarly, it seems to me that, if anything far-reaching and real is to be discovered about the actual grammar of the child, then rather devious kinds of observations of his performance, his abilities, and his comprehension in many different kinds of circumstance will have to be obtained, so that a variety of evidence may be brought to bear on the attempt to determine what is in fact his underlying linguistic competence at each stage of development . . .

The second of these passages, from Chomsky (1965), is as follows:

(2.2)

[1] One may ask whether the necessity for present-day linguistics to give such priority to introspective evidence and to the linguistic intuition of the native speaker excludes it from the domain of science. [2] The answer to this essentially terminological question

seems to have no bearing at all on any serious issue. [3] At most, it determines how we shall denote the kind of research that can be effectively carried out in the present state of our technique and understanding. [4] However, this terminological question actually does relate to a different issue of some interest, namely the question whether the important feature of the successful sciences has been their search for insight or their concern for objectivity. [5] The social and behavioural sciences provide ample evidence that objectivity can be pursued with little consequent gain in insight and understanding. [6] On the other hand, a good case can be made for the view that the natural sciences have, by and large, sought objectivity primarily insofar as it is a tool for gaining insight (for providing phenomena that can suggest or test deeper explanatory hypotheses).

[7] In any event, at a given stage of investigation, one whose concern is for insight and understanding (rather than for objectivity as a goal in itself) must ask whether or to what extent a wider range and more exact description of phenomena is relevant to solving the problems that he faces. [8] In linguistics, it seems to me that sharpening of the data by more objective tests is a matter of small importance for the problems at hand ...

One of the first characteristics of these passages to strike the reader is the high traffic in evaluations of various sorts. The clause relation of *Situation–Evaluation* can be seen as the most fundamental relation in discourse organization (for discussion of this, see Winter 1977; 1979; 1982; 1994; Hoey 1979; 1983; and Bolívar 1986); the use of evaluations in themselves does not therefore distinguish Chomsky's style from those of other writers. What does make Chomsky's use of evaluations significant are (i) the quantity of them; (ii) the interweaving of them with the situational elements; and (iii) the presentation of them without basis.

The more normal practice in scientific argumentation is that either an evaluation is offered and then a reason for that evaluation and basis follow, or the situation is presented first and then evaluated. The effect of this is to enable the reader to question the evaluation.[1]

In the Chomsky passages selected for analysis, however, we find that the two patterns of *situation–evaluation of situation* and *evaluation–basis of evaluation* are less clearly present. The evaluation and what is evaluated are instead interwoven in a much more complex way, and this allows him to offer more such evaluations. In the first passage quoted above (Example 2.1) we have at a conservative estimate ten instances of evaluation; in the second, we have five. Examples of evaluations embedded in premodifier position within nominal groups are:

---

[1] Consider, for example, the following brief passage from Ullman (1962). '[1] Statements like "le mot n'est que par le contexte et n'est rien par lui-même" [footnote omitted] which are frequently heard nowadays are neither accurate nor realistic. [2] While it is perfectly true, and even a truism, that words are almost always found embedded in specific contexts, there are cases when a term stands entirely by itself, without any contextual support, and will still make sense. [3] A one-word title such as Tolstoy's *Resurrection*, Ibsen's *Ghosts* or Jane Austen's *Persuasion* can be heavily charged with meaning, and even such elliptical titles as Kipling's *If* and Henry Green's *Nothing* will conjure up some sort of idea.' Oversimplifying slightly, we can say that sentence 1 is evaluation, sentence 2 provides the reason for the evaluation, and sentence 3 provides a basis for the reason.

(2.3)

For anyone concerned with intellectual processes, or any question that goes beyond *mere* data arranging, it is the question of competence that is fundamental.

(2.4)

These *rather obvious* comments apply directly to study of language, child or adult.

(2.5)

The answer to this *essentially terminological* question seems to have no bearing at all on any *serious* issue.

In all the cases just quoted, the evaluation is not the main point of the sentence of which it is a part. The question that elicits Example 2.3, for instance, is not: *What is your opinion (or evaluation) of **data arranging***? nor anything like it. The evaluation of *data arranging* as *mere* is embedded within a nominal group with *anyone* as its head which is in itself part of a prepositional phrase functioning as adjunct. It would be difficult therefore for a reader to question it; likewise, the depth of its embedding in the sentence exempts Chomsky from the need to follow it with a basis. In short, the inclusion of his evaluations in such a form allows him to present a running commentary without at any stage forcing him to justify his commentary as he gives it. Also, where the evaluation takes the form of the premodification of a noun as opposed to the complement position in a sentence, it is more readily regarded by writer and reader as given information or common ground. It is therefore for this reason also less subject to careful scrutiny.

If we examine carefully the evaluations that thus avoid direct scrutiny, we find that in some cases there is more room for argument than is in fact being allowed. The phrase *these rather obvious comments* for example, in sentence 5 of Example 2.1, conceals a potential disagreement. The phrase refers to the comments that 'one can find out about competence only by studying performance, but [that] this study must be carried out in devious and clever ways, if any serious result is to be obtained'. But why are these comments obvious? Leaving aside the controversial nature of the distinction made between competence and performance, I would suggest that for any intelligent layperson who accepted the distinction it would be far from obvious that the data gained from the study of performance in a *direct* way would be useless in the study of competence, since the two are intimately related. The obviousness of the remarks only becomes apparent if the reader has already accepted the theory to which he or she is being encouraged to subscribe.

Why has a potentially contentious evaluation been deliberately defused of its power to create argument by its placement at a rank lower than the sentence? The answer seems to be that, for Chomsky, calling his comments *rather obvious* makes it more difficult for a potential opponent to oppose him. It is a classic case of the Emperor's new clothes gambit. It will be recalled that in Hans Andersen's tale two imposters persuade a whole population to see clothes where there is only nakedness by warning everyone that if they cannot see the clothes they are unfit for their posts or hopelessly stupid. The effect of the *rather obvious* is to make anyone who does not find the comments obvious suspect his or her own judgement rather than

Chomsky's and to make potential critics frightened of opening themselves to the charge of missing the obvious. I shall return to this point later.

Sometimes the effect of embedding the evaluation is to shield aspects of the theoretical framework from questioning. Consider the following sentence from 'Linguistic theory' (Chomsky 1966) which again has evaluation by premodifier (the emphasis is mine):

(2.6)
Repetition of fixed phrases is a rarity; it is only under exceptional and *quite uninteresting* circumstances that one can seriously consider how 'situational context' determines what is said, even in probabilistic terms.

As with the previous example, the embedding of the evaluation protects Chomsky from having to provide a basis for a contentious viewpoint; the evaluation might well be disputed by, among others, those who are interested in the adoption of social roles or exploring the mechanics of phatic communication. Such matters need not be of negligible interest to sociolinguists: the point is that they are to generative grammarians. Calling circumstances *quite uninteresting* where situational context determines what is said has the effect of removing the necessity of incorporating any contextual features in generative grammar. It also leaves unthreatened his contention that the problem of creativity is central to linguistic theory (Chomsky 1964*b*).

The presentation of these two evaluations is in such a way that evidence is not required to support them and that the reader is unable to focus attention on them without breaking the flow of the argument with which he or she is being presented. It would be a distortion of the facts, however, to suggest that all Chomsky's evaluations are of this submerged type, though many are. It is instructive to examine those in the two passages quoted that are not submerged, as it would be these that the reader might expect to be supported by a basis or to follow a situation. The first example in Example 2.1 is in the first sentence, repeated here as Example 2.7 :

(2.7)
It seems clear that the description which is of greatest psychological relevance is the account of competence, not that of performance, both in the case of arithmetic and the case of language.

Although it is not apparent from the extract quoted, this sentence in fact answers the question: *what conclusion can you draw about the relative relevance of competence and performance from the illustration just given (and how certain are you of this conclusion)?* and not the evaluative question: *what is clear?* The evaluation is therefore serving much the same function as a disjunct (such as *Clearly*) and is in no sense central to the sentence. As with the previous examples, therefore, the reader does not expect a basis to follow. It is worth noting at this juncture that this is a common formula in Chomsky's writing, usually used as it is here to reinforce a conclusion by making it seem subject to no doubt. Other examples, drawn from 'Current issues in linguistic theory' (1964*b*), are:

(2.8)

In any event, whatever the antiquity of this insight may be, *it is clear* that a theory of language that neglects this 'creative' aspect of language is of only marginal interest.

(2.9)

Perhaps this notion . . . is related to the equally strange and factually quite incorrect view . . . that current work in generative grammar is in some way an outgrowth of attempts to use electronic computers for one or another purpose, whereas in fact *it should be obvious* that its roots are firmly in traditional linguistics.

(2.10)

It seems natural to suppose that the study of actual linguistic performance can be seriously pursued only to the extent that we have a good understanding of the generative grammars that are acquired by the learner and put to use by the speaker or hearer.

The same basic omission is present in the relation that holds between sentences 7, 8, and 9 of Example 2.1. Sentence 8 is an evaluation as *not surprising* of sentence 7, which does not evaluate the truth but the degree of unexpectedness of the truth. Sentence 9 is the reason for this evaluation and also for the evaluation of the conference tape-recordings as *totally false*. This reason does not contain and is not followed by basis, though it might be argued that sentence 10 in part serves that function. Once again, the two evaluations are arguable, but in this case they are given further emphasis by the use of the intensifiers *totally* and *in the least bit*. Contrary to what is suggested, it would be surprising to any educated non-linguist that a record of people's speech gives a totally false picture of the conceptions of linguistic structure that produced that speech; as before, the evaluation is only unsurprising to those who have already accepted the theoretical approach being outlined. As with *rather obvious*, Chomsky's calling his claim *not in the least bit surprising* puts the onus on his opponents to demonstrate why their *surprising* claims should be listened to. In other words, Chomsky is saying of his own claim that it is the expected or the unmarked and therefore that alternatives need the greater justification.[2]

Evaluating Opponents

We have seen that for the most part evaluations supporting or protecting Chomsky's own thesis are given without basis. The same is true of those of his evaluations that attack alternative positions. We have touched on this already in our discussion of *rather obvious*. We must now examine this in more detail.

It has been observed that, in his attack on Skinner (reprinted in Fodor and Katz 1964), Chomsky introduced a new note into linguistic debate. There, however, his target was one man who had himself made large claims. It is regrettable that throughout Chomsky's later writing he adopts the same tone towards anyone whose view of linguistic theory or method is different from his own. In Example

---

[2] It is reasonable to argue that sentence 7 in part offers a basis for the evaluation in sentence 6, but since it is an evaluation in itself, this does not meet the objection being made.

2.1, there are six insults directed at any potential dissenters; in Example 2.2, which is only seven sentences long. there are seven. We will look at each in turn.

Sentence 3 of Example 2.1 refers to *anyone concerned with intellectual processes or any question that goes beyond mere data arranging*. There are two stings to this. First, if the reader is involved in data processing, he or she is dismissed as being involved in *mere* data arranging. The word *beyond* underlines the fact that Chomsky's opponents have already damned themselves by concerning themselves with far more trivial issues. Secondly, anyone who disputes the main claim of the sentence—that it is the question of competence that is fundamental—is laying him or herself open to the charge that he or she is not a person who is concerned with intellectual processes or any question that goes beyond mere data arranging. In short, anyone who disputes Chomsky's claim is a mere data arranger. This is the Emperor's new clothes gambit with a vengeance.

Essentially the same device has been used in the next three sentences. If a reader carries out studies of performance that are not devious and clever in their execution, then his or her results are not serious; anyone who disputes the claim is in danger of having his or her results not taken seriously. Anyone who attempts to construct a grammar that describes observed linguistic behaviour directly is attempting the absurd; anyone who defends such a position is doing the same. (The significance of *rather obvious* in this respect has already been discussed.) Exactly the same is true of sentences (11) and (12). Potential defenders of the use of an actual corpus are discouraged from speaking out by the charge that their type of linguistics is the most superficial kind; potential defenders of direct observation of performance are discouraged by the implication that they have not discovered anything *real*.

In the second passage (2.2), the attack is more obvious. The question that is posed in sentence 1 is first dismissed as *essentially terminological* and then not answered, although, to those who ask it, it represents a question about the fundamental validity of the whole enterprise of generative linguistics.[3] He evaluates, however, the answer he does not give as having no bearing on any serious issue. Thus anyone who pursues the question is interested only in trivial issues. Then he pursues the advice described by Trollope in *Barchester Towers*: 'Wise people, when they are in the wrong, always put themselves right by finding fault with the people against whom they have sinned'. Instead of answering the question 'which has no bearing on any serious issue', he suggests that those who pose it pursue objectivity at the expense of insight and understanding. We are told that *the social and behavioural sciences provide ample evidence that objectivity can be pursued with little consequent gain in insight and understanding* (sentence 5 of Example 2.2). No data are given, no papers quoted, no notorious examples held up to view. The statement is deemed self-evident. If this is difficult to justify, still more so is its sequel: *on the other hand, a good case can be made for the view that the natural sciences have, by*

---

[3] Botha (1973) is devoted to this question.

and large, sought objectivity primarily insofar as it is a tool for gaining insight (sentence 6). But no good case is made or even attempted; we are expected to take Chomsky's unassisted word for it. Finally, having challenged thus his challengers, Chomsky resorts to the Emperor's new clothes gambit once more. Anyone who persists in his concern at the generative grammarian's over-reliance on the intuition of the native speaker (usually the linguist himself) is liable to be branded one whose concern is for objectivity as a goal in itself rather than for insight and understanding (sentence 7).

Conclusion

In this chapter I have examined two factors, closely related, that enter into Chomsky's success as a rhetorician. Both had been delineated by Botha (1973), though neither was illustrated or described in any detail. It has been found that Chomsky uses evaluation both as a running supportive commentary on his own arguments and as a device for cowing opposition. In connection with the latter point I have argued that an absence of basis to back his more controversial evaluations is disguised by means of embedding and references to unspecified work. While these features are intermittent in all his later writings, they are almost wholly absent in *Syntactic Structures*; it is clear therefore that Chomsky's initial influence was not dependent on them. It is all the more to be regretted therefore that he felt it necessary to resort to such measures in his subsequent writings, particularly as his influence has been felt as much in matters of debating style as in content.

3

Corpus-Based Analysis of Evaluative Lexis

Joanna Channell

EDITORS' INTRODUCTION

* * *

This chapter presents examples of words and phrases (such as *fat, par for the course*, and *right-on*) which have connotations of positive or negative evaluation. Channell uses concordance lines from the Bank of English corpus to show how these connotations come about. Concordance lines bring together many instances of a given word from many sources, allowing us to observe the typical contexts of that word, in particular, the other words that it most usually occurs with. Channell demonstrates the importance of this collocational information and uses it to provide evidence for connotations that the reader may not have been aware of previously.

Channell uses the term 'pragmatic meaning' (in preference to 'connotation') for those aspects of meaning that are associated with how a word or phrase is typically used, rather than those which are inherent in the word or phrase itself. There are strong links between this research and earlier work on what Sinclair and, later, Louw (1993) refer to as 'semantic prosody'. The notion of semantic prosody (or pragmatic meaning) is that a given word or phrase may occur most frequently in the context of other words or phrases which are predominantly positive or negative in their evaluative orientation ('polarity' is the term that Channell uses). As a result, the given word takes on an association with the positive or, more usually, the negative, and this association can be exploited by speakers to express evaluative meaning covertly. A commonly quoted example is the phrasal verb *set in* (Sinclair 1991), which is typically used with a subject indicating something undesirable (an illness or bad weather, for example). Consequently, *set in* has connotations of negativity which can be exploited to hint at an attitude or feeling. For example, *the hot weather set in early that year* suggests that, for this writer, hot weather is something to be disliked, even though the writer does not say this openly.

One of the key points that Channell makes is that pragmatic meaning is often hidden from the intuitions of speakers of the language in question. (Most speakers of English are not consciously aware of the semantic prosody of *set in* until it is pointed out to them, even though it must be part of their daily language experience.) Not only is the information apparently hidden from introspection, but it is equally hidden from observation, if only one or two samples of the word or phrase in question are available. (We could not tell from the *hot weather* example above by itself that *set in* has the pragmatic meaning it does.) We need to have available a large number of instances of the word or phrase to appreciate the evidence for positive or negative evaluation. As Channell shows, such samples are most easily obtained and examined as concordance lines from a large corpus. (Channell's use of a corpus as a research tool may be compared with that of Conrad and Biber, this volume.)

Because pragmatic meaning is hidden from introspection, identifying which words have it can be a matter of chance: someone may just happen to come across such a word while studying something else. Chance is a poor basis for linguistic research, however. Channell's research, by contrast, is based upon a systematic study of all the most frequent lexis of English, carried out during the compilation of the *Collins* COBUILD *English Dictionary* (CCED) (1995). Pragmatic meaning is coded in that dictionary, and this gives Channell a comprehensive database from which to select her examples.

* * *

Introduction

The work reported in this chapter is intended to show how analysis of the evaluative function of a word or expression can be derived from concordanced examples extracted from a corpus of language data. I want to argue (and demonstrate) that analysis of evaluation can be removed from the chancy and unreliable business of linguistic intuitions and based in systematic observation of naturally occurring data.

In doing this I will argue not only that a corpus-based analysis produces a sound description of this aspect of language, but also that it allows observations which go beyond what intuitions can achieve, in revealing evaluative functions which intuitions fail to pick up (see Louw 1993 for similar points).

Having discussed examples, I will then briefly allude to the implications and applications of such work as well as outlining the theoretical questions raised.

Approach

In this work, the evaluative function is taken to be whatever carries the expression of the speaker's or writer's attitude or emotional reaction to the content of their text. The focus is on that function where it is carried by individual lexical items, or by semi-fixed expressions, rather than on examples where the function is carried by whole sentences or stretches of text (for example, the creation of implicatures which show attitude). A further narrowing of focus is that I shall discuss lexical items which encode evaluation as part of their meaning, alongside other features, rather than those whose overt and only purpose is to evaluate. The following two examples show items whose sole function is to give a subjective evaluation:

(3.1)

The Australian press thought he was an *idiot*. (*Guardian*)

(3.2)

I waver between wondering why everyone finds him so *scrumptious*, and finding him so myself. (*Independent*)

By contrast, in the next example, *self-important* conveys additional information apart from the disapproving evaluation:

(3.3)

They were, are, the most plodding, bloated, *self-important* slop-bucket in rock history. (Review of a band in a magazine on popular music)

In spirit this is broadly a Firthian programme, intended to be descriptive; and approaching the description of meaning through consideration of occurrences in context. Firth stated that: 'the complete meaning of a word is always contextual, and no study of meaning apart from a complete context can be taken seriously' (1935: 37).

Stubbs (1996: 22–78) provides a succinct account of the debt of current corpus linguistics to Firthian linguistics, which he concludes with the observation that: 'the detailed descriptive work now being done in corpus linguistics will bring far-ranging revisions to many received ideas in syntax and semantics' (1996: 49). He might equally have added pragmatics, since recent research, and the examples in this paper, make it clear that many pragmatic phenomena can only be revealed by study of a large corpus. They are not accessible to introspection and not visible from the study of single examples.

Unlike Firth, however, I make the assumption that broadly there are two aspects to the description of meaning such that:

semantics + pragmatics = meaning

(this is similar to Gazdar's formulation, 1979: 2). The encoding of attitude can be either semantic or pragmatic. In the case of *scrumptious*, it is semantic; in the case of *self-important* (discussed below) it is pragmatic, and present in addition to the semantic meaning, which is defined in the Oxford Advanced Learner's Dictionary (OALD) as 'thinking that one is much more important than one really is'. The type of meaning to be described is sometimes also referred to as connotation. This use of the term *connotation* is what Lyons (1977: 176) is careful to designate the 'non-philosophical use'. He defines the connotation of a word as 'an emotive or affective component additional to its central meaning'.

The analysis consists of two techniques taken from two different areas of language analysis. First, collocational analysis uses computational techniques to identify words which typically co-occur with the lexical item under investigation. Secondly, an adaptation of Conversation Analysis is used here to analyse the information about the meaning and function of an item which is observable from consideration of its particular effect on what follows in a text or conversation.

Data

The data are drawn from what was at the time 200 million words of spoken and written English in the Bank of English corpus,[1] which is used in the preparation of Collins COBUILD publications. The examples chosen for discussion are just a few from the many hundreds identified and analysed during the two and a half years when I worked on the preparation of the new Collins COBUILD English Dictionary (CCED 1995). (For more information on corpus work, see, for example, Barnbrook 1996; McCarthy 1990; Sinclair 1991; Stubbs 1996.)

Method

The method is 'bottom up' in the sense that to establish the evaluative polarity of an item researchers must have in front of them a large number of examples. Secondly, evaluative polarity is not usually accessible to intuition, so the researcher cannot start by 'thinking of an example' and then look for citations of it. Hence the observations here could only arise during a project (such as the compilation of a new dictionary) which involved looking in detail—and individually—at most of the lexis of current English. The team of CCED compilers followed a specific methodology for pragmatics (developed by Alice Deignan and me) which asked them to look for (among other things) evidence of positive or negative polarity in the concordances for any word, and to construct the relevant entry accordingly. Their work resulted in a large number of hitherto unrecorded and, often, unexpected observations about English. CCED (1995: pp. xxxiv–xxxvii) gives details about how pragmatic aspects of language are treated in the dictionary.

I will begin by discussing an example which has an obvious and well-known evaluative function.

Examples

EXAMPLE 1: *FAT*

In a British context, it is clear that the word *fat*, because of the learned prejudices of British culture in regard to body weight, is neither a neutral descriptor, nor a compliment. Table 3.1 shows a short extract from the concordance data for *fat*, sorted to show the next word to the right in alphabetical order.

---

[1] The number of words in the Bank of English is constantly increasing. At the time the research for this paper was done, the total stood at 200 million. In July 1998 it was 320 million. The Bank of English includes British informal spoken language, British, American, and Australian newspapers and magazines, books published in Britain and the USA, and radio broadcasts from Britain and the USA.

Use concordance examples for n-good specific items?

Table 3.1. Concordance examples for fat

I'll fall for that. My inner thighs are growing **fat**. Me and God I've been
chastise yourself for eating and end up feeling **fat**. If your hand — or your mind — moves towards
Well, I met with Stanley Jaffe, and he saw I'm no longer **fat**.' Still, she had to do a screen test, the
and toads. In the middle sits my duck, Jeffrey, sleek and **fat**, and utterly calm despite my sudden appearance
Schopenhauer residence chanting 'Fat and old, **fat** and old' mourning the sexy flowering of her youth?
the end-all? Not even the Ex smells bad? It's an ex with a **fat** ass? A squint? What are you, a moron?
at them with quiet eyes and an enigmatic smile. A short, **fat**, brown proprietor with a bald head and a gray
out across the front seat trying to coax out our big **fat** cat, Pooch. Pooch hates anything that involves
— whenever he went — from old Maria Ivanovna, a **fat** crafty old woman, or from her deputy anna
and equally bellicose Middlesex side. The once-**fat** Gatt says he threatens real business this summer
with a teasing grin. 'You're going to be the best dressed **fat** lady in town. Would you believe most of it is
into the dining room. We debated leaving, but a party of **fat** people beside us told us not to give up because it
fat people? A: It could be. I mean perhaps you should ask **fat** people. B: Do you think that's a reason that it
on the way out the door. Drive all the way down to that **fat,** pompous lunatic's castle on the hill. He checked
you can remember some of these — one is, 'Your mom is so **fat,** she on both sides of the family.
To the problem which broke up his marriage. 'I was a **fat** slob, a pig hooked on cocaine,' said one headline.
Bollag reporting: A pig shed, housing dozens of large, **fat** sows surrounded by their little piglets
FATHER: It is a wonder you don't get **fat,** the amount you eat between meals.

I invite readers to scan these lines and see what impressions they gain of the word *fat*. My analysis would be that:

(a) *fat* collocates with words which are negative descriptors: *old, ass, bald, slob, crafty, pompous*;

(b) that to be fat is undesirable is shown by structures which allude to *not* being fat (*end up feeling fat, it is wonder you don't get fat, he saw I'm no longer fat*);

(c) fatness is humorous (*best-dressed fat woman in town, your mom is so fat, she . . .*).

In all the examples where the item being characterized as fat is human, the evaluation is negative.

An important observation about evaluative functions can be seen from this word: that polarity can shift depending on the referent to which the attribute is being applied. In this case, where the referents are animals, it is fine to be fat (*dozens of large, fat sows surrounded by their little piglets—oh, how cute!*). Indeed, it may be very positive (*my duck, Jeffrey, sleek and fat*). Note also that where *fat* collocates with inanimate referents, it is also often negative, for example, *fat salary, fat profits, fat cats* (see Carter 1987: 53–4 for discussion).

These data show us concrete evidence for something which everyone living within a British cultural framework takes for granted, that for a person to be fat is to be unattractive and bad. This is of course not true of other cultures. So *fat* provides an example of a culturally agreed or culturally motivated evaluation, which depends on shared values within the culture. I have used *fat* as a clear example, in order to show how corpus data substantiate the intuition that some uses of *fat* are negative.

A large category of examples noted during our work on CCED is about personal behaviour. This is not wholly surprising, since as Thompson and Hunston propose in their introduction to this volume, evaluative language is concerned with the expression of individual judgement and socially defined notions of good and bad, and evaluation of personal behaviour is in many cases a matter of individual judgement. In particular, there is a large set of negative words which relate to a striking and perhaps definitional aspect of British culture and that is that the British are critical of any kind of self-importance or self-aggrandizement. The following example illustrates this in detail.[2]

EXAMPLE 2: *SELF-IMPORTANT/SELF-IMPORTANCE*

It is hardly necessary to show examples to convince readers of the awful disapproval with which British English speakers use the expression *self-important*. Here are a few examples (selected from 134 citations):

---

[2] Other items with similar evaluative functions include *grand, social climber, pontificate*. A related category are words and expressions which convey that someone has got more rewards than they deserve: *flavour of the month, get something handed to him/her on a plate.*

```
     the tender egos of a bunch of self-important reporters.
   boy—boy, insincere, overwrought, self-important, retro indie swill
head bobs forward and back in that self-important, self-adoring way
     the most plodding, bloated, self-important slop-bucket in
there is a swipe at David Owen: so self-important, so naked in his ambition
caught up in New York's alarmingly self-important social circles,
```

Negative items in the immediate linguistic context are:

nouns   tender egos, swill, slop-bucket, swipe
adjectives insincere, overwrought, self-adoring, plodding, bloated, naked (in his
                ambition)
adverbs   alarmingly

The negativity of each of these items could be demonstrated by a similar search for their own typical collocates. Hence we can see that part of what happens in evaluation (either negative or positive, but in this case negative) is that speakers and writers cluster negative items so that there is a mutually supporting web of negative words. Louw (1993: 172) finds that: 'in many cases semantic prosodies "hunt in packs" and potentiate and bolster one another'.

Returning to *self-important*, the features which come out are that the writer or speaker is deeply critical of the person described as self-important, because they act as if they are more important than the speaker judges they are. A positive judgement of possibly the same personal attributes could be achieved by such epithets as *confident, assertive, effective* and could well describe the same person— Lord Owen (a former British politician), referred to in the penultimate example above, has had marked success as an international negotiator, which would suggest that many people evaluate his qualities positively.

Having looked at two examples of lexis which have obvious and intuitively accessible polarity (in both cases negative) I now come to the first of my less obvious examples.

EXAMPLE 3: *RIGHT-ON*

Right-on appears to be a new usage, since it was not included in the 1989 edition of OALD or the 1987 *Collins COBUILD English Language Dictionary* (CCELD). It is in OALD (1995) with the following definition:

adj (infml) aware of and sympathetic to current social and political issues, esp involving groups who are not well represented: a right-on feminist.

Corpus data suggest, however, that the Oxford compilers missed something. In most examples *right-on* carries a negative evaluation, as in the following:

(3.4)
There are those on the side of the tediously right-on as well as with the yob squad who will regard this . . .
(3.5)
. . . very short hair, checked shirt, men's trousers, loads of 'right-on' badges with a strident, assertive personal style . . .

(3.6)

The Times says 'the right-on Ben Elton and Stephen Fry are about as funny as tofu', which I thought was rather severe . . .

(3.7)

April De Angelis's selection of right-on wimps and screwballs is . . .

(3.8)

I'm bloody sick of your right-on, wishy-washy, liberal idealism.

(The source of examples 3.4–3.8 is British magazines and newspapers, selected from 1,333 occurrences, frequencies range from 14 per million in magazines to 5.3 per million in *The Times*.)

These examples show a negative attitude to the referent to which right-on-ness is attributed. Collocates such as *tediously, strident, wimps,* and *screwballs* support this claim. However, the use of *right-on* seems more complex and more subtle than, say, *fat.* It names a political point of view with which one may or may not agree. In the above examples, the writers do not agree.

In the corpus data for *right-on,* some apparently positive examples appear on closer examination to be ironic or to be creating implicatures which accomplish disapproval off the record (cf. Louw 1993), for example:

(3.9)

. . . a re-release of their debut from last summer. Easy-going, right-on but brilliantly off-beat post-daisy age hip-hop, and . . .

Here, the presence of *but* indicates that 'to be brilliantly off-beat' is placed by the writer in pragmatic opposition to *right-on,* leading to the meaning that right-on-ness is not, by itself, a favourable attribute for a piece of music.

The following two examples are clearly positive uses of *right-on*:

(3.10)

Yoghurt is the right-on product for the forward-looking dairy trade. The mark-ups are restrained and health benefits well tabulated.

(3.11)

Virago is a triumphant combination of right-on thinking, impeccable literary taste and commercial know-how. Happy birthday! Here's to the next 20 years.

Where *right-on* collocates with other negative words, it carries a negative attitude to the political stance referred to. Where it is surrounded by a positive context, it reads positively. In the preponderance of negative instances in the Bank of English, what we are perhaps seeing is some evidence, rather more subtle than that usually cited, of the right-of-centre bias of the British media (the newspaper sample in the Bank of English is itself not balanced, since it includes more right-of-centre papers than left-of-centre ones—this however is itself a reflection of the relative numbers and positions of British newspapers).

The next word for discussion is a good example of negative polarity which does not appear to be open to conscious introspection. I have shown these data to several hundred people in different audiences and it seems that while people readily

accept (and add to their stock of conscious knowledge) that the word *regime* is negative, many report that they had not consciously realized it until they saw the data.

EXAMPLE 4: *REGIME*

The following definition, from OALD (1995) gives a definition of *regime* which
seems to accord with intuitions:

regime n (a) method or system of government: a socialist, fascist, totalitarian, military
regime.

Consideration of any single example in isolation suggests that this is an adequate
definition, thus:

... the collapse of Communist regimes in Eastern Europe (CCED)

However, once we move on to a large number of instances, something additional
emerges. *Regime* also includes in its meaning that a speaker disapproves of the government or system of authority so designated. Note that *regime* has two other
meanings, related to the first but not showing the same polarity: one which refers
to diets, fitness, exercise, and so on, and one about business management and
administration. Concentrating on the political meaning, the COBUILD corpus
revealed over 6,500 instances of *regime*. The most frequent left collocates for these,
in descending order,[3] are: '*military, communist, ancien, nazi, Soviet, Vichy, fascist,
present, Iraqi*' which from a British perspective represent those types of government which are generally disapproved of.

   Within Britain, *regime* is used to attack one's political opponents. The following
example reports political debate in the British parliament (Jack Cunningham is a
Labour politician and Mr Ashdown the leader of the Liberal Democrat Party. John
Major was at the time the Prime Minister and leader of the Conservative Party):

(3.12)
Jack Cunningham was left to complain that Mr Ashdown had said nothing new and
spent more time attacking Labour than John Major's discredited regime. (*Guardian*)

The following example is somewhat surprising, since it comes from the *Guardian*,
a newspaper which is usually sympathetic to the Labour Party:

(3.13)
The breakdown of services in the London borough of Lambeth was nothing to do with
underfunding but the result of years of political feuding, mismanagement and incompe-
tence by the Labour regime, according to an independent inquiry by Elizabeth Appleby
QC, who published her report yesterday.

A different kind of evidence that *regime* is a negatively loaded descriptor was
provided by a legal case in which the government of Singapore brought a con-
tempt of court action against the *International Herald Tribune* newspaper. The

[3] 'Left collocate' means a word frequently occurring immediately before the word under discussion.
'In descending order' means in order of frequency. Thus *ancien regime* is less frequent than *communist
regime* but more frequent than *nazi regime.*

paper's opinion page had carried an article which referred to 'intolerant regimes' and claimed that they use 'a compliant judiciary to bankrupt opposition politicians'. The article did not name any particular countries, but we must assume that the government of Singapore believed that it was being obliquely referred to, and that the reference was prejudicial to it. Defending himself in cross-examination, the paper's editor:

... said he believed the article referred to 'Asian communist and military regimes' such as China, North Korea, Vietnam or Burma, not to Singapore. He argued that the word 'regime' meant 'a system of government which is totalitarian or has major totalitarian characteristics'. He denied that it could be applied to democratic governments. (The *Guardian*)

Corpus evidence does not support the editor's analysis. What it does support is the notion that the choice of the word *regime* invokes a critical stance.

The next example for discussion is another case in which intuitions do not immediately suggest anything negative.

EXAMPLE 5: *PAR FOR THE COURSE*

I begin again with a single example and a dictionary definition.

(3.14)

She was about an hour late but I'm told that's about par for the course for her.(OALD)

be par for the course (infml) to be what one would expect to happen or expect sb to do. (OALD)

Introspection would suggest that the definition is adequate. This metaphorical use of *par for the course* derives clearly from its use in golf to describe a score which is the expected one for the golf course involved. In golf, therefore, it is a positive evaluation of someone's performance (though to be 'under par' is even better). Once we look at numbers of examples, however, a different picture emerges. The metaphorical uses have developed a new aspect of meaning, not derived from the golfing original. The following are all the citations found in the British Books corpus:

```
      and then she started wailing.' <p> Par for the bloody course,' the Duchess
      S African interference in Namibia—par for the course, despite that place's
an insubstantial presence in her life. Par for the course. <p> Study after
            vulture-like in the corridor—par for the course with RTAs. You won't
plays, the vicious infighting that was par for the course around a woman who
he took it with a flick of his wrist. 'Par for the course. I done this trip so
nights a week is quite acceptable and par for the course. Trying to break with
The third was out of order, which was par for the course. The fourth was on
missed it. This turns out to be about par for the course this night. When I
will being contested was pretty well par for the course too. Nobody expected
hers were not. Which had always been par for the course, according to her
A for sexuality and E for subtlety. Par for the course out here. (Would he
      and was, as a golfer might say, par for the course. Aysgarth smiled at
was cancelled at the last minute: par for the course. Athenagoras'
<o> Michelle seemed rather put out, par for the course, as I went outside
their pregnancy. Disturbing dreams are par for the course in pregnancy. It must
```

The actions evaluated here as 'par for the course' are the following:

> wailing, South African interference in Namibia, an insubstantial presence, vulture-like behaviour, vicious infighting, something which is out of order, something missed, a contested will, scoring E for subtlety, something cancelled, Michelle being put out, disturbing dreams.

Without looking at further context for any of the examples, it can be seen that *par for the course* appears to be restricted to contexts where an event or behaviour is being evaluated negatively. It does not itself provide a negative evaluation, but rather the evaluation of a bad event or circumstances as 'to be expected'.

The eleven examples of this expression in the corpus of spoken British English (frequency 0.5 per million) also show only negative evaluations. In speech it is used in two ways: either by the speaker to self-evaluate the point they have just made, or by a second speaker to offer their own evaluation of the first speaker's point. Where a second speaker uses *par for the course*, it has an affiliative function of expressing sympathy or agreement. The following example from a female speaker shows a self-evaluation:

(3.15)
C. And I think the worst thing I do suffer from is—harassment from single male guests in the hotel who think you're fair game. I mean I've had such crude comments lewd — comments just aimed at me since I've been stopping at the—hotel. And it's every single holiday I go I get it so I accept—it as sort of par for the course.

This shows that *par for the course* is a useful resource in the performance of what Boxer and Pickering (1995) call 'indirect complaints'. An indirect complaint is one where the addressee is not responsible for the perceived wrong as in the reported sexual harassment here. When an indirect complaint is performed, the addressee can use *par for the course* in their reply to show sympathy or understanding. The following two examples show this:

(3.16)
D. That was nasty wasn't it Eve
E. Yeah but it's par for the course [laughter]
(3.17)
[difficulties in printing a computer file]
F. . . . bombs the machine when you go to print. Soon as you hit er—'Okay' that's it. [laughs] Terminal. So erm I can only think there's something in the file that's doing it.
G. Oh shit. Well it's par for the course for today I think.
F. Is it. Oh dear. [laughs]
G. It's been a real shit day.
F. Oh well I'm glad somebody else is having one.

In the next example text, a conversation, *A* is attempting to persuade B to his point of view. Both work for a building society, and *A* believes it would be quite acceptable to ask for particular kinds of personal financial information in connection with applications for new accounts. *B* appears reluctant.

(3.18)

B. Well we could do it on a voluntary basis. I mean we can ask them if they would like to fill this form in. You probably can't make it compulsory. You might put people off you see.

A. I was just assuming that it would only be if it was sort of Mafia money—sort of stuff— People aren't really reluctant about giving—I mean this is fairly [B: Oh] rudimentary kind of information.

B. I don't know. Maybe—Maybe not. Maybe people expect to fill in f- lengthy forms [A. Mm]—th-these days if they open accounts.

A. It seems all sort of par for the course in a way.

B. Yeah. Yeah. Er.

A. —find out you've got a lot of accounts with the Mafia or something.

B. [laughs] I hope not.

A uses *par for the course* to support his own argument that 'people find this kind of thing normal' and to draw *B*'s contribution in as a support as well ('people expect to fill in lengthy forms'). *A*'s use is therefore affiliative, but in a more complex setting than those above. He needs to do repair work (because there is a disagreement) and this is shown by the hedging around *par for the course* and by his joke. *B* accepts the repair by laughing at the joke.

American English data suggest that the metaphorical use of *par for the course* is not as well established in US contexts and, in particular, is hardly used in books. All the examples, are, however, still negative contexts. Here are two out of nine from National Public Radio:

(3.19)

REPORTER. . . . needled Democrats noting that she was one of only two women ever to address the convention.

GOVERNOR ANN RICHARDS [Democrat, Texas]. And two women in 160 years is about par for the course. But if you give us a chance, we can perform. After all, Ginger Rogers did everything that Fred Astaire did. She just did it backwards and in high heels.

(3.20)

REPORTER. Lafayette really has gotten by with relatively little damage. I mean, we had 75 mile-per-hour gusts and there's leaves and branches all over the streets, and—and power is out. But, I mean, that's all kind of par for the course in a hurricane.

Returning to the British examples, there are a small number where *par for the course* occurs in a context which is apparently not negative and its meaning appears to be exactly that described by OALD. The three clear cases are all from the same newspaper (*Today*) and on the same topic (the entertainment industry) which raises at least the possibility that they were all written by the same journalist. In two of the three extracts, *par for the course* is used to attribute acceptability to a claimed 'normal' behaviour, which is then contrasted with a specified unacceptable behaviour (in the first case, blatant self-publicity, and in the second, marital infidelity).

(3.21)

For Claudia Schiffer, who has been publicising her autobiography and revealing lots of fascinating personal details, such as the fact that she once ate a whole bar of chocolate. A good plug is par for the course on this sort of exercise, but Ms Schiffer went further, insisting on appearing in most photos with her masterwork clamped firmly to her bosom.

(3.22)

In an interview last year, Pru spoke frankly about the temptations which accompany work and separation. 'As far as I know, Tim hasn't strayed,' she said, 'though I'd be very surprised to know for certain that he hadn't. I'm sure both of us have had lots of flirtations. That's just par for the course, isn't it? Tim would be extremely angry if he ever thought I'd been unfaithful—but he'd also be profoundly bored if he thought I never fancied anyone else.'

In both cases, it is possible that the writer/speaker in fact orients negatively to the described behaviour, and reveals this covertly through the choice of *par for the course.* Both 'a good plug' and 'lots of flirtations' are behaviours which some would find unacceptable.

We have seen that *par for the course* has an established association with negative evaluations which would allow writers to code in their evaluation without making it explicit. There is however no other evidence from these two texts that the writer holds a negative view. The third example is more clearly a positive evaluation on the surface, but again describes behaviour which some at least would be critical of:

(3.23)

Reinforcing his image as a sexual athlete, Jack Nicholson has been working hard in London . . . 'If Jack isn't in bed by 3am he always goes back to his hotel,' giggles one of the starlets who have danced attendance as his publicity caravan moved around town this week. All of which is pretty much par for the course for a high profile 57-year-old roisterer who's making darn sure his Jack-the-lad image stays intact. And, hell, why shouldn't a footloose superstar have a little fun now and again?

To summarize, therefore, we can note that *par for the course* has developed a meaning which, while still related to its parent use in golf, has departed from that because it is almost always used about events or behaviours which are reported as 'bad' and then claimed to be 'expected'.

Thus far, all the examples considered have showed negative evaluations, or situations where negative evaluations are taking place (although *fat* can also be positive). Here, to redress the balance, are two examples of expressions which evaluate positively, and again are not intuitively obvious as doing so.

EXAMPLE 6: *OFF THE BEATEN TRACK*

This expression refers to an area where not many people live or go. Rather than being a neutral descriptor, all the occurrences in the Bank of English indicate a positive evaluation, for example:

(3.24)

Colfiorito, at 760 metres, is cool in the summer, off the beaten track, and as a result becoming ever more popular with visitors. This fine hotel has every facility, including tennis-courts and the obligatory swimming-pool. (British Books)

(3.25)

My perfect day; Sophie Lawrence.

EastEnders star Sophie is appearing in The Rocky Horror Show at the Duke Of York Theatre, London. Where? 'I'd be living off the beaten track in the South of France, in an old stone farmhouse surrounded by meadows, in the hills near the sea.' (*Today*)

(3.26)

Aghios Georgios was off the beaten track—in fact there was hardly a track at all. The rough, loose-stone road gave our hire car some heavy stick. Escape. But that's the charm of this island. (*Today*)

For comparison, I have found two other expressions, with broadly the same cognitive meaning, but the opposite (negative) polarity:

Out in the sticks

(3.27)

[*Today* reporting a train breakdown]

But five minutes after leaving Nuneaton that also broke down. Regional Railways Central said: 'Passengers were stranded out in the sticks so it was not possible to walk them along the line or pick them up by road.'

(3.28)

[*Times* personal finance pages]

'We are finding that whereas properties right out in the sticks would have been snapped up a few years ago, nowadays some people are thinking twice about them.' Bedford reckons that the best bet is to buy a property . . .

In the boondocks

(3.29)

. . . any prolonged stint in those boondocks is pretty demoralizing.

(3.30)

. . . would rescue whatshisname from the boondocks and everything would go back to . . .

(3.31)

. . . from God-knew-where in the boondocks . . .

(3.32)

. . . rednecks from the boondocks looking for action.

My final example, again about social behaviour, introduces a further interesting angle on evaluative function, by considering how corpus study can reveal words and expressions which are in the course of changing their meaning to acquire a new sense or new polarity.

EXAMPLE 7: *TO ROAM*

Levinson (1983: 165–6) summarizes research on language change which shows that new senses for existing words often start as implicatures (i.e. as pragmatic aspects of meaning). However, he states that 'we do not know exactly how it works'. The current behaviour of the verb *to roam* may throw some light on the process.

Corpus data post-1988 shows it in a semi-fixed expression which exchanges the positive polarity of earlier uses for a negative one. I speculate that this represents a lexical change which is currently taking place.

Beginning with the long-standing uses, *roam* has somewhat similar definitions in both the 1974 edition of OALD and the 1987 CCELD:

roam walk or travel without any definite aim or destination over or through (a country, etc.): go — ing; — about the world; — the seas; settle down after years of — ing. (OALD)

If you roam an area or roam around it, you wander or travel around it without having a particular purpose. (CCELD)

From these, we can see that the word is neutral, in fact often positive, creating connotations of leisure, beautiful countryside, and so on. The current Bank of English shows clearly, however, alongside the well-established uses, the emergence of a new pattern, with a different meaning and a different set of connotations. This is the expression *to roam the streets*. In 1,020 occurrences of the lemma *roam* (i.e. *roam, roamed, roaming, roams*), there are 113 occurrences of *roam/roamed/roaming the streets*. Table 3.2 shows a sample of them.

The majority of these examples involve a negative evaluation of the activity described. Listing the nouns which are found as the subject of *roam the streets*

TABLE 3.2. *Concordance examples for* roam the streets

```
         potato peel and sawdust. Children  roamed the streets  searching for food.
           how many prostitutes actually  roamed the streets  then since the idea of
         three thousand vagrant children  roamed the streets  and docks ready for
      of armed men are reported to have  roamed the streets  attacking people and
  and return home immediately as mobs  roamed the streets  stoning cars and
        let him down completely. This boy  roamed the streets  until eventually he
    the ambling American servicemen who  roamed the streets  in twos and threes
          Public Morality Committee who  roamed the streets  of Riyadh in an effort
      last summer, about 60 teenagers  roamed the streets  randomly beating people
        the city as bands of looters  roamed the streets  during the night. By 9
  Hotel in Bangkok as bands of people  roamed the streets,  burning and looting
       fires. ABC reporter Steve Bell  roamed the streets,  talking to the rioters.
  Right-wing youth gangs and neo-Nazis  roamed the streets  again overnight for the
      As people left, vandals moved in  roaming the streets  and sometimes sleeping
     in particular who are out there  roaming the streets  right now..
  township schools to spend their days  roaming the streets  or joining marches.
   ve got packs and packs of wild dogs  roaming the streets,  which further is
  perhaps thousands of armed men now  roaming the streets  of the capital,
        here. The dog had been found  roaming the streets  with some very very
    er neutered which aren't gonna be  roaming the streets  anyway there'll
    how many 12 and 13-year-olds are  roaming the streets  and council estates,
      Africa when we have such bigots  roaming our streets.
  who spent the last years of his life  roaming the streets  and port and Cartagena
      would be indoors rather than out  roaming the streets  making up their own
     Nancy did not approve of her pet  roaming the streets,  but she did not want
      to 3:4, where she finds him after  roaming the streets  in the middle of the
   that while jobless stockbrokers are  roaming the streets  of London, their
   Some 27,000 classic cabs are still  roaming the streets  of Britain, 17,500 of
```

makes the point clearly: *prostitutes, vagrant children, armed men, mobs, looters, right-wing youth gangs and neo-Nazis, vandals, wild dogs, bigots.* Activities undertaken while roaming the streets include: *searching for food, attacking people, stoning cars, randomly beating people, burning and looting, rioting.* In the collocation *roam the streets, roam* is therefore seen to acquire the following characteristics which it does not have in its original uses:

(*a*) dangerous;
(*b*) threatening;
(*c*) disapproved of;
(*d*) purposeful.

That this change is currently happening is shown by the occurrence of a small number of examples where *roam the streets* does not have the negative characteristics which the bulk of examples have, for example:

(3.33)
ABC reporter Steve Bell roamed the streets, talking to the rioters.

This example is interesting because the reported situation makes *roam the streets* appropriate, while the referent in subject position does not. Notice however that this roaming is clearly purposeful.

(3.34)
. . . that while jobless stockbrokers are roaming the streets of London . . .

While the writer implies that for stockbrokers to be jobless is a bad thing, I doubt that s/he equates them with armed gangs or wild dogs. The following example is clearly not negative:

(3.35)
Some 27,000 classic cabs are still roaming the streets of Britain . . .

On the basis of these data, I would predict that *roam the streets* will settle in to having only a negative meaning and that positive uses will disappear. The next stage would be for all uses of the lemma *roam* to become negative.

Returning to Levinson's question—how does the process of change work?—it seems that it is gradual. The data show that most current writers are avoiding *roam the streets* when the described activity is positive but it is doubtful that any would be consciously aware of that. Those who use *roam the streets* in a positive setting could be hypothesized to be taking the verb *roam* and collocating it with the location *the streets*. The negative meaning is not clearly enough established for everyone to be aware of it (and we don't know that it will become so, though my claim is that it will). Currently the two meanings (for *roam the streets*) co-exist, but with the negative by far in the ascendancy. This would suggest that what we see is a snapshot of the process of change. Stubbs (forthcoming) points out further aspects of the process in that *the streets* (without *roam*) appears in many negative contexts (*a growing menace on the streets* and *not safe to walk on the streets* are two of his examples). The predictions made here will become testable against fresh corpus data at a later date.

Discussion and Conclusions

The examples I have described show a variety of evaluations, based on political views, moral views, and aesthetic judgements. The implications of these kinds of analyses are far-reaching in several related areas: for theories of lexical meaning, for psycholinguistic accounts of the mental lexicon, and, on the applications side, for dictionaries and language teaching. I will now briefly touch on each of these.

First, the method shows that the analysis and description of evaluative functions is possible in a systematic way. Without recourse to intuitions, quantitative data show clear evidence of where there is an evaluative polarity to an item.

On the theory of lexical meaning, it is disturbing to discover that important aspects of the use of lexical items are not open to conscious reflection, particularly when these concern something as important to meaning as positive versus negative orientation. The situation in fact brings lexis into line with syntax and phonology: theory recognizes that in those two areas, speakers manipulate rules of which they have no conscious knowledge (e.g. to produce the correct form of the plural morpheme in *dogs* versus *cats*). The lack of awareness seems perhaps surprising in connection with meaning, since underlying linguistic theory is the assumption that the act of meaning is a conscious one (and therefore *unlike* the act of constructing a grammatical utterance) and that therefore speakers will know why what they say means what it does.

What has been observed about lexical change implies that:

- the same word has different meanings for different speakers at the same moment; and
- speakers continue to learn new meanings and new uses for words they already know; and hence
- that speculating about the content and structure of the human mental lexicon becomes correspondingly more difficult.

Turning now to applications, the development work for CCED, on which this chapter is based, made it clear that the notion of evaluative function was central to the description of a sizeable but as yet unquantified proportion of words. We saw several examples of dictionary definitions which are incomplete because they fail to specify the polarity of a word or expression. I would argue that descriptions of lexical meaning, including those found in dictionaries, cannot ignore this aspect, or restrict it to a few items marked 'derog.', if they claim to be full descriptions of the items concerned.

The work also raises some uncomfortable questions for language teaching. Learners must be given information about the evaluative functions of words they learn (where relevant), which in turn means that teachers need access to correct information about these (Brown 1995 sketches the problems). Since we know that introspection is not just unreliable, but inadequate, this would suggest that serious improvements are needed in the description of vocabulary in textbooks, readers, and dictionaries.

Finally, the material in this chapter raises many questions which cannot yet be answered. The first and most crucial is: why are the evaluative polarities of many items not discernible from introspection? No possible reason, or explanation, has so far suggested itself. The fact itself adds substantially to the potential for language to be used manipulatively, in order to say things without really saying them, and this would suggest that research on such items could become a central focus for those interested in critical linguistics (cf. Stubbs 1997 for further examples and similar points).

Secondly, there is the observation that negative polarities seem more obvious, and more frequent, that positive ones. During the writing of CCED, compilers noted more than double the number of negatively loaded words to positively loaded ones. It is too early to know why that might be, or even if it is a substantive observation. It might be, for example, that compilers were more sensitive to negative items because the social consequences of an error with a negative item are much greater than those arising from misuse of a positive item. The whole area of evaluative language seems to require tying up with the notion of 'facework' employed by Brown and Levinson (1987) in their explanation of politeness.

Thirdly, how do speakers learn about the evaluative function of lexical items? It must be the case that frequency plays some role, particularly for those not open to conscious reflection, such that the journalist who wrote about classic cabs 'roaming the streets' had not yet seen enough examples of the negative use of *roam the streets* to have made the necessary adjustment to his or her mental lexical entry for *roam*.

Finally, in the business of theory building, it is customary to seek generalizations. This raises the question of whether there is anything in common between linguistic items which display evaluative polarities not accessible to intuition. On the evidence in this chapter, the conclusion is 'not so far' but I guess that is par for the course in the study of naturally occurring language.

Appendix: dictionaries cited

Collins COBUILD *English Language Dictionary* (CCELD) (1987). London: HarperCollins.
Collins COBUILD *English Dictionary* (CCED) (1995). London: HarperCollins.
Oxford Advanced Learner's Dictionary (OALD) (1995). Oxford: Oxford University Press.

4

Adverbial Marking of Stance in Speech and Writing

Susan Conrad and Douglas Biber

EDITORS' INTRODUCTION

＊　＊　＊

Conrad and Biber's chapter is a statistical study of three collections of texts: one of conversations, one of academic writing, and one of news reportage. In this corpus they identify adverbials with a variety of grammatical forms: mainly adverbs such as *probably*, prepositional phrase such as *in most cases*, and subordinate clauses such as *I think*. These adverbials express meanings associated with the speaker or writer's attitude, or stance, towards what he or she is saying. Three kinds of meaning are identified:

(1) epistemic stance, which indicates how certain the speaker or writer is, or where the information comes from (e.g. *probably, according to the President*);
(2) attitudinal stance, which indicates feelings or judgements about what is said or written (e.g. *surprisingly, unfortunately*);
(3) and style stance, which indicates how something is said or written (e.g. *honestly, briefly*).

Conrad and Biber are able to identify which meanings are most frequently found in each register, and which grammatical forms are most frequently associated with each meaning in each register. They can tell us, for instance, that adverbials of stance are more frequent in conversation than in academic prose or news reporting; that adverbials indicating epistemic stance are more frequent than any of the others, in all three registers; and that in conversation stance is most frequently indicated by an adverb, followed by clauses, followed by prepositional phrases. They also identify the most frequently occurring words and phrases in each category. For a teacher of English, for example, this information is immediately useful: if you are teaching learners how to express stance in conversational English it is important to know that the most useful words are *probably, of course, perhaps*, and *maybe* and that useful phrases include *I think* and *I guess*.

It is interesting to compare Conrad and Biber's use of a corpus with Channell's (this volume). Conrad and Biber work with corpora in which each instance of a particular meaning or function (the expression of stance) has been marked (tagged). They then use statistics to provide a comprehensive picture of how that meaning is expressed through adverbials in each register. Channell's starting-point, by contrast, is the individual word or phrase, and she reveals unexpected meanings by discussing sets of concordance lines. The outcome of Conrad and Biber's work is a broad picture of the most typical adverbial realizations of stance in various contexts. The outcome of Channell's work is a detailed picture of the stance (evaluations) associated with particular lexical items.

The two approaches complement each other, and not only because Conrad and Biber's focus is grammar whereas Channell's is lexis. In fact, towards the end of their paper, Conrad and Biber comment that their work has thrown up interesting observations about individual lexical items that would warrant further research using, presumably, a method similar to Channell's. Conversely, Channell's work identifies items that might fruitfully be subject to statistical analysis. Importantly, both approaches give us the kind of information that is not obtainable from intuition. We cannot calculate the relative frequency of a given set of words and phrases, as Conrad and Biber do, through intuition alone. And in many cases, as Channell points out, we cannot identify the connotation of a word through intuition alone.

*   *   *

Introduction

Over the last several years, linguists have become increasingly interested in the ways that speakers and writers convey their personal feelings and assessments in addition to propositional content. Such investigations have been carried out under several different labels, including 'evaluation' (Hunston 1994), 'intensity' (Labov 1984), 'affect' (Ochs 1989), 'evidentiality' (Chafe 1986, Chafe and Nichols 1986), 'hedging' (Holmes 1988, Hyland 1996), and 'stance' (Barton 1993; Beach and Anson 1992; Biber and Finegan 1988, 1989). Investigation of personal expression has also been conducted with a variety of complementary methodologies, ranging from detailed descriptions of a single text sample to empirical investigations of general patterns in large computer-based corpora.

In the present chapter, we apply corpus-based methods to studying the differing ways in which speakers and writers use adverbials to mark their personal 'stance'. We use the term 'stance' as a cover term for the expression of personal feelings and assessments in three major domains:

(1) epistemic stance, commenting on the certainty (or doubt), reliability, or limitations of a proposition, including comments on the source of information;

(2) attitudinal stance, conveying the speaker's attitudes, feelings, or value judgements;

(3) style stance, describing the manner in which the information is being presented.

We restrict our study of stance to grammatical devices used to frame a proposition.[1] For example, in Example 4.1,[2] the stance adverbial *maybe* is used to express the speaker's uncertainty about the following proposition (*she put grease in it*):

(4.1)
Maybe she put grease in it. (Conv)

The matrix verb or adjectival predicate controlling a complement clause can similarly be used to express speaker stance. Thus, in the following example the adjective *sure* marks the speaker's certainty about the following proposition:

(4.2)
I'm sure I've spoken to him. (Conv)

Other grammatical devices, such as modal verbs and some nominal expressions, can also be used to mark stance.

In the present study, we focus exclusively on adverbial markers of stance. By applying corpus-based analytical techniques, we are able to document the differing ways in which speakers and writers mark stance using the grammatical resources available in the adverbial system of English. These same techniques can be applied to studying the full range of stance features, but such a study is beyond the scope of this chapter.

One of the primary findings resulting from a corpus-based approach is that global generalizations regarding stance are inadequate. Further, it is not the case that stance is marked in spoken registers but avoided in written registers. Rather, each register has distinctive patterns of use: specifically, each register favours a different set of stance adverbials, prefers different grammatical types of adverbials, and tends to distribute adverbials in different clause positions. As we briefly show, these patterns of use can be interpreted functionally, in relation to the distinctive communicative characteristics of each register.

Characteristics of Adverbial Stance Markers

Adverbial stance markers can be characterized with respect to three major parameters: (1) semantic class, (2) grammatical realization, (3) placement in the clause. In addition, most stance adverbials are similar in having scope over an entire clause and presenting the speaker's attitude or framing towards the proposition in

---

[1] We thus exclude purely lexical expressions of stance, where an entire clause is used to directly express an attitude or feeling. For example, the following sentences clearly express personal feelings and judgements through the use of value-laden verbs, adjectives, and nouns: *I hate him and his cardigan.* (Conv); *You're so stupid.* (Conv); *What an absolute jerk!* (Conv). However, these examples do not illustrate the grammaticalized expression of stance: the use of a grammatical device to provide a personal framing for some other proposition.

[2] All example sentences given in the paper are from naturally occurring discourse. The register of the example is given in parentheses: Conv (Conversation); Acad (Academic Prose); News (News reportage).

that clause. However, we also describe a special sub-class of stance adverbial that has scope over a phrase.

In terms of their meaning, stance adverbials can be grouped into the three major semantic classes identified in the last section: epistemic stance, attitudinal stance, and style stance.

Epistemic stance adverbials provide speaker comment on the status of the information presented in the main clause. Under epistemic stance, it is possible to distinguish among several sub-classes.

(*a*) Indicating the degree of certainty or doubt concerning the proposition

(4.3)
Well *perhaps* he is a little bit weird ... (Conv)
(4.4)
About 12–20 pigs per pen is *probably* the ideal number ... (Acad)
(4.5)
Some potentialities for bettering rice yields by this method *undoubtedly* exist, but their magnitude remains unknown. (Acad)

(*b*) Commenting on the reality or actuality of the proposition

(4.6)
You can *actually* hear what she's saying. (Conv)
(4.7)
You're wise to lock it *really*. (Conv)
(4.8)
For a little while it was not clear that wave mechanics and matrix mechanics were different expressions of the same basic physical theory, but *in fact* that proved to be the case. (Acad)

(*c*) Indicating that the proposition is somehow imprecise

(4.9)
It seems to clean it up *if you call it that*. (Conv)
(4.10)
'We were both dancing and then she *sort of* fell over and went into a fit.' (News)

(*d*) Identifying the source of information, either specifically or by implication with words such as *apparently* and *evidently*

(4.11)
Egypt's nuclear power industry is still in the design phase, but *according to Mr. Kandil*, nuclear power was the only clean energy alternative for Egypt ... (News)
(4.12)
they just *apparently* built up huge quantities of dry bird droppings and these were staggeringly high. (Conv)
(4.13)
Durkheim's emphasis upon the importance of constraint is *evidently* directed primarily against utilitarianism. (Acad)

(*e*) Marking limitations of the information or identifying the perspective from which the proposition is true

(4.14)

In most cases the stacking of bands is such as to produce a monoclinic cell similar to that in tremolite . . . (Acad)

(4.15)

From our perspective, movement success is paradoxical. (Acad)

Attitudinal stance adverbials also include a wide range of meanings, conveying attitudes, feelings, value judgements, or expectations; but it is more difficult to group these into sub-classes. Examples include:

(4.16)

but *fortunately* I put it in a folder so the folder was destroyed. (Conv)

(4.17)

Most surprising of all, at a quarterly delegate meeting at the end of 1873, it was generally held that there could be no reasonable objection to their [women's] employment . . . (Acad)

(4.18)

The extent to which insect flight-muscles are developed is, *as one would expect*, correlated with the capacity for flight. (Acad)

(4.19)

Unfortunately, IPC as proposed is applicable to only a relatively small number of pollutants. (News)

(4.20)

Sensibly the presenter, matinée idol-manqué Richard Jobson, kept his dinner suit on. (News)

(4.21)

Amazingly, Adam walked away from the crash with just a graze on his left shoulder. (News)

Finally, style stance adverbials comment on the manner of speaking. That is, they state the way in which information is being presented or is meant to be understood, such as:

(4.22)

Honestly, I've got a headache. (Conv)

(4.23)

If his—desires were carried out we'd, well we'd be talking about thousands of pounds. *Literally*. (Conv)

(4.24)

More simply put, a feedback system has its inputs affected by its outputs. (Acad)

(4.25)

Briefly, the aim was to encourage particular schools to develop and implement learning resources plans . . . (Acad)

A cross-cutting descriptive parameter for stance adverbials is grammatical realization, as a single adverb, adverb phrase, noun phrase, prepositional phrase, finite subordinate clause, or non-finite subordinate clause. These are exemplified below.

(*a*) Single adverb as stance adverbial

(4.26)

A message *actually* belongs to exactly one communication act. (Acad)

(*b*) Adverb phrase as stance adverbial

(4.27)

I assume you're right Lynda, but *quite frankly* I don't know. (Conv)

(*c*) Noun phrase as stance adverbial

(4.28)

The enthusiastic housekeeper will *no doubt* be pleased to hear that the carpet retailers are going back to the twist. (News)

(*d*) Prepositional phrase as stance adverbial

(4.29)

I'll tell you *for a fact* that Steven won't go for Ollie tonight . . . (Conv)

(*e*) Finite subordinate clause as stance adverbial

(4.30)

She, she's in hospital here *I think*. (Conv)

(*f*) Non-finite subordinate clause as stance adverbial

(4.31)

We feel that if we did not pursue this second transplant it would be like, *to put it bluntly*, pulling the plug on her. (News)

Finally, most stance adverbials can occur freely in different clause positions: initial, pre-verbal, post-verbal, and final. We illustrate the positions here with occurrences of *actually* in conversation. In initial position, the adverbial is placed before the subject of the clause:

(4.32)

Actually I can't blame her. (Conv)

In pre-verbal position the adverbial occurs between the subject and main verb, including placement between an auxiliary and main verb:

(4.33)

Well I *actually* said thank you for that. (Conv)

(4.34)

I'll *actually* go round there. (Conv)

(4.35)

. . . he didn't *actually* do them. (Conv)

Post-verbal position has the adverbial between the main verb and an obligatory final element such as a subject predicative or direct object:

(4.36)

I'm *actually* cold. (Conv)

In final position, the adverbial follows all obligatory elements of the clause:

(4.37)

They look good *actually*. (Conv)

Certain stance adverbials are exceptional in often being restricted in their clause position. These adverbials, which are sometimes used on the clausal level, can also be used to have scope over a following phrase, and therefore must be placed just before the phrase. These include markers of imprecision, such as *sort of*, and even style adverbials, such as *literally*:

(4.38)
There's such . . . you know . . . *sort of* appalling need. (Conv)
(4.39)
At the centre, visitors can see not only the trees flourishing on *literally* the world's richest compost. (News)

We include these as stance adverbials because they mark stance, presenting the speaker's assessment of imprecision or style, even though they have more local scope in these cases.

Patterns of Use for Adverbial Stance Markers

The overview of stance adverbials summarized in the last section is itself corpus-based, presenting the distinctions that are identified through consideration of hundreds of adverbials in natural discourse contexts. However, given the appropriate analytical tools, a corpus can reveal much more about a grammatical feature, enabling investigation of the actual patterns of use in addition to structural descriptions. The following sections outline such an investigation, considering the distinctive ways that speakers and writers use stance adverbials.

CORPORA AND METHODS OF ANALYSIS

The analysis of stance adverbials reported here was carried out as part of the *Longman Grammar of Spoken and Written English* (Biber *et al.* 1999: chapter 10). We report findings based on two of the main registers in the Longman Spoken and Written English Corpus: conversation[3] and academic prose, with about 5 million words of text for each register. For some patterns of use, we also report findings from news reportage, since it provides a useful point of contrast to both conversation and academic prose.

Corpus-based grammatical investigations utilize a range of sophisticated computational techniques and analytical tools. For the Longman grammar project, the entire corpus was grammatically tagged and then analysed using a series of computer programs specially tailored for each set of grammatical features being studied. More detailed study often required interactive analyses based on smaller sub-samples from the corpus.

Adverbials are among the most difficult grammatical features to analyse using computational techniques, because they are so pervasive and flexible in their distribution, and because the same forms commonly serve other grammatical

---

[3] For this paper, the conversation and news reportage registers are comprised of British English.

functions. Therefore, we used an interactive text analysis program, similar to a spellchecker in a word processor. All adverbials were first identified in a 100,000 word sample from each register. Then, the interactive program cycled through each text, stopping when it reached an adverbial. The program prompted the user to select the correct codes for that adverbial. The interactive program provided an initial analysis of the use characteristics of each adverbial (e.g. semantic class, grammatical realization, and clause position). When the initial analysis was correct, the user simply accepted that code. However, the interactive program also provided a list of other possible analyses to choose from, so when the initial analysis was not correct, the user selected the option corresponding to the correct analysis.

Following the interactive coding of each stance adverbial, other programs and statistical packages were used to compile frequency counts and to analyse the association patterns among contextual characteristics.

REGISTER DISTRIBUTION OF STANCE CLASSES

Figure 4.1 displays the frequency of stance adverbials in conversation, academic prose, and news reportage. As this figure shows, there are almost twice as many stance adverbials in conversation as in the written registers.[4] This distribution fits

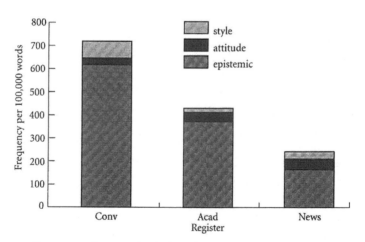

FIGURE 4.1. Frequency of stance adverbials in three registers

[4] Compared to some other grammatical features, stance adverbials are relatively rare in all registers. For example, circumstance adverbials (with meanings such as time, place, and manner) are over ten times more common than stance adverbials, occurring around 8,000 times per 100,000 words.

well with the expectation that conversational partners are personally involved with their messages and therefore commonly frame propositions with their personal attitudes and assessments. However, it is more surprising to discover that academic prose writers use stance markers almost twice as often as newspaper writers.

Epistemic stance adverbials are much more common than the other semantic classes in all three registers. In fact, the most common stance adverbials all mark epistemic stance; Table 4.1 lists all stance adverbials that occur more frequently than 10 times per 100,000 words in a register.

TABLE 4.1. *Most common stance adverbials across registers*

	Conversation	Academic Prose	News Reportage
Epistemic—doubt/certainty			
certainly¹	*	*	*
definitely	*	—	—
maybe	**	—	*
of course	***	*	*
perhaps	**	***	*
probably	******	**	**
Epistemic— actuality			
actually	*******	*	*
really²	***********(***)	*	*(*)
in fact	*	*	*
Epistemic—imprecision			
like	**	—	—
sort of	******	—	—
Epistemic—source of information			
according to	—	*	**
Epistemic—limitation/perspective			
generally	—	**	—

Notes:

[1] Each * = more than 10 per 100,000 words.

[2] Marks enclosed in parentheses denote occurrences which could, alternatively, be interpreted as adverbs of intensity. Such ambiguity occurs with *really* particularly in post-verbal position before a subject predicative, for example, *It's really wonderful* (Conv). In such cases *really* could be interpreted as meaning 'in reality' or as an intensifier of *wonderful.*

As Table 4.1 shows, there are relatively few stance adverbials that are notably common. However, some of these forms are extremely common in conversation. Because of this, there is very little diversity in the choice among stance adverbials in conversation, despite the fact that the use of stance markers overall is by far the most common in conversation. That is, four stance adverbials are extremely common in conversation, each occurring more than 60 times per 100,000 words: *prob-*

ably, actually, really, sort of. Taken together, these four adverbials account for about 70 per cent of all epistemic stance markers in conversation.

The frequent occurrence of these particular adverbials is consistent with several contextual characteristics of conversation, particularly the focus on interpersonal interactions, the conveying of personal assessments and opinions, and the lack of time for planning or revision which makes precise word choice difficult. Thus, participants often use *probably* as they give their assessments of situations and people and make future predictions:

(4.40)
It's *probably* what smelled. (Conv)
(4.41)
That's what I mean with that Jean you *probably* won't need vitamins. (Conv)
(4.42)
Yeah, but he could *probably* do a two till ten shift . . . (Conv)
(4.43)
He'll *probably* buy the Pioneer speakers. (Conv)

The actuality stance adverbials *actually* and *really*, on the other hand, are used to claim that what is being said is not just an opinion but a true reflection of reality:

(4.44)
A. Let's hope I've got my keys. My—
B. It's alright, I've got mine.
A. *Actually*, I've got yours. (Conv)
(4.45)
Catherine was *actually* a year lower than Suzannah. (Conv)
(4.46)
You don't *really* need to drink constantly. (Conv)
(4.47)
Well it's all called tea *really*. (Conv)

All three of these items also reflect the imprecision common in conversational discourse. They have a generalized meaning; the exact likelihood of *probably*, for example, remains indeterminate.

The other common stance adverbial, *sort of*, overtly marks imprecision. Typically, it is used to show imprecision in word choice:

(4.48)
So we're all *sort of* in the same, very close vicinity. (Conv)
(4.49)
Yeah you couldn't *sort of* get at anywhere near him to start with. (Conv)

It turns out that the same kinds of epistemic meanings are marked in academic prose. That is, academic authors pay considerable attention to overt assessments of certainty, actuality, and imprecision. However, unlike conversation, there is a relatively wide range of different epistemic stance markers used in academic prose, with no individual marker being extremely common.

(4.50)

Certainly it can be shown that for an isentropic expansion the thrust produced is a maximum when complete expansion to P occurs in the nozzle . . . (Acad)

(4.51)

There is *perhaps* no more important index of the social condition. (Acad)

(4.52)

Probably the conditions that would allow life to flourish anywhere in the universe do not differ much from those that have allowed life to evolve on Earth. (Acad)

(4.53)

It is, *of course,* of a complexity far beyond our power to solve. (Acad)

(4.54)

But the unexpected was what *actually* happened. (Acad)

(4.55)

These alignment rules mean that such computers do not *in fact* operate as pure byte-oriented machines . . . (Acad)

In addition, academic prose has a greater emphasis on marking the limitation of propositions, reflected in the higher frequency of the stance adverbial *generally*:

(4.56)

Generally, early varieties are insensitive or of low sensitivity while long-duration varieties are very sensitive. (Acad)

(4.57)

The mature females are large white worms with pointed tails which may reach 10.0 cms in length (fig. 56) whereas the mature males are *generally* less than 1.0 cm long. (Acad)

Finally, in comparison to the other two registers, news reportage rarely marks epistemic stance. The contrast with academic prose is especially interesting: while it is relatively common for academic prose to overtly flag propositions for their degree of certainty or actuality, news reportage more commonly reports propositions as simple fact. However, news reportage does occasionally include epistemic stance adverbials—especially in quotations from interviews, but also in explanations of past or future conditions which cannot be known with certainty, in analyses of events and people, and in imprecise reports of amounts:

(4.58)

'However, no one should be frightened,' she added. 'I would *certainly* stay the night without any fears.' (News)

(4.59)

And he insists: 'Paul is a nice lad, *really* . . . ' (News)

(4.60)

. . . detailed records of the security police, if they ever existed, have *probably* long since been destroyed. (News)

(4.61)

Upstairs in the Hampton Room Kawak was preening and strutting his stuff with a worried frown, pondering *perhaps* in which language to prepare a winner's speech. (News)

(4.62)

Maybe the Food Safety Bill will be useful damage-limitation: pre-empting public terror that almost nothing in the supermarket is safe to eat. (News)

It is also interesting to note that news reportage is the only register to make relatively common use of a stance adverbial marking the source of information: *according to*. This corresponds to the emphasis in news reportage on identifying the source of information. *According to* is used with sources that range from specifically named people and publications to sources identified only by their location:

(4.63)
By Friday night, *according to the prominent Paris-based Romanian human rights activist, Mr Mihnea Berindei*, the chain around the pastor's house was 200 strong. (News)
(4.64)
According to the French art magazine, Connaissance des Arts, the Picasso painting has belonged for more than 50 years to a collector who kept its existence secret—even from members of his family. (News)
(4.65)
According to Washington sources, the first step towards this new world order for steel has been agreed in principle by Brussels and Washington . . . (News)

Overall, attitude and style stance adverbials are much less common than epistemic stance adverbials. However, these classes are moderately common, with somewhat surprising distributions. Style stance adverbials are similar to epistemic stance adverbials in being most common in conversation, to emphasize that the speaker is being, among other things, 'serious', 'honest', 'truthful', 'frank', or 'hopeful':

(4.66)
No *seriously*, I can't I can't sing that song. (Conv)
(4.67)
Honestly, it's so hard when you make him cry. (Conv)
(4.68)
I don't think they'll be enough nuts *to tell you the truth*. (Conv)
(4.69)
The hangers could in fact go, go in there because that looked to be rather a good hanger, *frankly*. (Conv)
(4.70)
Hopefully something better will come along. (Conv)

It is more surprising that style adverbials are also moderately common in news reportage. In this register, they generally are used in articles which review sports or entertainment performances, and in quotations:

(4.71)
Frankly, few societies would have tackled even the choreography of this week's presentation, not to speak of the rest. (News)
(4.72)
Hopefully team owner Frank Williams—rumoured to be courting Ayrton Senna as Prost's team mate for 1994—will have noticed. (News)
(4.73)
However, Mr Leeder said: '*Quite honestly* I don't hold out much hope, but this is the first time the church has agreed to visit us . . . ' (News)

It is also surprising that attitude stance adverbials are moderately common in news reportage and academic prose, but relatively rare in conversation. In news, many of these occur in reviews, where the purpose of the text is largely to convey attitude:

(4.74)
As one might expect of such an assembly of talent, Sahara Blue is a stately, tasteful listen, but only at its best captures the poet's urgency and potency. (News)

(4.75)
Here, *unfortunately,* no restaurant area is yet available to allow customers to eat what they buy where they buy it, but the time spent waiting for a takeaway sandwich will be an invaluable education in Italian food. (News)

Quotes from interviewees also contain attitude adverbials:

(4.76)
Instructor Graham Marley, 33, said yesterday: 'It was a freak accident but *fortunately* Terry kept his bottle.' (News)

However, attitude stance adverbials occur in some news reports as well:

(4.77)
Ironically, before Monday night's murder in north Belfast, the only other woman to be killed by terrorists this year was singled out at a flat a short distance away. (News)

(4.78)
. . . 72 per cent of respondents think that a further cut in business rates would have a favourable effect on their company, though, *surprisingly,* 4 per cent believe it would have an adverse impact. (News)

Within academic prose, some author attitudes are overtly included in manuals and textbooks, and even technical reports may include comments about what is surprising or expected:

(4.79)
My account of political integrity takes the personification much more seriously, as if a political community really were some special kind of entity distinct from the actual people who are its citizens. *Worse,* it attributes moral agency and responsibility to this distinct entity. (Acad)

(4.80)
Fortunately, reheat systems for commercial supersonic transports are only required to produce about 10 per cent increase in thrust . . . (Acad)

(4.81)
In general, somewhat stout, short-strawed varieties are more resistant, *as may be expected,* but some of the long-strawed varieties are also resistant. (Acad)

(4.82)
Somewhat surprising, there are more accidents than near-accidents occurring in clear weather and in daylight. (Acad)

GRAMMATICAL REALIZATION OF STANCE ADVERBIALS

Although stance adverbials can be realized by many different grammatical structures (see 'Characteristics of Adverbial Stance Markers' above), only three of these are commonly used: single adverbs,[5] prepositional phrases, and finite subordinate clauses. Taken together, these three grammatical realizations account for over 90 per cent of all stance adverbials in these three registers. As Figure 4.2 shows, however, the three realizations are not at all equally common across registers.

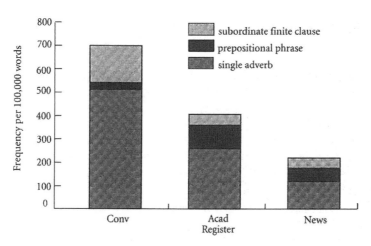

FIGURE 4.2. Grammatical realizations of stance adverbials

All three registers use single adverbs far more commonly than any other grammatical realization of stance adverbials. However, these forms are by far the most prevalent in conversation, where they account for 70 per cent of all stance adverbials. Single adverbs can express the meanings associated with all major semantic sub-classes of stance adverbials, for example:

(4.83)
You *definitely* pay the penalty don't you, for leaving your children? (Conv; epistemic—certainty/doubt)
(4.84)
The airline *actually* withdrew special security precautions shortly before the DC10 went down. (News; epistemic—actuality)
(4.85)
It's Friday today so everyone's . . . *sort of* relaxed and good. (Conv; epistemic— imprecision)
(4.86)
Evidently the degree of reaction increases markedly from root to tip of the blade. (Acad; epistemic—source of information)

---

[5] Included as adverbs are fixed, multi-word expressions such as *sort of* and *of course* in which the noun and preposition no longer have independent meaning. Included as prepositional phrases are expressions such as *in fact*, in which the component words maintain their individual meaning and modification of the noun can occur (e.g. *in actual fact*).

(4.87)
Generally, however, a functional model explicitly reflects the internal structure of the system. (Acad; epistemic—limitation/perspective)
(4.88)
But, *amazingly,* most men quizzed don't believe the conspiracy theory. (News; attitude)
(4.89)
Technically all definitions should be in 'iff' form. (Acad; style)

Table 4.1 also shows that the vast majority of the most common stance adverbials are single adverbs, including all four of the most common stance adverbials in conversation.

In contrast, stance adverbials realized as prepositional phrases are by far the most common in academic prose, although news reportage also shows a heavy reliance on these forms (accounting for *c.*25 per cent of all stance adverbials in both registers). Prepositional phrases perform a more limited range of semantic functions than adverbs, though they can be more elaborated. They are particularly useful in limiting the generalizability of claims or explicitly stating that the author's perspective is being presented—functions more commonly marked in academic prose than the other registers. Examples include:

(4.90)
On the whole, however, philosophers have ignored this possibility. (Acad)
(4.91)
The motivations or sentiments which lead individuals to participate in social activities are not *in most cases* coterminous with the functions of those activities. (Acad)
(4.92)
From our point of view the most important types of physical equilibria are phase equilibria . . . (Acad)
(4.93)
From our perspective, it went too far in narrowing the original Schelerian ambition to a sociological subfield. (Acad)

Surprisingly, finite subordinate clauses are by far the most common as stance adverbials in conversation, in contrast to the stereotypical expectation that conversation is structurally simple. The majority of these forms are comment clauses, which typically have a first person pronoun subject and are used to explicitly mark a proposition as the speaker's opinion or to convey some level of doubt:

(4.94)
It'll come out in the wash *I guess!* (Conv)
(4.95)
It's a good job I've got two. So I shall have one of them *I think.* (Conv)
(4.96)
She'll do that for a long time *I bet.* (Conv)

Other finite clauses show doubt or possibility:

(4.97)
Well *you never know,* Vic might even phone if she can get near a phone. (Conv)

(4.98)
Who knows I might even get a chance to try one of these days. (Conv)

Finally, a relatively rare but notable use of finite subordinate clauses as stance adverbials in conversation concerns clauses with the subordinator *because.* These clauses, rather than giving the reason for the proposition in the main clause, report the source of evidence for the speaker's comment, for example:

(4.99)
He's seriously deficient in what he should be learning *cos . . . he should know that at least.* (Conv)

CLAUSE POSITION OF STANCE ADVERBIALS

Figure 4.3 displays the proportional distribution of stance adverbials according to clause position. As this figure shows, stance adverbials tend to come early in a clause (initial or pre-verbal position), especially in the two written registers. From a processing perspective, these positions are 'user-friendly' in that they provide the author's framing for a proposition before actually presenting the proposition. In addition, stance adverbials in initial position often serve a secondary function as linking adverbials. This is particularly true for the adverbial *in fact* and for style stance adverbials, as in the following:

(4.100)
I can hear actually. *In fact,* I can hear everything you're saying. (Conv)
(4.101)
Through gossip we learn from other people's lives without undergoing the pain or danger of their experiences. *In short,* gossip is a chronicle of humanity. (News)
(4.102)
The two experimental set-ups were different, incompatible, and so could not act together. *In a word,* they were complementary. (Acad)

Stance adverbials such as these serve to intensify or condense previous statements. The adverbial marks not just the nature of the upcoming clause (e.g. that it is an actual fact or that it is being presented briefly), but also its connection to the previous discourse (and cf. Thompson and Zhou's chapter, this volume).

Stance adverbials in post-verbal position are also relatively common in academic prose and conversation. Often adverbials in this position modify noun phrases rather than whole clauses, functioning as markers of imprecision, for example:

(4.103)
This is *about* the fourth time we've played. (Conv)
(4.104)
[They] account *roughly* for 57 per cent and 43 per cent of group sales respectively. (News)

However, especially in clauses with *be* as the main verb and no auxiliary verbs, a variety of stance meanings are marked in post-verbal position:[6]

---

[6] As an alternative analysis, these cases can also be considered placement immediately after the operator (in this case *be*), and are thus similar to pre-verbal position when the adverbial follows an auxiliary verb.

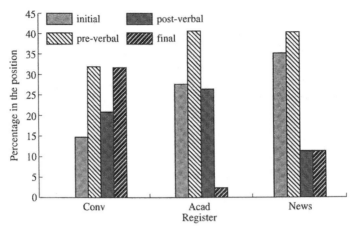

FIGURE 4.3. Clausal positions of stance adverbials

(4.105)
Well I think it was *actually* different places . . . (Conv)
(4.106)
. . . they were *definitely* not respectable in the eyes of most clerks. (Acad)
(4.107)
It is, *in a word*, more modernist. (Acad)
(4.108)
Characters are *apparently* motiveless, compulsive liars, who shy from eye contact. (News)
(4.109)
These are *literally* bandits. (News)

Surprisingly, stance adverbials in final position are particularly common in conversation. These are less efficient for listeners, since the proposition has been processed before hearing the speaker's stance; but they are convenient in on-line production circumstances, since they allow speakers to amend or qualify a proposition after it has been completed. Finite clauses are used most commonly in this position, such as those illustrated above and the following:

(4.110)
But it's hard luck *I suppose.* (Conv)
(4.111)
That one's quite hot *I think.* (Conv)
(4.112)
. . . treatments and preservation of the rain forest and all this sort of thing, *I imagine.* (Conv)

Overall, then, while it is true that many stance adverbials appear early in the clause, a variety of factors are associated with their placement, including the grammatical realization of the adverbial, the structure of the clause, the register of the text, and the primary and secondary semantic roles of the adverbial.

Conclusion

In this chapter we have provided only a brief introduction to the major characteristics of the adverbial marking of stance in English. Much more could be said about the details and complexities involved in the use of stance adverbials. However, even this overview provides valuable contributions to the study of stance marking—both in content and in methodology, illustrating the role of corpus-based analyses.

Perhaps most importantly, the findings presented here show the importance of register to analyses of stance marking. Across the three registers included here, there are distinct differences in the use of stance adverbials—in their typical meanings, grammatical realizations, clausal positions, and the most commonly used items. The different preferences of each register are associated with the communicative purposes and production circumstances of the register. Thus, generalizing from any one register to others or to English as a whole would be misleading.

In addition to demonstrating the differences among registers, corpus-based analyses are important in revealing specific areas that deserve more intensive study. For example, in contrast to both written registers, conversation was found to have a high frequency of particular stance adverbials marking doubt, imprecision, and actuality. In analysing occurrences of these stance adverbials, it is clear that they have important social functions beyond simply marking the speaker's stance. Markers of doubt such as *perhaps* and *maybe* are used in making suggestions, while actuality adverbs such as *really* and *actually* also serve to soften disagreements. Thus, the social roles played by such very common stance adverbials in conversation would be an interesting area for further investigation.

In sum, corpus-based analyses complement more intensive studies of particular texts. Studies such as the one presented here provide the background necessary for understanding both the structural variants of language features and the actual patterns of use of these features. Through corpus-based analyses we gain a perspective on what is truly distinctive about language use in particular contexts and identify useful directions for future investigations.

5

A Local Grammar of Evaluation

Susan Hunston and John Sinclair

We mentioned in the introduction to this volume the generally accepted view that, except in the case of modality, evaluation does not have its own grammar and can most efficiently be explored in lexical terms alone. This bias arises partly at least because, from the viewpoint of a general grammar of the language, evaluation appears parasitic on other resources and to be somewhat randomly dispersed across a range of structural options shared with non-evaluative functions. If, however, we start from the expression of evaluation and identify the set of structures that are involved, we may well end up with a more systematic and coherent picture. That is what Hunston and Sinclair set out to do in their chapter: to provide a local grammar of evaluation.

They argue, following Sampson (1992), that there are a number of areas of language which fit uneasily, if at all, into a generalized description of the grammar of a language. These are areas such as idioms and names which clearly have a patterning of their own but which can be handled within a generalized description only as exceptions or 'leftovers', because this patterning is frequently different in kind from that seen when the traditional perspective of the verb-centred clause is taken. For such areas, a local grammar is needed. Local grammars do not need to squeeze the description into ill-adapted general categories but use a categorization and terminology that is developed specifically for each area. The loss in generalizability is compensated for by the gains in qualities such as accuracy, transparency, and cumulative coverage.

Given that evaluation is, as is consistently argued in this volume, a central function of language, and yet general grammars have been unable to present a coherent account of it, it is clearly an ideal area to try out the concept of local grammars. Focusing on evaluative adjectives, Hunston and Sinclair devise highly specific and transparent categories such as *thing evaluated* and combine them with categories which are equally non-traditional but which have wider potential applicability, such as *hinge* (cf. Barnbrook and Sinclair 1995), to establish a set of patterns in which these categories occur. It is interesting to compare this chapter with that of Conrad and Biber (this volume), which also focuses on the use of a particular structural/semantic class, evaluative adverbials, though taking a rather different approach that works within traditional categories.

Hunston and Sinclair justify their approach primarily in terms of the applications in automatic parsing, but there are also potentially much wider implications both for linguistic description as a whole and for the development of a 'natural' grammar which reflects more closely than traditional ones the ways in which users experience patterning in language. In an age when decentralization and devolution are burning issues in the political field, it seems appropriate that a similar movement should be under way in the linguistic field. The search for overarching language universals can all too easily lose touch with its essential starting-point in the individual experience of language use (Toolan 1996); local grammars are one way of redressing the balance. It yet remains to be seen how far they can beneficially take over the functions traditionally served by generalized grammars: Hunston and Sinclair's chapter suggests that the inroads may be greater and more illuminating than is generally realized at present.

*   *   *

Introduction

This chapter argues that there are gaps in the coverage of grammatical structures achieved by a generalizable system of structural analysis and that these gaps require the development of an alternative approach in order to achieve a comprehensive treatment. The alternatives will be simpler than the general system, and therefore, since they are needed anyway, it is prudent to make them do as much of the analytical work as possible—an approach which finds support in the long-established tradition of work on sub-languages (see discussion below). Once embarked on this policy, links are readily established with speech acts and pragmatics, and the possibility arises of a novel kind of functionalism. The communicative behaviour of evaluation is used as an example of this kind of analysis. Examples are given of the patterns in which evaluative adjectives and nouns are used, and these examples are parsed to show how the categories of a grammar of evaluation might be mapped on to open text.

Grammars, Local Grammars, and Sub-languages

The grammar of a language offers, implicitly at least, to provide the categories and organization necessary to describe to a satisfactory standard any text that is composed in that language. In recent years a new resource has begun to be used in order to check how reliable grammars are at providing a categorization of anything that arises in the actual business of speaking and writing; this is the electronically held corpus. Corpora are now routinely used in training new software, and are likely to be increasingly used to compare, validate, and evaluate automatic analytical systems. Training means trying out prototypical software on a small corpus, studying the results and from there improving the performance of the software; the process is conducted cyclically.

Even when using the latest parsers, corpus grammarians continue to find that, once the software has done its best with open text, there is still a lot left over. By this they do not mean the errors and problems which can in principle be resolved by further development of the system, but the observation that there remain segments of text which will never be adequately described by whatever parser is developed for the main body of the text. This prediction that there will always be 'leftovers' can be confidently made because the organization of the leftovers appears to be substantially different from the organization of the rest. Sampson (1992) points this out forcibly, and refers to Fillmore *et al.* (1988) for supporting evidence of areas not covered by conventional grammar. The areas referred to include punctuation, variable idioms, speech representation, and special conventions for expressing such things as names, addresses, titles, amounts of money. For many of these leftovers, Gross's (1993) concept of local grammars and finite automata seems a useful suggestion. Gross argues that neither phrase structure rules nor transformational rules are suitable for specifying these structures, but that finite automata, with all their limitations, can be used. Indeed, the limitations are what make the automata suitable for these fairly modest pieces of description, on the principle that the best grammar is the 'simplest' one (Chomsky 1957: 14 n.) that achieves the targets set.

Both Gross and Sampson consider that the quantity of open text given over to such structures makes it necessary for them to be tackled in a grammar. Sampson says, and Gross hints, that these structures are neglected because they do not exhibit interesting generalities—many of them are social conventions reflected in the language, highly specific and unpredictable from any general perspective. They come low in the priorities of a grammarian seeking certain kinds of universal truths. User demands, however, provide a counterweight to these theoreticians' priorities. Language policy-makers and international funding agencies use grammars in applications such as translation, speech recognition, document retrieval, and so on. For this they demand systems that are near-perfect in terms of accuracy (better than 99.5%);[1] that work without human pre-processing or intervention; and that work at a high enough speed to be applied in real time (i.e. while the researcher waits). If general grammars cannot meet these criteria, local grammars might. Thus, since local grammars are going to be necessary, it is sensible to explore what can be done with them; since provision must be made for them in any comprehensive grammar, and since they are inherently simpler, weaker, more limited than the other kinds of rules, it is in the interests of efficiency to make the greatest possible use of them.

---

[1] Such a measure begs the question of how the results of analysis are assessed. For the purposes of this chapter it is sufficient to define accuracy as correspondence to the decisions taken by human analysts.

One descriptive area worth exploring briefly is the perplexed one of sub-languages. For thirty years, since Harris (1968), linguists have been trying to identify convincing examples, as Pearson (1998) records in a valuable critique. Although the original idea of sub-languages implied that they were something special, perhaps revealing the structure of scientific knowledge, the actual criteria seemed to overlap a lot with local grammars. Lehrberger's (1986) criteria, quoted by Pearson, are readily applied, say, to the writing down of sums of money. They are:

limited subject-matter;
lexical, syntactic, and semantic restrictions;
'deviant' rules of grammar;
high frequency of certain constructions;
text structure;
use of special symbols.

It is possible, then, to see the items described by local grammars as small (but not insignificant) sub-languages, and sub-language descriptions as extended local grammars. Since the search for genuine sub-languages in text of ordinary occurrence has proved singularly unsuccessful to date, there could be point in building up a view of specialist uses of a language from the humble levels of local grammars.

In Barnbrook and Sinclair (1995), it was claimed that the language of the definitions in the COBUILD dictionary series constituted a sub-language. It met Lehrberger's criteria with ease, apart from the 'limited subject-matter', which suggests that this criterion should be reassessed.

This idea of specialized content has been intuitively perceived as central to sub-language thinking from the start, but on examination it looks to be unreliable as a criterion. Certainly we may expect that small, specialized interest groups would gradually evolve distinctive ways of expressing themselves in talking and writing about their specialisms, partly no doubt for the sake of efficiency, partly for differentiation, and partly from unconscious copying from others. But the definition of a sub-language does not exclude widely accessible types of communication if they otherwise fit the specification. Newspaper headlines, sometimes offered as an example of a sub-language, support this position, since they range over the whole of human experience. A general dictionary, too, has to span the sum of human affairs, and this seems to be a different matter from the kind of discourse that is used in it. There are specialized dictionaries which meet the criterion of limited subject-matter, but lexicography is not altered by a restriction on subject-matter. It would be strange if a dictionary of science, using the same defining techniques as COBUILD, should be considered as a sub-language, but not the general dictionary.

There are two reasons for pressing the claim that the 'full-sentence' definitions used by COBUILD constitute a sub-language, regardless of their subject-matter. One is that, since it is not the kind of register that was thought of as typical of sub-languages, its acceptance would widen the scope of sub-language argumentation; the other is that the definition sentences of a dictionary are by no means the only types of linguistic structure found within its pages. There are also statements about such things as the rules of pronunciation and word-class, notes on usage and sometimes etymology,[2] and examples of words in use. Therefore, in identifying the sub-language we are accepting that it is a selection from a more varied discourse, and has to be separated from it.

The original idea of a sub-language included, by implication at least, that it was a variety with its own integrity, used continuously on appropriate occasions; that it constituted the language of complete events, not that it was a recurrent style within a more general discourse. But the reality of text is that it does not remain strictly conformant to any set of sub-language constraints for long; specialist language and general are mixed together seamlessly. To avoid sub-languages being relegated to the margins of linguistic interest, it became necessary to pick out from a whole text stretches of text which constitute examples of a sub-language. Dictionaries use a wide range of language variety, some of it quite complex, and none sustained for any length of text—but the repetitive structure of a dictionary entry guides the user to expect the appropriate variety at each point. As a result the extraction of just the defining language from a dictionary is a simple job. In the case of the extraction of sub-language from text with a less pronounced surface organization, there is always the danger of circularity in the method.

We can now draw attention to the similarity between sub-languages and stretches of text that require local grammars. The distinction turns out to be largely a difference in the method proposed to describe them, rather than serious differences in the patterning to be described. If one prefers to adapt a general analytical tool to account for all instances of sub-languages, there will have to be so many adaptations and so much detail that is specific to each sub-language that one might eventually feel that the initial endeavour, to show that a single general grammar can account for all text, is fundamentally eroded. If, on the other hand, one opts for several local grammars, then a diversity of analysis is built into the grammar from the outset. Returning to the position taken by Sampson and Gross, we could accept that local grammars are necessary anyway, and consider how a virtue might be made of this necessity. Can local grammars offer descriptive features that are superior to general ones?

There is one important practical point to deal with before attempting an answer to this question. Stretches of text to be handled by local grammars have to be identified in some way, whereas a general grammar does not select (or at least should not select). So for each local grammar there will have to be a test applied to each text unit to see if it qualifies for analysis. We can predict that some units will be wrongly selected by more than one grammar, at least until the test procedures

---

[2] Each of these other fields qualifies as a sub-language also. The idea of them as sub-languages has fuelled a good deal of interest in the automatic extraction from natural running text of entries for dictionaries (Fontanelle 1995).

become very sophisticated. If a sentence which superficially has the same structure as a definition, but is not one, is analysed in this way, it appears to be simply a bad definition. We can use Barnbrook and Sinclair's instance 'A dog is a damned nuisance' to show this. As a definition it is regularly structured (the word *dog* is defined as *a damned nuisance*): the fault is in the initial assignment rather than the analysis itself. Ultimately, Barnbrook and Sinclair (1995: 17) envisage a battery of specialized parsers, each one analysing only those sentences which have a particular function, and each one using its own set of terms. In addition to these, routeing software would be needed to identify the function of each sentence and so to send the sentence to the correct parser.

Let us return, then, to the question of whether local grammars are superior to general grammars. The local grammar produced by Barnbrook and Sinclair (1995) offers an alternative analysis to the regular one; an analysis that is significantly different and is capable of being expressed as a finite automaton. Any qualifying sentence then has two analyses, one when its function (definition) is not taken into consideration, and one which takes as its starting-point that the sentence is a definition. On the one hand, sentences can be described by a general grammar that points primarily to their structural relations; this grammar will be very complex and powerful because it needs to cover all the general patterns. On the other hand the same sentences could have an alternative analysis once their discourse function is assigned; the grammatical analysis will be much simpler because of the selection process. There is little doubt which analysis will be the more useful and effective. To talk about a definition in terms of 'subject', 'verb', and 'object' is much less helpful than to talk in terms of '*definiendum*', 'superordinate', 'discriminator', and 'contextual residue' (see below for details of the analysis). The latter analysis is 'functional' in a different way from the tradition of functional grammars, and incorporates some valuable pragmatic parameters.

Functional grammars (Dik 1968; Halliday 1994) describe the internal functioning of the components of a grammar, how they relate to each other, and how they create units of meaning, but it is characteristic of the meaning so produced that it remains internal to the grammar. The use of a semantically suggestive terminology indicates the area of meaning and gives a rough guide to the operational sense of a choice, but it does not reach precision of description. Words like 'past', 'present', 'future', or 'active', 'passive', or even 'material process', 'goal', 'circumstance' have this quality; words (for English) like 'subject' or 'object' have lost most of their relevance. Categories such as these have a vast range of use; it is thus not surprising that their application is restricted to linguistic analysis itself. The difficulty that students experience when learning to use the terminology is evidence for its esoteric nature.

The prospect of an alternative analysis based on a local grammar for each type of sentence is that it will assign category labels that are far more transparent and trustworthy than the highly general ones. Hence it is worthwhile to explore how far the concept of local grammars can be extended at the level of the sentence.

Unlike the development of a general grammar, there is no onus on this investigation to achieve total coverage. A number of discourse types may be realized with such variety and overlap with each other that the development of a local grammar is not worthwhile, and a number of individual sentences may be too deviant from any pattern to be classifiable. But the gains from even a partially successful application of the local grammar make the investment of effort worthwhile.

In the remainder of this chapter we consider the language of evaluation. How do we recognize it, and describe it in a way that brings out its discourse function? The term is often ill-defined and much overused, and yet it is of great importance in human communication. There are two aspects to the categorization of language units—their constituency and their structural position. The second of these often overrides the first, as the example bogus definition above makes clear; if 'A dog is a damned nuisance' occurred in the definition position of an entry *dog* in a dictionary, one would have no choice but to accept it as a definition. Similarly, one view of spoken interaction is that each short exchange contains structural provision for an evaluation as a final element; after the main business of the exchange, to pass information, have a question answered, or a request or instruction complied with, there is an opportunity for participants to agree about what the exchange was worth to them. Often this element is no more than a simple acknowledgement or murmur of thanks by one of the participants, accepted by the other(s) by default; hardly strong evaluative language, but because of its structural position, interpreted as a positive evaluation.

In this chapter, however, we consider only the constituency aspect of evaluation. We offer a description of sentences that are likely to be interpreted as evaluations without recourse to evidence of their structural roles. Although this is only a partial picture, it is a start, and from it we may be able to assess the penetration of local grammars as alternative descriptive tools to the general grammar.

The Local Grammar of Definitions

The sub-language analysed by Barnbrook and Sinclair consists of the definitions used in the Collins COBUILD English Dictionaries. Specifically, Barnbrook (1995) developed a parser to analyse the definitions in the *Collins COBUILD Students Dictionary* (CCSD). These definitions use full sentences, of a kind that might be used spontaneously by a teacher or anyone else seeking to define a word for a learner. They might therefore be seen as a form of natural language, in contrast with the cryptic and highly conventionalized definitions found in traditional dictionaries (Hanks 1987: 116; Barnbrook and Sinclair 1995: 13). The human reader of one of the COBUILD dictionaries has no difficulty in identifying what is being defined (the *definiendum*) and what it is being defined as (the *definiens*), in effect paraphrasing the natural language definition into a virtual equation. We might abstract this simple equation as shown in Table 5.1 (though this represents only part of the information found in the definitions).

TABLE 5.1. *Definitions as equations*

Word	COBUILD definition	Equation
biggish	Something that is biggish is fairly big; an informal word.	biggish = fairly big
bloodstock	Horses that are bred for racing are referred to as bloodstock.	bloodstock = horses bred for racing
calve	When a cow calves it gives birth to a calf.	calve = give birth to a calf

In order to develop a computer program that would allow a machine to replicate this human skill, Barnbrook (1995) divided the COBUILD definitions into seventeen types (three of which are illustrated in Table 5.1), mapped functional terminology onto each part of each type, and wrote software which would parse each definition automatically. The equation referred to in Table 5.1 is expressed as a 'left-hand side', which contains among other things the *definiendum*, the thing defined, a 'right-hand side', which contains among other things the *definiens*, the definition, the two sides being connected by a *hinge*. The COBUILD definition of the first sense of *run* is analysed as shown in Table 5.2.

TABLE 5.2. *A parsed definition*

Hinge	Left-hand side		Right-hand side	
		Definiendum		*Definiens*
When	you	**run**	you	move quickly, leaving the ground during each stride.

Source: Adapted from Barnbrook (1995: 179).

In Table 5.2, *you* on the left-hand side is matched by *you* on the right-hand side. These matches are omitted from both *definiendum* and *definiens*.

A more detailed description of parser output is given in Barnbrook and Sinclair (1995). This paper does not include the terms *definiendum* and *definiens*, but in the examples below these terms have been added. For example, the definition *An **orbit** is the curved path followed by an object going round a planet, a moon, or the sun* is parsed as follows:

left-hand side:
    an   match₁
    orbit   headword—***definiendum***
    is   **hinge**
right-hand side:
    the   match₂
    curved   discriminator }
    path   superordinate }—***definiens***

followed by ⎫
an object . . . ⎬   discriminator ⎱
or the sun ⎭

The definition *If you* **apply** *a rule, system, or skill, you use it in a situation or activity* is parsed like this:

left-hand side:

if	**hinge**
you	match$_1$
apply	headword—***definiendum***
a rule . . . skill	match$_2$

right-hand side:

you	match$_1$
use	superordinate ⎫
it	match$_2$ ⎬—***definiens***
in a situation	discriminator ⎭
or activity	

(Adapted from Barnbrook 1995 and Barnbrook and Sinclair 1995: 32, 34)

Although Barnbrook and Sinclair developed their grammar and parser using only those definitions found in the CCSD, one of the eventual applications of their work lies in the automatic retrieval of information from non-dictionary texts. A computer could search, for example, technical manuals to find definitions and could convert them into equations of the type illustrated in Table 5.1, thereby producing a dictionary automatically. Investigations along these lines are currently being carried out by Pearson (1998). The local grammar would then be being applied, not to a set of sentences which naturally occur together and which are identifiable via the organization of the dictionary database, but to isolated sentences occurring here and there throughout a text.

Local Grammar and Evaluation

We have seen above that the sentence *A dog is a damned nuisance* is open to analysis in the terms of two local grammars. As a definition it is analysable as *definiendum, hinge, definiens*. To analyse it as an evaluation we might use the terms *thing evaluated, hinge, evaluative category*. Apart from that change in terminology, the operation of the parser would be essentially identical. Can we deduce from this easy transposition that evaluation will be as amenable to analysis with a local grammar as definition seems to be?

To answer this question, we have to remember the characteristics of definitions that made the project of parsing them automatically a feasible one. Definitions are expressed in a restricted number of patterns (as identified by Barnbrook and by Pearson). It is this restriction that qualifies the language of definition as a sub-language and that allows for automatic parsing.

Are evaluations restricted in a comparable way? We begin with the most straightforward case of evaluation: where an entity is attributed with evaluative qualities, through the use of an adjective, such as *This building is really beautiful*. Adjectives that might play this role are easily identified intuitively. The adjectives *beautiful, nice, great, interesting, terrible, despicable* and *important*, for example, are taken by most people to indicate evaluation, simply because it is clear that their meaning is both subjective and value-laden. As such adjectives do not constitute a closed class, however, it is not possible to program a computer with a list of them. Instead, for a search program to be able to recognize when an entity is being evaluated with an adjective, whatever that adjective is, we must be able to specify the patterns of language that are used in this way. Here are some examples (taken from the Bank of English) which illustrate the variety of patterns that the adjective *beautiful* occurs in:

(5.1)
[before a noun] She was a beautiful and considerate young girl.
[following a link verb] She is both beautiful and charming . . .
[with a comparator] She was just as beautiful as she had been 30 years before . . . I wasn't beautiful enough for the movies . . . I had forgotten how beautiful she was
[patterns with the superlative] . . . wintry Bosnia was at its most beautiful . . . He works in a winery complex that is one of the most beautiful in Australia . . . Elba is the largest and most beautiful of the Tuscan islands.
[patterns with 'about'] There is absolutely nothing beautiful about dying for a cause . . . there's a great deal that is beautiful about Ian Sellar's moving film . . . What's beautiful about lying in mud and acting like a cockroach on its back . . . [their] team embody all that is bright and beautiful about the game
[followed by a to-infinitive] Her face is beautiful to look at . . . it was beautiful to see the land so green after years of drought.

Recent work in corpus linguistics (e.g. Sinclair 1991; Francis 1993; Hunston and Francis 1998), has focused on the importance of patterns in the grammar and lexis of English. This work has culminated in two major surveys of words and their patterns, one focusing on verbs (Francis *et al.* 1996), the other dealing with nouns and adjectives (Francis *et al.* 1998). Two observations have been made: first, that every sense of every word can be described in terms of the patterns it commonly occurs in; and secondly, that words which share a particular pattern typically also share a meaning.

For example, the noun *invitation*, in the sense of a request to attend something such as a party or a meal, is often followed by a to-infinitive, as in *The ambassador has refused an **invitation** to attend the inauguration ceremony*. There are many other nouns which have this pattern, one sub-set of which indicates that a future course of action is being instigated or allowed. As well as *invitation* these include: *appeal, call, cue, incentive, instruction, leave, licence, mandate, plea, proposal, request, suggestion, warning*. As the *Collins* COBUILD *Grammar Patterns* series shows, this is not an isolated case but it illustrates a general rule of language: each word occurs in a limited set of patterns, and words which share pattern also share meaning.

Two things follow from this. First, it should be possible to specify, from the total range of patterns that adjectives occur in, the limited set of patterns that typically occur with evaluative words. Secondly, from those patterns and the adjectives that are used with them, it should be possible to distinguish between evaluative and non-evaluative adjectives. Provided we limit our discussion to evaluations which are explicit and which use typical evaluative words, we should be able to write a local grammar of evaluation.

Identifying and Parsing Evaluation: Some Examples

We consider here some patterns which are typically used to evaluate. Our aim will be to ask whether patterns like these can be used to identify evaluative adjectives and to demonstrate that it is possible to parse sentences which contain the patterns using a local grammar of evaluation.

FIRST PATTERN: IT + LINK VERB + ADJECTIVE GROUP + CLAUSE

This pattern (or rather, it is a collection of several patterns) begins with an introductory or anticipatory *it*, followed by a link verb, an adjective group, and a finite or non-finite clause (a that-clause, wh-clause, to-infinitive clause, or -ing clause). According to the metalanguage used in Francis *et al.* (1996, 1998), the patterns are expressed as *it* **v-link ADJ that**, *it* **v-link ADJ wh**, *it* **v-link ADJ to-inf**, and *it* **v-link ADJ -ing**. As Francis (1993) has noted, the adjectives that are used in these patterns belong to one kind of evaluative meaning or another. Examples include: *fortunate, heartening, splendid, wonderful; awful, stupid, terrible; important, necessary; common, odd, interesting, relevant, significant, surprising.* The thing that is evaluated is realized by the clause following the adjective group, and the adjective itself places the 'thing' into an evaluative category. We can show this partial parsing as in Table 5.3.

This pattern is clearly a good 'diagnostic' of evaluative adjectives, as all adjectives that occur in the pattern are evaluative. In addition, the parsing is straightforward; there is only one configuration mapping the pattern onto the parsing categories. The only problems are those caused by pattern concatenation: adjective patterns change when they follow verbs that also have patterns. For example, if an adjective such as *strange*, which has the pattern *it* **v-link ADJ that**, itself occurs as part of the pattern **V n adj** with a verb such as *think*, the pattern of the adjective is changed by omission of the link verb, as in *I thought it very strange that no one else had heard the news.*

TABLE 5.3. *Parsing first pattern*

		Evaluative category	Thing evaluated
it	**link verb**	**adjective group**	**finite or non-finite clause**
It	was	certain	that he was much to blame.
It	was	surprising	how many on that course had disabled children.
It	seemed	important	to trust her judgement.
It	was	wonderful	talking to you the other day.

SECOND PATTERN: *THERE* + LINK VERB + *SOMETHING/
ANYTHING/NOTHING* + ADJECTIVE GROUP + *ABOUT/IN* + NOUN
GROUP/-ING CLAUSE

This pattern begins with the 'dummy subject' *there*, followed by a link verb, followed by *something, anything*, or *nothing*, followed by an adjective group, followed by the preposition *about* or *in* and either a noun group or an -ing clause. Examples are:

(5.2)
There's something rather appealing about being able to spend the evening in a town.
There is nothing sacrosanct about this unit of analysis.
There is something ironic in seeing the Dalai Lama surrounded by burly security guards.
There isn't exactly anything romantic about trying to do a love scene under ruthless studio lights.
There is something very American about the National Archives collection of presidential libraries.

Its function is to give a subjective judgement about something, and this is typically a judgement of good or bad. Usually, then, the adjective in this pattern is an evaluative adjective, although nationality adjectives are also used. Nationality adjectives in this pattern have the sense of 'being typical of a national group' rather than 'being a citizen of a particular country', and are thus subjective. The adjective is often modified by an adverb such as *rather* or *particularly*. The 'thing evaluated' is always realized by the noun group or '-ing' clause following *about*, and the 'evaluative category' is always realized by the adjective group following *something*. By analogy with Barnbrook and Sinclair's (1995) analysis of definitions, we refer to the parts of the pattern that connect these two as the 'hinge'. We may present a partial parsing of the pattern as shown in Table 5.4.

How successful would a search program be that used the pattern in Table 5.4 to identify evaluative adjectives and to parse the sentences of this pattern that they occurred in? To answer the second question first, the parsing would clearly be expected to be very successful, as the configuration of pattern and categories is straightforward—there are no exceptions. As for success in identifying evaluative adjectives, it has to be said that whereas most of the adjectives that occur in this pattern are evaluative, many represent subjectivity though not necessarily a

TABLE 5.4. *Parsing second pattern*

		Hinge	Evaluative category	Hinge	Thing evaluated
there	link verb	*something/ anything /nothing*	adjective group	*about* or *in*	noun group or -ing clause
There	's	something	rather appealing	about	being able to spend the evening in a town.
There	is	nothing	sacrosanct	about	this unit of analysis.
There	is	something	ironic	in	seeing the Dalai Lama
There	isn't	anything	romantic	about	trying to do a love scene . . .
There	is	something	very American	about	the National Archives collection . . .

judgement of good or bad. The *American* example above is a case in point. In addition, it would be necessary to identify 'adverb' *American* as the subjective adjective, as this adjective is subjective only when modified. The same is not true of *appealing*—in that case the adjective is evaluative whether modified or not.

This pattern is very productive. Although some adjectives are used in it very frequently (e.g. *American, appealing, attractive, beautiful, British, comforting, compelling, curious, depressing, different, disconcerting, disturbing, endearing, English, equivocal, exciting, extraordinary . . .*), many, many more are found only once or twice in a very large corpus. Probably no corpus would ever be large enough to allow the grammarian to make a definitive list of the adjectives used in this pattern. This is even more true of a variant of the pattern, which has *nothing* instead of *something*, and which is often used with adjectives that do not normally have an evaluative or subjective meaning. A famous example comes from Douglas Adams's *The Restaurant at the End of the Universe* in which a character says of the End of the World, *There's nothing **penultimate** about this one!*

THIRD PATTERN: LINK VERB + ADJECTIVE GROUP + TO-INFINITIVE CLAUSE

In this pattern the adjective is followed by a to-infinitive clause. As linguists have often noted, the relationship between the subject of the main clause and the verb in the to-infinitive clause varies: with some adjectives, the subject of the main clause is also the (understood) subject of the to-infinitive clause (e.g. *John is eager to please*) while with other adjectives, the subject of the main clause is the (understood) object of the to-infinitive clause (e.g. *John is easy to please*). From the point of view of the pattern as evaluation, however, there is another parameter of variation: the adjective may be one that places a person or thing into an evaluative category (e.g. *Horses are **pretty** to look at, You are **right** to say that*) or it may be one that indicates a personal response to a situation (e.g. *Benjamin had been rather **overawed** to meet them*). The first type can be further subdivided. In most cases, the noun group at the beginning of the pattern is the thing evaluated, the adjective group realizes the evaluative category, and the to-infinitive clause indicates a restriction on the evaluation, as in *Horses are pretty to look at (but they are terribly dim)* or *People are slow to learn (but they never forget what they have learned)*. Examples of this type can be parsed as shown in Table 5.5.

TABLE 5.5. *Parsing third pattern (i)*

Thing evaluated	Hinge	Evaluative category	Restriction on evaluation
noun group	**link verb**	**adjective group**	**to-infinitive clause**
Horses	are	pretty	to look at.
The car	was	terrible	to park.
People	are	slow	to learn.
He	is	unworthy	to utter her name.
Certain women	were	appropriate	to join the trial.
This book	is	interesting	to read.

Some adjectives, however, indicate that a particular form of behaviour is morally right or wrong, foolish or wise, and the person who carries out that behaviour is only instantially good, bad, foolish, or wise, not inherently so. In these cases, the to-infinitive clause realizes the 'thing evaluated'. The noun group at the beginning of the pattern, which also carries some evaluation and stands in the place where the 'thing evaluated' is expected, may be termed the 'evaluation carrier'. The parsing may be shown as in Table 5.6.

TABLE 5.6. *Parsing third pattern (ii)*

Evaluation carrier	Hinge	Evaluative category	Thing evaluated
noun group	**link verb**	**adjective group**	**to-infinitive clause**
You	are	right	to say that.
I	wasn't	stupid	to go there.
They	would be	sensible	to say 'yes'.

The second case, where the adjective indicates a personal reaction, not a quality, is somewhat more complex, as the evaluation is not averred by the speaker but is attributed to the person identified in the first noun group in the pattern. The thing evaluated is indicated by the to-infinitive clause, and the adjective group indicates a personal response, that is, it indicates that someone is evaluating something, though the evaluative category is not named. The parsing may be shown as in Table 5.7.

TABLE 5.7. *Parsing third pattern (iii)*

Evaluator	Hinge	Evaluating response	Thing evaluated
noun group	**verb group**	**adjective group**	**to-infinitive clause**
Benjamin	had been	rather overawed	to meet one of the Billington family.
He	is	most anxious	to avoid appearing weak.

Again we can ask, how successful would a search program be that used this pattern to identify evaluative adjectives and to parse the sentences in which they occurred? The parsing here would be more difficult, as the configuration depends on the particular adjective. The search program would have to be given lists of adjectives that identified a sentence as belonging to the *You are right to say that* type or the *Benjamin had been overawed to meet the Billingtons* type, to differentiate these from the more common *Horses are pretty to look at* type. However, this pattern is also fairly productive, in the sense that a very large number of adjectives are used only occasionally in it. However large the corpus, then, it would be impossible for a grammarian to state absolutely all the adjectives like *right* and *overawed*. It is possible, however, (see Francis *et al.* 1998), to list the most frequent adjectives of that type. The parser might then be expected to make some, but not many mistakes. Similarly, the identification of evaluative adjectives could be done with some, but not total, success, in that two types of adjective, as mentioned above, occur with this pattern.

FOURTH PATTERN: LINK VERB + ADJECTIVE GROUP + THAT-CLAUSE

In this pattern the adjective is followed by a that-clause (with or without the word *that*). Most of the adjectives in this pattern indicate a personal reaction to a state of affairs (e.g. *amazed, angry, disappointed, envious, horrified, pleased, worried*), or someone's degree of certainty or awareness of something (e.g. *aware, certain, confident, doubtful, ignorant, sceptical*), or an attitude towards the future (e.g. *afraid, anxious, eager, hopeful, nervous, pessimistic, worried*), or a way of talking about a state of affairs (e.g. *adamant, categorical, definite, emphatic, insistent, resolute*). As a result, this pattern is most often used to attribute evaluation to someone. It may be parsed as shown in Table 5.8.

TABLE 5.8. *Parsing fourth pattern (i)*

Evaluator **noun group**	Hinge **link verb**	Evaluating response **adjective group**	Thing evaluated **that clause**
He	was	very angry	that she had spoken to to people about their private affairs.
I	'm	fairly certain	he is an American.
Doctors	were	optimistic	that he would make a full recovery.
He	is	adamant	that he does not want to enter politics.

There is a smaller group of evaluative adjectives that classify a state of affairs as desirable or not (*fortunate, lucky, unlucky*) or that indicate that something is true (*correct, right*). These may be parsed as shown in Table 5.9.

TABLE 5.9. *Parsing fourth pattern (ii)*

Evaluation carrier **noun group**	Hinge **link verb**	Evaluative category **adjective group**	Thing evaluated **that clause**
They	were	lucky	that we scored when we did.
You	are	right	that he didn't go to the apartment when he said he did.

FIFTH PATTERN: PSEUDO-CLEFTS

Pseudo-cleft clauses begin with *what*, a link verb, and an adjective group. This is followed by the verb *be* and a noun group or a finite or non-finite clause of some kind. The adjective group may be followed by a prepositional phrase, often beginning with *about*. Examples include:

(5.3)
What's very good about this play is that it broadens people's view . . .
What's interesting is the tone of the statement.

In the first example, it is debatable whether what is evaluated as *good* is the play itself or the fact that 'it broadens people's view'. We regard the second of these alternatives as being the case, on the grounds that if the second example were altered to read *What's interesting about this statement is its tone*, the thing evaluated would still be 'the tone' rather than 'the statement'. We therefore introduce the term *evaluative context* to classify the prepositional phrase beginning with *about*. The examples may be parsed as shown in Tables 5.10 and 5.11.

TABLE 5.10. *Parsing fifth pattern (i)*

Hinge	Evaluative category	Evaluating context	Hinge	Thing evaluated
***what* + link verb**	**adjective group**	**prepositional phrase**	**link verb**	**clause or noun group**
What's	very good	about this play	is	that it broadens people's view.

TABLE 5.11. *Parsing fifth pattern (ii)*

Hinge	Evaluative category	Hinge	Thing evaluated
***what* + link verb**	**adjective group**	**link verb**	**clause or noun group**
What's	interesting	is	the tone of the statement.

Another pattern with *what* attributes evaluation. In this pattern, *what* is followed by a subject-verb sequence, as in *What I find so amazing is that my Dad is a very strict Hindu*. This may be parsed as shown in Table 5.12.

TABLE 5.12. *Parsing fifth pattern (iii)*

Hinge	Evaluator		Evaluative category		Thing evaluated
what	**noun group**	**verb group**	**adjective group**	**link verb**	**clause of noun group**
What	I	find	so amazing	is	that my Dad is a very strict Hindu.

SIXTH PATTERN: PATTERNS WITH GENERAL NOUNS

In these patterns, the adjective modifies a general noun such as *point* or *thing*. The noun group is followed by a link verb and another noun group or finite or non-finite clause of some kind. The first noun group may be followed by a preposition phrase, often beginning with *about*. Examples include:

(5.4)
The surprising thing about chess is that computers can play it so well.
The important point is to involve them as much as possible in the decision.

In the first of these examples, we again find a context for the evaluation in the prepositional phrase with *about*. These examples can be parsed as shown in Tables 5.13 and 5.14.

TABLE 5.13. *Parsing sixth pattern (i)*

Evaluative category	Evaluative context	Hinge	Thing evaluated
adjective + general noun	***about* + noun group**	**link verb**	**clause or noun group**
The surprising thing	about chess	is	that computers can play it so well.

Note: It is of course essential to point out that in these as in other examples of parsing, the table has been simplified. There should be more columns so that the *evaluative category* is shown to be 'surprising', not 'the surprising thing'.

TABLE 5.14. *Parsing sixth pattern (ii)*

Evaluative category	Hinge	Thing evaluated
adjective + general noun	**link verb**	**clause or noun group**
The important point	is	to involve them in the decision.

How Adjectives Behave

The brief look at the patterns above gives reason for cautious optimism. It seems that patterns may be used to identify evaluative adjectives, although in some cases at least it seems that the search may not be 100 per cent reliable. Once a pattern with an evaluative adjective has been identified, it can be parsed, although the parser may need a considerable amount of information to do this, as adjectives with different meanings command different configurations. Before continuing to examine the various patterns that adjectives have, it is worth pausing to consider other aspects of adjective behaviour and asking how these relate to evaluation. The relationship appears to be far from simple. Features of behaviour are associated with particular kinds of meaning; some of these meanings are in turn associated with evaluation, but the correspondence is not one-to-one. For example, the feature of 'gradedness' is associated with comparison against a norm or scale. Gradedness is a *necessary* feature of evaluative adjectives (i.e. all evaluative adjectives are graded, e.g. *fairly interesting*) but it is not a *sufficient* feature (i.e. not all graded adjectives are evaluative, e.g. *fairly tall*). Clearly there is not necessarily a one-to-one correspondence between features of behaviour and evaluation. Here we will consider some features of adjective behaviour and discuss their relation to evaluativeness.

Affixes

Some affixes are sometimes, but not always, associated with evaluative adjectives. The prefixes *hyper-*, *ill-*, *mal-*, *once-*, *over-*, and *well-* , when used to form adjectives, appear to be overwhelmingly associated with evaluation (e.g. *hyperactive, ill-advised, maladjusted, once-famous, over-confident, well-adjusted*), as do the suffixes *-ant*, *-off*, *-proof*, *-rich*, *-ridden*, *-some*, *-stricken,*, and *-worthy* (e.g. *arrogant, badly-off, bullet-proof, mineral-rich, guilt-ridden, loathsome, famine-stricken, creditworthy*). Most of these adjectives are relatively rare, however. The following affixes are often, but not always, associated with evaluation: *-able* (the evaluative *admirable* but also the non-evaluative *arable*), *-ary* (*extraordinary* but *auxiliary*), *be-* (*befuddled* but *bereaved*), *-bound* (*class-bound* but *north-bound*), *dis-* (*discourteous* but *dissimilar*), *-free* (*crime-free* but *duty-free*), *-ful* (*beautiful* but *lawful*), *-headed* (*big-headed* but *bareheaded*), *-ible* (*accessible* but *collapsible*), *il-, im-, in-, ir-* (*illegible, immature, inadequate, irrelevant* but *informal, inbuilt, ingrowing*), *-ish* (*amateurish* but *feverish*), *-ive* (*aggressive* but *alternative*), *-less* (*flawless* but *childless*), *-ly* (*costly* but *earthly*), *-minded* (*bloody-minded* but *career-minded*), *near-* (*near-impossible* but *near-identical*), *non-* (*non-aggressive* but *non-human*), *off-* (*off-balance* but *off-peak*), *-ous* (*advantageous* but *continuous*) *sub-, super-, ultra-* (*subhuman, super-abundant, ultra-cautious* but *subsonic, supersonic, ultrasonic*), *un-* (*unacceptable* but *unpainted*), *under-* (*underdeveloped* but *undersea*), *-y* (*dirty* but *grassy*) (Information from *Collins* COBUILD *English Guides 2: Word Formation*).

Gradedness

An adjective which has comparative and superlative forms, and which is sometimes or often used with a grading adverb, such as *rather, fairly, more, most, so, too*, or *very*, is likely to be evaluative, though it is not necessarily so. An adjective which is not graded in these ways is unlikely to be evaluative. As mentioned above, gradedness indicates comparison, and comparison with a norm or scale is often a matter of subjectivity. Subjectivity is one of the contributors to evaluative meaning. When an adjective has two senses and is graded in one sense and ungraded in the other, the graded sense is often evaluative. For example, one sense of *original* is ungraded and not evaluative—*The original building was destroyed in the Great Fire*—another sense is graded and evaluative—*Newsweek called it 'the most original horror film in years'*.

There are several patterns that are associated with graded adjectives; here are some examples:

(5.5)
He looks much too *young* to be a grandfather/for parenthood.
Their relationship was *strong* enough to accommodate a mistake [or for anything].
It's about as *interesting* as the Chelsea Flower Show.
The memories are more *important* than the music.
The race was one of the *greatest* in modern times.

They do not come more *stubborn* than the small landholders of Smithfield.
There's nothing *better* than natural light to bring out the colour of paintings.
In autumn it is unquestionably at its most *beautiful*.
Most of this work was middle-class propaganda of the *crudest* kind.

Many of these examples can be parsed using terminology we have already met
(see Tables 5.15, 5.16, and 5.17).

TABLE 5.15. *Parsing patterns with graded adjectives (i)*

Thing evaluated	Hinge	Evaluative category	Restriction on evaluation
noun group	link verb	adjective group with 'too' or 'enough'	to-infinitive or prepositional phrase with 'for'
He	looks	too young	to be a grandfather.
Their relationship	was	strong enough	for anything.

TABLE 5.16. *Parsing patterns with graded adjectives (ii)*

Thing evaluated	Hinge	Evaluative category	Restriction on evaluation
noun group	link verb	superlative adjective group	prepositional phrase
The race	was	one of the greatest	in modern times.

TABLE 5.17. *Parsing patterns with graded adjectives (iii)*

Thing evaluated	Hinge	*at*	possessive	Evaluative category
noun group	link verb			superlative adjective group
It	is	at	its	most beautiful.

In some cases, greater generalization can be achieved by combining grammatical patterns into notional ones. In Table 5.18 the phrases *they do not come* and
there's nothing are treated as similar because they share the characteristic of negativity.

In some cases where comparatives and superlatives are used, two things are
effectively evaluated (see Tables 5.19 and 5.20).

Position

Adjectives occur typically either before a noun (the attributive position) or following a link verb (the predicative position). Some adjectives typically or always
occur only in one position or the other (*an **electric** fire*; *the boy is **asleep***). As is well

TABLE 5.18. *Parsing patterns with graded adjectives (iv)*

Hinge **negative**	Evaluative category **comparative adjective group**	Hinge ***than***	Thing evaluated **noun group**	Restriction on evaluation **to-infinitive clause**
They do not come	more stubborn	than	the small landholders of Smithfield.	
There's nothing	better	than	natural light	to bring out the colour of paintings.

TABLE 5.19. *Parsing patterns with graded adjectives (v)*

Thing evaluated 1 **noun group**	Hinge **link verb**	Evaluative category **comparative adjective group**	Hinge ***as* or *than***	Thing evaluated 2 **noun group**
It	's	about as interesting	as	the Chelsea Flower Show.
The memories	are	more important	than	the music.

TABLE 5.20. *Parsing patterns with graded adjectives (vi)*

Thing evaluated 1 **noun group**	Hinge **link verb**	Thing evaluated 2 **noun group**	Hinge ***of the***	Evaluative category **superlative adjective group**	**general noun**
Most of this work	was	middle-class propaganda	of the	crudest	kind.

known, however, close association between adjective and noun indicates an intrinsic quality (e.g. Halliday 1994: 185). Evaluation is an extrinsic quality, being a matter of judgement, and this is why evaluative adjectives usually come before other adjectives if a noun is multiply pre-modified (e.g. **beautiful** *white scented blooms*). Only adjectives indicating relatively extrinsic qualities are used in predicative position. Typically, then, only non-evaluative adjectives are restricted to the attributive position. Evaluative adjectives are typically used in either position: *one of the most* **original** *works; this is all true but not very* **original**.

When it comes to parsing, the configuration involved in each adjective position is as shown in Tables 5.21 and 5.22.

TABLE 5.21. *Parsing attributive adjectives*

| Evaluative category | Thing evaluated |
adjective	**noun**
interesting	statistic

TABLE 5.22. *Parsing predicative adjectives*

| Thing evaluated | Hinge | Evaluative category |
noun group	**link verb**	**adjective group**
They	're	interesting.

A prepositional phrase may be used to attribute the evaluation to someone else (see Table 5.23)

TABLE 5.23. *Attributing evaluation with adjectives (i)*

| Thing evaluated | Hinge | Evaluative category | Evaluator |
noun group	**link verb**	**adjective group**	***to* noun group**
Colonel Lewis	is	interesting	to historians.

or attribution may be achieved through the choice of link verb (see Table 5.24).

TABLE 5.24. *Attributing evaluation with adjectives (ii)*

| Evaluator | Hinge | Evaluating response |
noun group	**link verb**	**adjective group**
She	felt	miserable.

Complementation patterns

Many adjectives are often or always used with a complementation pattern. That is, they are followed (when in predicative position) by a prepositional phrase, or by a finite or non-finite clause. For example, the adjective *afraid* has the following complementation patterns:

- prepositional phrase beginning with *of*, for example, *He was not afraid of death*;
- prepositional phrase beginning with *for*, for example, *I'm afraid for her*;
- that-clause, for example, *Everyone was afraid that he would kill himself*;
- to-infinitive clause, for example, *His son isn't afraid to speak up.*

The patterns with that-clause and to-infinitive clause have been discussed above. As a general rule we can state that the adjectives with complementation patterns typically indicate either subjective judgement or what someone feels (Francis *et al.* 1998). In other words, it is evaluative adjectives that have complementation patterns.

For example, adjectives which are followed by a prepositional phrase beginning with *for* include the following groups:

- those which indicate how someone feels about a situation: *afraid, grateful, sorry, thankful*;
- those which indicate a desire: *avid, desperate, eager, hungry, impatient, raring, thirsty*;
- those which indicate that someone or something is judged (in)appropriate or (un)ready: *adequate, convenient, eligible, equipped, fit, ill-equipped, inappropriate, necessary, perfect, ready, sufficient, suitable*;
- those which indicate fame or notoriety: *famed, famous, infamous, known, notable, noted, notorious*;
- those which indicate that someone is judged responsible: *answerable, liable, responsible*;
- those which indicate shortage and need: *pressed, pushed, strapped.*

Adjectives that are followed by the preposition *about* include the following groups:

- those which indicate how someone feels about a situation, for example, *afraid, angry, ashamed, bitter, curious, guilty, enthusiastic, furious, happy, jealous, keen, nervous, optimistic, proud, pessimistic, sad, sorry, unhappy, wary*;
- those which indicate how certain someone is of what they think or say, for example, *categorical, certain, confident, doubtful, positive, sceptical, sure, uncertain*;
- those which indicate a judgement about what someone says about a person or situation, for example, *bitchy, catty, charitable, cynical, flippant, horrible, insulting, polite, rude, right*, and *wrong*;
- those which indicate a judgement about how someone has reacted to a situation, for example, *brilliant, excellent, fine, funny, good, heavy, lovely, marvellous, nasty, nice*;
- those which indicate a judgement about someone's behaviour, for example, *careful, careless, cautious, considerate, dumb, gentle, harsh, irresponsible, reckless*;
- those which indicate a judgement about someone's mind, for example, *discerning, forgetful, intelligent, modest, sensitive, serious, tolerant, wise.*

It is clear that parsing these patterns would require the same distinction that was made above with respect to that-clause patterns and to-infinitive patterns, that is, a distinction between adjectives which express judgement on the part of the speaker or writer, and those which attribute a judgement to someone else. These can be illustrated as shown in Tables 5.25 and 5.26.

TABLE 5.25. *Parsing adjective complementation patterns (i)*

| Thing evaluated | Hinge | Evaluative category | Restriction on evaluation |
noun group	link verb	adjective group	prepositional phrase
The pitch	is	perfect	for cricket.
Davies	was	insulting	about the play.

TABLE 5.26. *Parsing adjective complementation patterns (ii)*

| Evaluator | Hinge | Evaluative response | Thing evaluated |
noun group	link verb	adjective group	prepositional phrase
The people	are	impatient	for change.
The 11-year-olds	feel	guilty	about the homeless.

Refining the Patterns: Prepositional Phrases

Several of the patterns described above have variants in which the evaluation is attributed rather than averred, but it is worth also making the general point that prepositional phrases beginning with *to* or *for* are often used to attribute evaluation. They are found particularly when the pattern begins with a 'dummy' subject, such as *it* or *what*, or with a subject including a general noun. The evaluation may be, and often is, attributed to the self. Here are some examples:

(5.6)
It was very clear *to me* that they knew what was going to happen.
What is important *to them* is their own results.

Other prepositional phrases, like the examples with *about* or *in* above, indicate an evaluative carrier, as in *It was very nice **of you** to meet us.*

A *Nuisance* Revisited

Although the main focus of this paper is adjective patterns and evaluative adjectives, it is interesting now to return to the example *A dog is a damned nuisance* and to see how the patterns associated with an evaluative noun—*nuisance*—might be parsed. Here is a random set of thirty concordance lines from the Bank of English at COBUILD, with *nuisance* as the node word:

```
1 apologize to Finch for being such a nuisance. But it was his grandparents
2 <FOX>Well no.<FOX>He's just been a nuisance.<FOX> It's an annoying it's
3 n wearing any device which is not a nuisance.' <H> Shown the door; Tony C
4 on my own. I'm just a trouble and a nuisance # <t> Her mother reached for
5 inherently non-serious but can be a nuisance and disfiguring. It is alway
6 ungry and frightened and they are a nuisance and can be dangerous. More t
7 eople. In fact school was a beastly nuisance and had no influence on me i
8 taff, who regarded him as an unholy nuisance and felt that 'Mamba' was un
```

```
 9 her ornamentals, it can be a darned  nuisance because so many of the best
10 aviation sanctions would thus be a  nuisance, but they would not amount t
11 T aims to cut down the millions of  nuisance calls made every year and t
12 ally work, they turned out to be a  nuisance for match anglers and we ar
13 franchise-holder would merely be a  nuisance. In the short term, other fr
14 s all very well, but I know what a  nuisance it is. And my experience is
15 ove all others and supersede local  nuisance-law-based ordinances. Farme
16 e word. Mucho macho harassment and  nuisance litigation later, the book
17 he discomfort score because of the  nuisance of the whole thing, and bec
18 sleeping on the beach and making a  nuisance of themselves by spoiling ou
19 ed an Oxford education without the  nuisance of having to travel to Oxfo
20 on us. But the flies were the only  nuisance on this perfect day # so c
21 requiring the council to abate the  nuisance or allowing it a reasonable
22 ou are a bit of a social misfit, a  nuisance. People trying to pay for s
23 ticism of the toilets to noise and  nuisance, plus complaints from local
24 e been libelled and on the abiding  nuisance represented by the uncorrect
25 added # The pirates were more of a  nuisance than anything else. But on r
26 fog, snags, and pirates remained a  nuisance, the Ohio became an open tho
27 be neighbourly, but it was a damn   nuisance to have to put on clothes a
28 g Gondolas are creating a terrible  nuisance we'd better stop them recor
29 ilities. Her headaches, although a  nuisance, were at a tolerable level
30 incomprehensible lyrics is a minor  nuisance which should be brought to t
```

Many of these lines can be analysed using the three basic terms mentioned above: *thing evaluated*, *categorizer*, and *evaluative category*. Lines 2, 4–7, 9, 10, 13, 20, 22, 25, 26, and 30, that is, thirteen lines out of the thirty, have the pattern represented by *A dog is a damned nuisance*. That is, they have the pattern 'noun group followed by link verb followed by noun group'. The parsing may be represented as shown in Table 5.27.

TABLE 5.27. *Parsing noun patterns (i)*

Thing evaluated	Hinge	Evaluative category
noun group	**link verb**	**noun group**
He	's just been	a nuisance.
School	was	a beastly nuisance.
The pirates	were	more of a nuisance than anything else.
. . . pirates	remained	a nuisance.

In lines 17 to 19, the noun *nuisance* is followed by a prepositional phrase beginning with *of*. The preposition is followed by either a noun group or an '-ing' clause. The noun group or '-ing' clause is the *thing evaluated*. The parsing may be shown as in Table 5.28. Finally, there is the pattern represented by line 14, *What a nuisance it is*, where the mapping of the terms of the analysis on to the pattern is different again (see Table 5.29). Lines 1, 3, 24, 28, and 29 would require more complex parsing but fit the same categories.

TABLE 5.28. *Parsing noun patterns (ii)*

| Evaluative category | Hinge | Thing evaluated |
noun group	of	noun group/-ing clause
. . . the nuisance	of	having to travel to Oxford.
the nuisance	of	the whole thing.

TABLE 5.29. *Parsing noun patterns (iii)*

| Evaluative category | Thing evaluated | Hinge |
noun group	noun group	link verb
. . . what a nuisance	it	is.

We now turn to patterns where more terms of analysis are needed. The first (line 27) includes an *evaluation carrier*, that is, a 'dummy' subject that appears to take the role of *thing evaluated* but which in fact simply anticipates the actual *thing evaluated*, which comes later in the sentence (see Table 5.30).

TABLE 5.30. *Parsing noun patterns (iv)*

| Evaluation carrier | Hinge | Evaluative category | Thing evaluated |
it	link verb	noun group	to-infinitive clause
It	was	a damn nuisance	to have to put on new clothes and go out.

The next pattern (see Table 5.31) introduces a new term, which indicates that, although it is the writer or speaker who does the evaluation, it is not that person but a third party who is affected by the thing that is evaluated. The term *person affected* will be used for this. In the case of the noun *nuisance*, the person affected is indicated by a prepositional phrase beginning with *for* following the noun (line 12).

TABLE 5.31. *Parsing noun patterns (v)*

| Thing evaluated | Hinge | Evaluative category | Person affected |
noun group	link verb	noun group	for noun group
They	turned out to be	a nuisance	for match anglers.

Finally, we need to take account of examples where evaluation is attributed. These are lines 8 and 14, so our partial analysis of line 14 is extended here (see Tables 5.32 and 5.33).

TABLE 5.32. *Attributing evaluation with nouns (i)*

Evaluator		Thing evaluated	Hinge	Evaluative category
noun group	**verb**	**noun group**	***as***	**noun group**
who	regarded	him	as	an unholy nuisance

TABLE 5.33. *Attributing evaluation with nouns (ii)*

Evaluator		Evaluative category	Thing evaluated	Hinge
noun group	**verb**	**noun group**	**noun group**	**link verb**
I	know	what a nuisance	it	is.

Five lines (11, 15, 16, 21, and 23) are still unaccounted for. These use *nuisance* in a technical, legal sense, rather than an evaluative one, and would therefore not be analysed by the evaluation parser.

Conclusions

This chapter has attempted to test the applicability of a local grammar to the concept of evaluation. Although we have not attempted to build the grammar as a computer model, we have perhaps amassed enough evidence to judge whether such an enterprise might be successful or not. We have shown, for example, that it is possible to identify some patterns whose primary purpose is to evaluate, or to attribute evaluation to another speaker, and which therefore tend to select evaluative adjectives. These patterns may be used as a 'diagnostic' for evaluative adjectives. It is likely that adjectives that sometimes appear in particular patterns are evaluative even when they are used in other patterns. It is not possible to be 100 per cent certain of this, however, partly because some adjectives have one or more evaluative sense(s) and one or more non-evaluative sense(s), and partly because some evaluative patterns are used creatively, making a non-evaluative adjective temporarily evaluative.

We have also shown that it is feasible to parse a range of adjective patterns so that participating roles, such as *thing evaluated* and *evaluative category* can be automatically identified. As with the grammar of definitions with which we began the chapter, such parsing works on any candidate sentence, regardless of whether it actually belongs to the target group. In many cases, however, the working of the parser depends on the particular adjective used, and it is therefore necessary to make distinctions, particularly between adjectives which indicate speaker judgement and those which indicate a feeling or response on the part of someone else. These distinctions would depend on lists of relevant adjectives being available.

The concepts of 'necessary' and 'sufficient' are useful when evaluating this approach to the identification of evaluation. Some indicators, such as gradedness, are necessary for evaluative meaning, but not sufficient. Conversely, occurrence in an evaluative pattern (plus gradedness) may be said to be sufficient for evaluative meaning, but not necessary for it. This means that the ways of identifying evaluation that we have discussed above may not capture every evaluative adjective. On the other hand, we believe that there are grounds for optimism, and that the construction of a local grammar of evaluation seems a very feasible undertaking.

This study of evaluation offers some support for the assertion that large quantities of text would be amenable to analysis using local grammars, and that such an analysis would be more simple, more precise, and more useful than an analysis using a general grammar. It would be simple in that each local grammar would use a limited number of terms, although the number of local grammars might need to be fairly extensive. It would be precise in that each local grammar could be stated in its own terms, without the need to fit in with more general statements. It would be useful because the terminology used would be reasonably transparent and would immediately relate the grammar and lexis of each part of the text to its discourse function.

6

Evaluating Evaluation in Narrative

Martin Cortazzi and Lixian Jin

EDITORS' INTRODUCTION

* * *

We mentioned in the introduction to this volume that there is a well-established tradition of using the term 'evaluation' in a relatively specialized sense to refer to a semantic and/or structural element of narrative; and Cortazzi and Jin's chapter is set within that tradition. They start from Labov's model of oral narrative, in which the presence of evaluation—signalling to the audience the 'point' of the story—is not only crucial in determining the perceived effectiveness of the story, but also criterial in distinguishing narratives from other stretches of talk such as reports or summaries. They discuss ways in which evaluation can be recognized, noting that it is frequently context- and culture-specific, and may depend as much upon performance as upon any features of the language itself.

They then move on to argue that the primary focus of many studies of narrative on evaluation *in* the text is too narrow, and needs to be complemented by an examination of the way in which the narrative is received and how the point of the narrative is understood—that is, the evaluation *of* the text. They point out that this level of evaluation is normally jointly constructed, by teller and audience; and that, as a result, socio-cultural factors play an extremely important role. They give examples to demonstrate that a narrative may be evaluated very differently by audiences from different cultures, both in the simple sense of whether they find the narrative successful, but also in the related sense of whether they understand the point of the story in the same way (or, indeed, whether they see a point to it at all).

As the final step in their argument for a stronger sense of context in the study of narrative, they examine the ways in which narratives are used as a basis for the evaluation of the teller—evaluation *through* narrative. People tell stories partly in order to project a particular persona—the telling of a story is inherently intended as an invitation to evaluate the teller; but of course audiences may also evaluate the teller on criteria that the latter does not intend or is not aware of. At the same time, evaluation through narrative can be seen from a different perspective: stories can be used to evaluate situations in which the teller and audience find themselves. The meaning of the story can only be grasped if its relevance to the context of telling is seen. A full understanding of the role of evaluation in this field needs to take all three levels of evaluation—in, of, and through narrative—into account.

Cortazzi and Jin's approach highlights the fact that the studies of evaluation in this volume have been consciously chosen to cover a broad spectrum. Towards one extreme we can place approaches such as that of Channell, who focuses on the behaviour of individual lexical items (evaluation as a context-driven aspect of word meaning). Cortazzi and Jin represent the other extreme: they focus on the behaviour of language users, in particular storytellers and audiences (evaluation as the act of evaluating).

* * *

Introduction

Evaluation is a major criterion of narrative. Conversational stories are highly structured linguistic productions and a teller's evaluation of the meaning of such a story seems to be part of this structure. This is particularly the case with those who use Labov's (1972) model of narrative structure. It means that judgements about whether a stretch of talk reporting personal experience is a narrative or not depend on whether the speaker uses evaluation. It means that perceptions of how a particular narrative is effective depend on how the speaker uses evaluation. Evaluation is held to be the key to narrative; through evaluation, speakers show how they intend the narrative to be understood and what the point is. This analytical position may be particularly useful in examining conversational stories because it avoids some problems of content analysis relating to the 'real' meaning. Rather, one can use narrative analysis to explore speakers' meanings by paying attention to their own evaluations. This classic stance towards evaluation in narrative emphasizes that speakers use evaluation to underline the point of a story and that this evaluative point is either about the teller's attitude, emotions, or character or is a general point about the way the world is (Linde 1993). However, it can be argued that Labov's model leaves out the relationship between teller and listener, that it does not fully consider features of narrative performance or culture, and that in general it does not pay sufficient attention to context. Since such criticisms affect how the evaluation element of a narrative is noticed, received, and analysed, it is important to evaluate the concept of evaluation in narrative in the light of wider socio-cultural dimensions.

This chapter examines the nature of evaluation in narrative by considering the linguistic structure of evaluation in narratives as they occur in natural conversation or as they are elicited in research interviews. We see how evaluation is carried out. We argue that the evaluation is not only *in* the narrative itself. Analytic considerations need to be broadened out to take into account how evaluation is negotiated between speaker and hearers. Evaluation is not always from the teller but can be from a story recipient. Relevant questions, therefore, concern who evaluates the narrative and how narrative responses affect the teller. Since these questions go beyond what happens in the narrative *per se* we need to consider evaluation *of* narrative in previous or subsequent talk. This can be further explored by looking at some consequences of narrative evaluation in wider contexts. Evaluation *through* narrative is a further important layer. Here tellers and their situations are evaluated through the narratives they tell.

We therefore propose three layers of evaluation: *in*, *of*, and *through* narrative. We argue that to evaluate models of evaluation in narrative we need to understand more about the multi-layered and multi-functional nature of narrative and how linguistic means are used in relation to socio-cultural contexts. Evaluating evaluation in narrative turns out to be highly complex. While evaluation in narrative is essentially about point of view, how we evaluate this depends on our point of view: as participants or observers, commentators or researchers. What are the values of the evaluator? Much depends on the disciplinary perspective which is adopted and perhaps the most appropriate strategy to evaluate evaluation is to adopt a multi-disciplinary approach. In examining all of this, we hope to answer further questions of an applied linguistic nature: what is the use of evaluation in narrative? Why is it worth evaluating evaluations?

In this chapter we first outline the linguistic structures of evaluation in narrative by looking at Labov's widely cited model of narrative analysis. We consider some issues of research methodology by examining the role of performance in elicited narratives. We show how evaluation in Labov's model can be used for applied research to examine tellers' cultural perspectives on the topic or content of narratives. We demonstrate that such applications of analysing the evaluations in narratives will be limited unless other more conversational models of narrative are taken into account. By considering evaluation in narratives in different contexts and cultures, we look at *who* evaluates *what*, *in* and *through* narrative, and *why*. Since much evaluation turns out to be negotiated, the original formulation of how evaluation in narrative works turns out to be problematic unless it is broadened. We make links with wider aspects of narrative such as the narrative configurations that are often used by qualitative researchers and academic writers when they report research. Finally, we reconsider the concept of evaluation in narrative in the light of the distinctions made about types of evaluation.

Evaluation *in* Narrative

Labov and his co-workers developed a sociolinguistic model of narrative that outlines the formal structural properties of oral stories of personal experience in relation to the social functions of narrative. They claim that a fully formed narrative has a six part structure (Labov and Waletsky 1967: 32–9; Labov 1972: 363–9; Labov and Fanshel 1977: 104–10; Labov 1982: 225–8). The abstract summarizes the point in advance or states a general proposition that the narrative will exemplify (*Something terrible happened to me . . .*). The orientation gives the setting, with details of time, place, and so on (*. . . at the weekend. I locked my baby in the car*). The complication makes up the main narrative sequence of events. It commonly includes a problem, dilemma or change, which gives the story interest. (*The baby* *was locked in the car. I didn't know what to do.*) The resolution describes the outcome, result, or solution (*they opened the car in the end*). A coda brings listeners back to the present time and concludes the narrative (*I'll never do that again*). The orientation, complication, and resolution can operate recursively and combine in more elaborate patterns. Not all of them are necessarily present in a narrative. The sixth element is the evaluation, which underlines the point of the narrative, revealing the speaker's attitude to what has been recounted and how the teller thinks it should be interpreted.

The evaluation is a salient feature of Labov's model. The model proposes that there are two social functions of narratives: a *referential* function, which gives the audience information through the recapitulation of the teller's experience, and an *evaluative* function, which communicates the meaning of the narrative by establishing some point of personal involvement (Labov and Waletsky 1967: 33). The evaluation makes the narrated events reportable, repeatable, and relevant. It wards off the withering rejoinder, 'So what?' and 'Every good narrator is constantly warding off this question' (Labov *et al.* 1968: 301–4).

An important question which cannot be warded off is, of course, how we know what the evaluation is. Before we look at the range of evaluative devices cited in the literature we will locate the evaluations in the two examples below. The main principle is that the evaluation marks part of the narrative, giving it prominence in any way that shows a departure from the local norm of the text. This relativity is important and is seen in Labov and Waletsky's original definition of evaluation (1967: 37) as 'that part of the narrative which reveals the attitude of the narrator towards the narrative by emphasising the relative importance of some narrative units as compared to others'.

Both of the following examples are transcribed oral narratives. In the first, the speaker is talking in casual conversation about the difficulties of being a single parent.

(6.1)

Narrative: The Baby in the Car
Something terrible happened to me at the weekend. I locked my baby in the car. The baby was in the car and so were the keys but I got out just for a moment and the baby was locked in. It was awful. I didn't know what to do. I went round the estate asking if anyone knew how to open a car door. It's a pretty rough area and they all looked round [gestures of wary looking round to see if anyone else is listening] and went 'Well . . . er . . . you could try this . . .' and 'I always . . . I mean, I've heard that you can do that.' Anyhow, a whole crowd gathered round all with keys and bits of wire in their hands. I was panicking but they kept telling me about all the different ways to open a car. They did it in the end, with a coat hanger. I'll never do that again.

The main narrative categories in this story are fairly clear. The evaluation could perhaps be seen in the last sentence as an emphasis on learning from potential mistakes. But this sentence is also a typical coda. If we look at the stressed words, then the extent of the complication or problem is underlined (*It was awful* . . .) and so

is the neighbours' responses (*You could try this* . . .). In fact, if we see the clustering of this stress with the neighbours' hesitation (*Well* . . . *er* . . .), self-correction
(*I always* . . . *I mean, I've heard that* . . .) and the wary gestures, then the evaluation
would seem to be marked in several ways. Such a clustering of evaluation devices
marks the 'peak' of the story, in Longacre's model of narrative (1976: 217–31). 'Even
in a rough area neighbours can be helpful when you are in trouble' or more
exactly, 'People in my neighbourhood all know about how to get into cars. They
don't want to confess this (probably many of them are car thieves) but they will
still help when you are in trouble.' This implication emerged strongly in the way
in which the narrative was performed, but the performance does not feature much
in this transcription. Thus, although the evaluation seems clear, there is a measure
of interpretation in stating exactly what it is. Probably, in all interpretations of
evaluations commentators find themselves adding to the text and supplementing
their understanding through the use of 'extra' social and cultural information.
Labov and Fanshel give many examples of this in a step they call 'expansion',
which is to 'bring together all the information that we have that will help in understanding the production, interpretation, and sequencing of the utterance in question' (1977: 49). However, this particular narrative is self-contained and further
contextual information, say about the speaker, the car, or the neighbourhood, is
not necessary to see the main point.

In a second example, the speaker (Lady Olga Maitland) presents a narrative in
the House of Lords (November 1996), during a British parliamentary debate about
tourism, extracts from which were broadcast on the radio.

(6.2)

Narrative: The Hotel Room Door
At the last party conference I stayed in a hotel in Bournemouth. The manager showed us
our room. When he opened the door to the bathroom . . . [laughs] the door came off and
fell onto the bed . . . [laughter from other members]. You can laugh—and I laughed at
the time—but the point is there shouldn't be hotels like this. We need standards and
some system of recognizing *all* hotels so that visitors and tourists know where they are.

In this second story the main point is clearly labelled by the speaker (*there
shouldn't be hotels like this*). This would seem to be the evaluation so that the anec-
dote exemplifies a bad hotel; this exemplification is used to support the main
debating point about a system of recognizing hotels. However, there is another
level of meaning here which is evident in the laughter. As the teller laughs at the
memory and the audience laugh at the telling, the narration is interrupted by the
speaker's meta-comment on both types of laughter. Clearly, the laughter stands
out and is explicitly marked by the speaker; all participants recognize the humour
of the situation and this is an important part of the evaluation. There are further
levels to this humour: the fact that many of the audience would have attended the
same or similar conferences, and even stayed at the same hotel; the high social status of the speaker (the manager himself shows her the room); and the ambiguity
of 'knowing where you are'. Linde (1993: 21, 81) emphasizes how many narratives

offer moral comments on the kind of person the speaker claims to be. In this case, the evaluation shows the teller as a person who has a sense of humour, both in the hotel and in the parliamentary debate. As with the first example, the narrative evaluation can be understood without further contextual information.

Evaluation Devices

As these examples indicate, in many cases locating and understanding the evaluation may not be a problem but often there is more than one level of evaluation. There is a measure of ambiguity about the term 'evaluation'. On the one hand, the evaluation refers to a structural element that occurs after the complication and before the resolution. It emphasizes the break between them, delaying the forward movement of the narrative and holding the listener in suspense (Labov and Fanshel 1977: 108), or it is said to interrupt the recounting to tell listeners what the point is, in an 'external' evaluation (Labov 1972: 371). This might be termed a primary structure. On the other hand, it is a functional element that is spread throughout various points of the narrative and overlaps with other elements. This 'internal' evaluation (Labov 1972: 370–5) is a rhetorical underlining that marks off the evaluated element grammatically, semantically, or prosodically. The speaker can mark almost any element to make it stand out from the rest of the text in this way. The evaluation thus forms 'a secondary structure' which is 'concentrated in the evaluation section' but may be found almost anywhere else in the narrative (ibid. 369). Both this secondary structure and the primary evaluation section are important elements: 'Unevaluated narratives lack structural definition' (Labov and Waletsky 1967: 39).

The problem with labelling evaluation a 'secondary structure' is that, unlike the other elements of narrative, evaluation does not have an easily specified set of forms or specified location in the overall structure (Polanyi 1989: 22–3; Linde 1997: 154). The evaluation can appear anywhere in a narrative and may be realized by any level of linguistic structure (phonological, lexical, syntactic, discoursal) and to interpret it a hearer or analyst may have to use contextual or cultural knowledge. Furthermore, with some narratives combinations and clusters of these are employed.

It is true that Labov (1972: 370–5) and Peterson and McCabe (1983: 222) give a comprehensive list of evaluation devices. The list includes such external devices as direct explanatory speech attributed to the narrator either as teller or story participant, or to a story character. There are other external devices like narrating an evaluative action ('he was shaking like a leaf'). Internal devices include the use of a range of intensifiers (adjectives, adverbs, lexical or phrasal repetitions) or modal verbs and negatives to refer to events which did not occur, but which might have done. Phonologically, a narrator may use heightened stress, vowel lengthening, marked changes in volume, speech rate and pitch, or whispers, song, rhyme, and non-linguistic noises. Lexically, tellers may choose words from a different register, change degree of formality, or use profanities and words with rich connotations. Syntactically, any marked change in complexity or use of tense may signal evaluation. In particular, the switch to the 'conversational historical present' in narrative ('He goes . . . this lady says . . . ') has been much studied as a feature of evaluation (Wolfson 1978, 1982; Schiffrin 1981; Johnstone 1987) to the extent that it has been called the 'evaluative present tense' (Fludernik 1991: 387). At the discourse level, the wide range of evaluative devices includes repetition, reported thought or speech, flashbacks and flashaheads, or explicit meta-comments. There is even some mention of 'culturally defined' evaluation like the use of symbolic action ('I crossed myself') (Labov and Waletsky 1967: 38), a category which we will illustrate later. From an analytic point of view, such a list specifies too much—there are too many categories—yet it is exemplified too little in the literature (but see Cortazzi 1991 for many examples). However, it is helpful to be aware of the enormous range of evaluative possibilities. Ultimately, though, evaluation in narrative is text-specific since the evaluation can use any linguistic device (or para-linguistic and non-verbal communication) to make the meaningful part of the story salient. We also argue that some evaluation is context- and culture-specific.

There are a large number of models of narrative analysis in different disciplines (Cortazzi 1993) but Labov's is one of the few to draw attention to evaluation as a key feature. Some assistance in using this model for narrative analysis can found in the concept of 'lexical signalling' (Hoey 1983; Jordan 1984) in which clause relations (e.g. situation, problem, solution, evaluation) are commonly signalled by key words in a text. Thus, such words and phrases as 'success', 'worse', 'excellent', 'disappointed', 'great', 'terrible', 'passed the exam', 'they did it in the end', 'it works wonders' may, depending on the context, be clear signals of evaluation in narrative.

From one point of view, Labov's model of narrative has been positively evaluated: it has been widely used in a number of different fields and it is probably the best-known model. It has been applied to literary analysis (Pratt 1977; Carter and Simpson 1982; Maclean 1988); in education, for analysing children's writing (Taylor 1986; Wilkinson 1986) and speaking (Hicks 1990); in developmental psycholinguistics (Kernan 1977; Peterson and McCabe 1983; McCabe and Peterson 1991; Bamberg and Damrad-Frye 1991); in mass communications (van Dijk 1988); and in anthropology (Watson 1972). It has been used to examine news stories (Bell 1991), stories of prejudice (van Dijk 1987, 1993), stories told by women (Coates 1996), by teachers (Cortazzi 1991), and international students (Jin 1992), besides conversational stories (Polanyi 1989) and life stories (Linde 1993). However, we will be arguing that, whatever its merits in the analysis of evaluation *in* narrative, it needs to be supplemented by other perspectives in order to gain a full picture of narratives and evaluation.

Evaluation *of* Narrative

The evaluation of narratives requires caution, perhaps using more than one approach. Not every narrative has the primary evaluation structure but it can be argued that all conversational narratives have secondary evaluation. Hymes (1996: 168–70) takes up a story analysed by Labov (1972: 367). Where Labov had not found evaluation, Hymes uses narrative divisions into lines, verses, stanzas, and scenes to seek the overall design of the story (see also Gee 1989). This ethnopoetic approach to narrative analysis draws on studies of the verbal art of other societies, notably societies traditionally studied by anthropologists. Using this approach to analyse the same story, it can be seen that evaluation is, in fact, present in recurrent parallels and culminating segments. Hymes emphasizes that narrative analysis to find evaluation is not just a matter of segmenting a story into narrative categories. It should be more inductive, he argues, seeking rhythms and repetitions in the overall patterning of the story verses and stanzas.

If 'narratives' do not have any evaluation, they are simply reports or summaries. Thus Linde (1993) proposes that evaluation is the major criterion of narrative. A major aspect of secondary evaluation is performance. As we have seen, this may involve stress, hesitations, gestures, or laughter, and it can also include vocal effects, different tones of voice, and emotional colourings. Like other features of narrative, performance is highly sensitive to the context of social interaction. Bauman (1993: 182) maintains that performance is a meta-communicative frame in which tellers assume responsibility to an audience for a display of communicative competence as part of a double contract: the narrator promises a performance; hearers promise to be an audience, even if the performance is fleeting or disclaimed. Wolfson (1976) found that narratives in research interviews lacked performance features; to this extent they were unevaluated and were essentially summary answers to interviewer's questions. She hypothesized (1982: 77) that narrative performance depends on whether participants share the norms for evaluation. If they do, the expression of performance (and therefore a major part of the point of the story) can be better understood and appreciated by the audience. This matters, of course, for researchers who obtain narratives in interviews; it affects their evaluation *of* the narrative as well as whether the narrative has an evaluation. Cortazzi (1991) and Jin (1992) found many examples of performed narratives in research interviews, presumably because the interviewers took pains to establish shared norms concerning interview topics.

Important aspects of the evaluation *of* narrative are the questions of who the narrative belongs to, and who does the evaluating. The ownership or authorship of conversational narratives is less obvious than it might at first appear. We can examine this by comparing narratives elicited in interviews with those that arise in casual conversation. The latter may seem more 'authentic' or 'spontaneous' until it is seen that interviews are also authentic, if particular, speech situations. While interviews generally involve asymmetrical roles, regarding questions and answers or turn-taking, many conversations do too since they can also vary in formality and in the rights and roles of participants. In both situations there is a joint construction of meaning. Thus Mishler (1986, 1997) has demonstrated that in interviews such as doctor–patient consultations *both* participants shape *both* questions and answers through their interaction by giving feedback and mutually constructing and reformulating meanings. Respondents learn from interviewers how to respond, how much detail to give, whether and how to tell a story. If respondents' answers contain narratives these are responses not just to interviewer questions but to an interviewer's assessments of previous answers and narratives. While 'investigators seem to assume that the story has been there all along, located inside the person, waiting to be expressed in response to the eliciting stimulus of a question . . . ', each respondent's 'story is co-produced, over the course of its telling' (Mishler 1997: 224–5). Awareness of the nature of this narrative context can counter the criticisms of Labov's model that it leaves out the relationship of teller and listener and seriously underestimates the effects of the interviewer and interview context (Mishler 1986: 82; Riessman 1993: 20).

The work of conversational analysts also shows how narratives are jointly produced (Sacks 1972, 1974; Jefferson 1978; Schegloff 1978). A story is frequently preceded by a 'proposal' in which the teller signals a forthcoming story and gets other people to be an audience ('That reminds me of something that happened at the conference . . . '; 'This is a story my grandfather told me'). This usually elicits 'acceptance' ('uh-huh . . . ', 'oh yes . . . ') but could be denied ('not that story again'). Many proposals are linked to abstracts, which can, in effect, evaluate the story in advance ('Something terrible happened to me . . . ') and which can also elicit acceptances. Story starts, and such pre-evaluations, are thus joint productions. More importantly, so are story endings. When the story is apparently finished the audience show appreciation of story content or narrative performance with a 'receipt' ('Incredible!' 'Really?'). Tellers do their utmost to get some sort of reaction otherwise the story falls flat or seems unfinished. Without a receipt the teller is likely to think the story has not been understood. The receipt is, of course, a kind of evaluation. Contrary to the previously cited criticism, Labov and Fanshel (1977: 109) recognize this listener's evaluation; listeners must indicate to tellers *that* and *how* they have understood. Sometimes the receipt repeats or even re-evaluates the teller's evaluation as participants negotiate their understanding of the meaning of the story. Thus the evaluation *in* the story may elicit evaluation *of* the story, and *both* of these may be joint productions. This happens in interviews, too. This is an important consideration for narrative researchers. Meanings and evaluations that are actually mutual constructions may be attributed solely to the respondent; the interviewer's contribution may be unacknowledged.

The co-construction of evaluation can have implications for entitlement and power. People generally think of the initial teller as having the right to tell the story and hence to the ownership of the evaluation. But some narratives are group tellings in which several speakers may re-orientate each other to narrative problems in the course of the narrating. This happens, of course, when a group have shared an experience but hearers 'who have not directly experienced the narrative events can acquire entitlement through expanding, querying, correcting, or challenging existing formulations of the narrative problem' (Ochs *et al.* 1996: 109). The evaluation in such cases is jointly owned and is evidence of a sharing of power.

The evaluation *of* narrative is more complex when there is a series of stories. Each story has a relationship to the previous one, which is more than that of simple adjacency (Ryave 1978). A second story, in itself, evaluates the first. It shows receipt of the first and firmly endorses it by relating more of the same kind of thing. A third story will evaluate both the previous ones. These story-evaluations may be positive or negative, as counter-stories. In either case, there is a strong tendency for tellers to make later stories more exaggerated than earlier ones, to cap the previous evaluations. Later stories thus exercise power over previous ones so that early narrators can feel put down. The evaluations *in* later stories become evaluations *of* early stories, and, therefore *of* the earlier tellers.

A series of stories may build up meanings in a larger text, an overarching narrative. This larger co-construction can, again, be a group entitlement. The evaluation of the series is not necessarily the same as the evaluation in the last story. More likely, the series evaluation belongs to all tellers and all hearers who provided receipts. The general sense of the global evaluation of the series is likely to be unduly influenced by any stories that were felt to have been particularly successful. The evaluations of these outstanding stories may thus exercise an evaluative power retrospectively over the entire series, wherever these particular stories were positioned in the series. The global evaluation also needs to take account of any counter-stories. These interweavings of evaluations of narratives can be seen to be more complex in inter-cultural situations.

Evaluation *of* Narrative in Different Cultures

Since narrative reflects culture, and at the same time constitutes culture, it may be expected that evaluations of narratives may vary cross-culturally. When Tannen (1980) compared the stories of Greek and American women, told after they had seen a silent film, she found clear differences. The Greeks focused on personal involvement; they were concerned with characters' motives and offered many judgements. The Americans, in contrast, focused on context and gave detailed objective reports. It is not difficult to imagine how the two groups might evaluate each others' stories.

Another example: after collecting the life stories of over a hundred Chinese speakers, Zhang and Sang (1986: 368) concluded that tellers generally used one of two storytelling approaches, 'one is a way of talking that is not Chinese, but like the narration in Greek tragedy: starting in the middle of the story. The other is that . . . the narrators mention the key point only very briefly and then pass on, while going into great and repeated detail about common experiences in shared time and place.' American listeners, perhaps with Labov's model in mind, might well fail to find the evaluation in either of these approaches. The listeners might therefore negatively evaluate the stories as being ill-formed. This would matter if, say, the Americans were teachers of the Chinese (or vice versa). It would be helpful to understand that Chinese speakers generally put high value on relationships and on collective harmony. Knowing this, the listeners might then see that the 'great and repeated detail about common experiences' is the evaluation, since this may be exactly the point of telling the story; it establishes commonality.

Further, the mention of the key point 'only very briefly' may reflect a cultural orientation towards the listeners which gives them credit for the ability to spot the main point after they have been carefully led towards it. This reflects a traditional Chinese discourse principle that is encapsulated in the saying: '*dian dao wei zhi*' (roughly: 'touch the point, then stop'). That is, the speaker points the way, to a certain extent, then stops, in the belief that a listener can work out the rest. In some narratives this means that the primary evaluation does not need to be mentioned since listeners can find it for themselves on the basis of the secondary evaluation. It is up to the listener to find the evaluative intention of the teller and how it may be realized in the story (see Shaul *et al.* 1987 for possible parallel notions in Hopi culture concerning Coyote stories). A Chinese storyteller may thus only have responsibility to tell the story; the hearer has the responsibility to evaluate it. This works when all participants share the same discourse values.

In many cultures narrative evaluations are bridges of one sort or another. This can be seen in the following example of a popular story from China.

(6.3)
Narrative: Wu Da Lang
In ancient times, a man called Wu Da Lang ran a guest house. He was short and ugly. He needed some new staff to help in the guest house. Experienced, smart and capable people turned up for to ask for the posts. In the end, he only employed those who were shorter than he was and were less capable than himself.

    Wu Da Lang kai dian—yi ge bi yi ge ai (Wu Da Lang runs a guest house—his employees are shorter than he is).

On the face of it, the evaluation of the story lies in the idea that the protagonist only employed those who were shorter and less capable than he was. However, what matters here is how the evaluation is used. The key is in the last line, which could also serve as a title, or pre-evaluation. In fact, it is this last line which is the evaluation, as used in conversation. The last line is a set phrase which can be used on any occasion to indicate those who are jealous of others who are more capable than they are and therefore only choose lesser people whom they can control. This story is an example of the Chinese genre of *chengyu*. These set phrases with terse meanings are usually of four characters in Chinese (like '*dian dao wei zhi*') and they generally represent the primary evaluation of a story. They are used in daily life with the evaluative functions to make moral, social, or professional judgements without even telling the story. Given general cultural knowledge of such stories, one does not need to actually tell the story to make the point about jealousy or social control; it is enough to use the last line. What happens, then, is that a speaker wishing to evaluate a situation simply quotes the first part, '*Wu Da Lang kai dian*' (Wu Da Lang runs a guest house), upon which the hearer responds with '*yi ge bi yi ge ai*' (his employees are shorter than he is). The two halves of the story evaluation are thus put together by separate speakers, who have then evoked the story without either of them telling it. They have thus established three bridges: a first one to the untold but remembered story; a second to a situation which has just been pungently evaluated by the story; and a third interpersonal one between themselves as a bond of common understanding. This genre is a well known one in China, such that many collections of written *chengyu* have been published (e.g. Yang 1991). The bridging only works, of course, when both parties know all of the above. Members of other cultures interacting with Chinese may not have access to the evaluation when they hear the exchange.

A further cross-cultural example, from a research interview, is given by a Chinese research student. The student is talking about his relationships with authority figures in Britain.

(6.4)

Narrative: Changing Research Supervisor

I spoke out what I thought. But it was awkward when I came here in the beginning. I wanted to change the research direction, so I had to change supervisor. When I talked to the Dean he vaguely suggested that I shouldn't change, but he also said he could allow me to change if I insisted on it. Eventually I decided to transfer here. Now this Dean is obviously not happy and is offended. He doesn't greet me when he sees me, ignoring me completely.

Here the evaluation concerns the absence of the greeting, which seems to worry the teller. It could be, as the teller apparently feels, that changing research direction and supervisor caused a bad relationship with the management. Perhaps the student has misjudged or misinterpreted the Dean's social manner, as many British students have thought when they read this transcription. British students do not see particular significance here. However, in China, when a leader shows awareness and recognition of the existence of a junior person this is an important signal of security and honour to the latter. In contrast, withholding such recognition could be demeaning, especially to a research student who is quite senior in his own country. Other Chinese students have evaluated the story as showing that going against the wishes of the authorities had caused a bad relationship. They think the Dean, as leader, believed the student had disturbed the harmony of a research team. Some of them think the story shows that while British culture apparently encourages directness or being straightforward, this is dangerous because it can lead to giving offence unwittingly. British students in their evaluations of the Chinese evaluations think that all this is highly unlikely; the Dean was busy or simply didn't see the student. For them, it is unlikely that any harmonic relationships have been disturbed. Clearly, the social issues have been differently evaluated. It is important for both parties involved in such apparently small incidents to be aware of other possible evaluations and of other evaluators' value systems.

The social practices of different evaluations of narratives across cultures can become a research issue, as well as a social issue. Brumble (1990) gives examples of how white researchers and editors imposed their own values on Native Americans telling their life stories. The latter's autobiographies were made to conform to Western ideas of what an autobiography should be and how it should be told. One editor is quoted (ibid. 80) as concluding: 'Indian narrative style involves a repetition and a dwelling on unimportant details which confuse the white reader and make it hard to follow the story. Motives are never explained—emotional states are summed up in such colourless phrases as "I liked it". For one not immersed in the culture, the real significance escapes.' Some respondents had their own evaluation of this narrative process and of the researchers' motives (Brumble 1990: 90): 'A lot of anthropologists, they come here and they say they want to be my friend, then they go away and put down what I say in books and make a lot of money'. We have found other Native Latin Americans who had their own defence against such researchers, a defence that dramatically affects evaluations in narratives. One confided to us, after a researcher had left with a bagful of recounted stories: 'That's not what really happens. That's only what we tell the anthropologists so they'll go away and leave us in peace.'

Evaluation *through* Narrative

Evaluation *through* narrative can mean that tellers, hearers, or their situations are evaluated through the telling.

In educational settings, for example, children have often been evaluated for fluency, confidence, or their learning of content knowledge through their ability to tell stories. More recently, teachers and teaching as a profession have been evaluated through narrative analysis. Teachers' stories of their work have become research-worthy. This is widely seen as being important because teachers' narratives give voice to their experience. Narrative evaluation can publicize the human qualities involved in teaching. It can give value to professional biography and self. It can give representation to minorities. It can be a key part of our understanding of teacher cognition in professional decision-making, classroom events, and interpretations of the teaching–learning process. Teachers' autobiographical stories can be evaluated to ascertain their needs for continuing professional development. Yet, among the valuable published works in this field (e.g. collections of articles by Holly and MacLure 1990; Thomas 1995; Cunningham and Gardner 1997; Gudmundsdottir 1997) there are few which use linguistic models of narrative. Cortazzi (1991) shows how collections of teachers' stories can be analysed in a Labovian framework combined with insights from conversational, psychological, and anthropological models. Large numbers of primary evaluations on the same topics can be examined. Cortazzi shows, for example (1991: 80–100), that evaluations in stories of teaching disasters and humorous classroom events both reveal that humour is a key quality in teaching. Laughing is sociable, shareable, and professionally sustaining; as one evaluation expressed it, 'I feel I've had a bad day if there hasn't been something to giggle about, I mean, *with* the children not *at* them'. Generally, in education there is plenty of evaluation through narrative but very little examination of how evaluation works in narrative.

In therapeutic settings, there is also much evaluation through narrative. Clients tell their stories to therapists or counsellors. They may tell their story in part to themselves as an audience: through the telling and reflection the past self is reconstructed using present perspectives and evaluations. Counsellors may tell stories from mythology, tradition, or life experience so that clients may evaluate their own life in relation to the storied evaluation. In mutual support groups, such as Alcoholics Anonymous, the telling of stories of personal experience may lead to a more realistic evaluation of the teller's situation. In such a group, the story itself is not news. In fact, it is probably the common experience of most of those gathered. However, the main effect of the narrative may be on the listeners. It is not so much that the listeners come to understand the teller and evaluate that story as that the listeners come to understand and evaluate their own stories better (Moore and Carling 1988: 161).

Van Dijk (1987: 71) found that in two groups of interviews about ethnic minorities in Holland, 66 and 59 per cent of stories had evaluations (presumably these were primary evaluations seen as separate structural categories). These generally portrayed minority group members as not only different, but as negative and inferior, so that van Dijk was able to draw up a schema of prejudiced talk through which, it is believed, racism is communicated interpersonally (van Dijk 1987, 1993). In terms of our schema, by locating the evaluation *in* narrative, researchers can analyse tellers' perceptions or evaluations *of* socially important issues and situations or culturally salient beliefs that are communicated, and perhaps engendered, *through* narrative.

Evaluation through narrative in a courtroom can be quite different. There is much telling of stories by witnesses, under particular conditions. The telling of their stories matters—trial outcomes can be affected by the narrative style of witnesses. A witness using a narrative style can be judged to be more credible than a witness using a fragmented style (Barry 1991). However, there are different narrative styles (O'Barr and Conley 1996). 'Rule-oriented' narratives tend to be circumscribed. They deal only with those issues that are directly relevant to the legal issue in hand. Rule-oriented tellers are probably more experienced in courtroom discourse. In contrast, 'relational' narratives follow more everyday narrative patterns. 'These narratives are typically rich in evaluation and personal details. They reflect a broad notion of relevance and thus include information from a variety of oral and written sources, much of which may be performed for dramatic effect' (O'Barr and Conley 1996: 119). 'Judges, however, react to such information as inappropriate and distracting, and often display considerable irritation toward narrators who offer it' (ibid. 117). When there are a series of narratives from different witnesses the evaluation of each and of the series as a whole can be serious— and a serious problem. Court judgments need to be given after evaluations of the evaluations in witnesses' narratives.

In all such fields, narrative is commonplace but professionally important. Some knowledge of the workings of narrative and of evaluation in, of, and through narrative is potentially very useful to practitioners and to those who train them or to those who carry out interpretative research into theories, processes, and professional practices.

Evaluation *in, of,* and *through* Narrative

The various levels of evaluation and narrative that we have outlined can be seen in the story of 'The Bull and the Saint' as presented by Carrithers (1992: 92–116). The story and its context can be interpreted in terms of evaluation *in, of,* and *through* the narrative. It is of some interest that the evaluation worked on all three layers simultaneously with the same story for the hearer, as will become clear later. We should point out that the evaluation schema we are using here is our own; Carrithers does not look at the story in terms of evaluation. While doing anthropological fieldwork among Jains in Kolhapur, in Maharashtra, India, Carrithers asked a number of urban businessmen about the teachings of the Jain religion. In one such research interview, a dealer in agricultural supplies, 'Mr P.', was philosophizing in his office at some length about key concepts of Jainism when he was called out to deal with a business matter. A shabby older man, 'Mr S.', who had been sitting silently in a corner then took up the discourse (Carrithers 1992: 96), telling the following story.

(6.5)

Narrative: 'The Bull and the Saint'
This is a story my grandfather told me. This is very important. Write this down [pointing to author's notebook]. There was a great man, a hero, a *mahapurus*, who lived right near here, and one time that man went out to the bulls. While [cleaning the dung out of the stalls] one of them stood on his hand. What did he do? He did nothing! He waited and waited, and finally the bull's owner came and saw what was happening! The owner struck the bull to make it move, and the great man told him to stop, that the bull did not understand! That is *dharma* [true religion]. That is genuine *jainadharma* [Jainism]!

Later, Carrithers read this story in a printed biography of Siddhasaga, who lived about a hundred years ago. The story of this local saint is known to around 30,000 Jains. The evaluation *in* the narrative is easy to locate in the last two sentences, in which the words '*that*' are heavily stressed. This is Labov's (1972: 371) external evaluation or what Polanyi (1989: 24) terms deictic evaluation. '*That* is **dharma** . . .' stands outside the recounting but points anaphorically to the meaning of the story. What exactly this meaning is may be more problematic, as we show later. Does it mean that we should understand animals or that they do not understand us? Or that we should be kind to animals? Why is it '*an important story*' of '*a great man*'? Carrithers states (1992: 99) that people unsympathetic to Jainism, both Europeans and Indians, after they have heard the story understand that Siddhasaga was either insane or stupid to let an Indian bull, nearly two metres high at the shoulder, stand on his hand without protest. That is, their evaluation of the narrative is negative.

Carrithers shows (1992: 97, 103) that this evaluation *of* the narrative is mistaken. Or, at least, this was not the evaluation of the participants in the office at the time. First, the narrative followed Mr P.'s philosophical explanation of *ahimsa*, the Jain teaching of harmlessness or non-violence. This central religious value includes vegetarianism; truthful, kindly speech; non-attachment to material goods; and helping all beings. Hence, for the teller, Mr S., the story portrays exemplary self-control and non-violence. In one sense the narrative was evaluated in advance by the preceding talk, without which (or without comparable cultural background knowledge) the evaluation in the narrative cannot be understood as intended. Secondly, the contextual relationships between Carrithers as enquirer or seeker and Mr P. were of a morally and spiritually pedagogic sort. The serious tone and teacher–student relation that had been negotiated with Mr P. were picked up by Mr S., the teller. The setting of the narration is a 'proper' setting to learn religious truths and can be thought of as a context of evaluation for the narrative. This negotiated teller–hearer relationship rules out the possibility of a negative evaluation of the internal meaning of the story. In fact, for both teller and hearer, this relationship and the circumstances of the narrating are part of the meaning of the story; evaluation without the setting of the narrating is impossible.

The evaluation *through* the narrative seems to work in several ways. First, the story follows a lengthy exposition of philosophical argument. Carrithers believed at the time, and still believes, that the evaluation, and the telling in general, implied that the example informs us in ways that philosophical exposition does not (ibid. 107). After the vehement words '*That is genuine Jainism!*', it is as if the teller had added, '*and not what Mr P. has been telling you*'. As Carrithers says (ibid. 92), 'Its import . . . was that a tale of such heroism is worth a thousand words of abstract doctrine'. Thus the teller and Carrithers juxtapose two modes of thought, which Bruner (1985: 11–43) calls 'narrative' and 'paradigmatic' thinking. The telling of the Bull and the Saint story implies a criticism of paradigmatic thinking (the traditional logico-scientific mode of knowing) in favour of narrative ways of making meaning which help us to understand human action. It is seen as a move in an argument about how to present Jainism. Secondly, the telling is clearly within the lived experience of the teller and his grandfather. Through the story Carrithers acquired a different orientation to the flow of relationships and interactions in the local villages. Through the evaluation he appreciated 'how the local Jain world often reverberates with stories of great or minor deeds' (Carrithers 1992: 108). Thirdly, Carrithers comes to understand that it is through the evaluations of such stories that the Jains themselves come to understand their cultural and religious heritage. Socialization takes place through narrative evaluation. We can say that the narrating not only informs the hearer of how a character in a story was but mirrors how the teller wishes to become or even, perhaps, wishes hearers to become. Telling such stories is therefore a key part of the process of self-realization of individual and collective identity. Carrithers concludes (ibid. 110), 'There is more to Jainism than stories but, I argue, it is through stories, through characters with states of mind living in a flow of action, that Jains themselves first and foremost understand Jainism'. Fourthly, Carrithers's own reporting of this ethnographic study is in a narrative format; through narrative he understands, presents, and evaluates his research. Carrithers (1992: 92) gives some meta-evaluation of his narrative of 'The Bull and the Saint' story: 'It is an ethnographic gem, the sort of illustration of the way of life that ethnographers happen across with pleasure and use in their books with immense satisfaction'.

As a postscript to this story and a final evaluation of the narrative, we asked Dr Ramesh Mehta of the Jain Centre in Leicester (personal communication 1998) what the story meant. He said that Jains have been reciting similar stories for well over 2,000 years. The stories are taught to children as part of moral and religious education. The stories socialize them into Jain ways of thinking. Many such stories are embodied in statues and symbols in Jain temples. Mehta evaluated Carrithers's evaluation as being essentially correct. His further evaluation was that the story embodies several levels of non-violence: in *action* (Siddhasagar doesn't push the bull away); in *mind* (he doesn't even think badly about the bull); in *relation to others* (he doesn't want to encourage the owner to push the bull away or for him to think badly of it); in *relation to his **karma*** (he endures the pain in silence to pay the price of possible bad actions which he may have committed in a previous reincarnation and thus hopes to break the cycle of the effects of past actions). An understanding of some of these levels depends, of course, on how the key words of Mr S.'s evaluation ('*dharma*' or 'religion' and '*jainadharma*' or 'Jainism') are understood. This implies an interplay between the linguistic aspects of evaluation (which words or which aspects of the text give the point to the story) and sociocultural aspects of the context and hearers' schematic knowledge. If hearers or re-tellers do not have an understanding of the keywords or of the evaluation as a whole it is not difficult to imagine that 'The Bull and the Saint' story might be greatly distorted in subsequent retellings, much as Bartlett's (1932) War of the Ghosts story has been distorted in classic experiments for memory of narratives.

Evaluation: Narrative Research and Life

This evaluation of data through narration illustrates the wider meaning of narrative as a research process, of eliciting, telling, translating, transcribing, selecting, analysing, reporting, and in general the whole business of carrying out this type of qualitative research and putting it into print. As Atkinson (1990: 104–28) demonstrates, the process of 'writing down' and 'writing up' ethnographic research often involves narrative construction of a tale of the researcher's exploration, a journey from outsider to insider, an account of the success of understanding others' understandings. In fact, Polkinghorne (1995: 12) actually calls this 'narrative analysis', a process in which 'researchers collect descriptions of events and happenings and synthesize or configure them by means of a plot into a story or stories'. Data are evaluated through narrativization, particularly in qualitative research. This evaluation requires researchers carrying out fieldwork to admit the reflexivity involved in their actions and story-making and, further, to carry this reflexivity through to the production of narrative texts (Okely and Callaway 1992). That is, in constructing the narratives of others, researchers need to evaluate their own ideas about narrative, about the processes of narrative construction, and about how their own autobiography might impinge on the story being told of others.

This last kind of story-making and its evaluation goes beyond research; it permeates our daily lives. The importance of recognizing the role of evaluation in such narrative can hardly be exaggerated. In effect, our life stories are put together in this way and our evaluations of them are our sense of moral selfhood and the creation of coherence of our lives (Linde 1993; Ludwig 1997). Leaders in many fields present a story (or counter-story). In a recent psychological study, Gardner (1997: 41–65) has argued, and convincingly illustrated, that a key—perhaps the key—to leadership is the effective communication of stories about self and group identity and about values and meaning. Gardner indicates the crucial role of evaluation in such group stories. Unless those who are led are prepared to adopt sophisticated or more critical stances to these stories a basic or biased story may prevail.

Throughout life, individuals hear stories and have to evaluate their merits consciously and unconsciously. There is always a chance that a more sophisticated story will prevail, particularly when the teller is skilled and the audience is sophisticated. However, my study provides abundant evidence that, more often than not, the less sophisticated story remains entrenched—the unschooled mind triumphs. (ibid. 49)

There is scope here for raising awareness of such narratives and for the teaching of critical evaluation of them, lest we become victims through them or find that our destiny is determined by them.

Conclusions

Evaluation *in* narrative, *of* narrative, and *through* narrative is clearly complex. Even a story of a few lines, such as 'The Bull and the Saint', can have many levels of meanings and the three layers of evaluation may function simultaneously. Some of these layers of meaning are in the text. Others are in the telling or in the setting of the narration and in the relationships established between participants in narration. Others emerge through the narrative process and in its reporting. Linguistic and socio-cultural elements may be interwoven across these layers and our evaluation of them may ultimately depend on the knowledge and experience (including experience of narrative and narrative analysis) which we bring to the narrative context.

A lot depends on *who* is evaluating *what kind of narrative* in *what kind of context.* In some cases, evaluation *in, of,* or *through* narrative is a self-evaluation. Speakers and hearers evaluate their individual and collective sense of self through the telling and hearing of stories. As we tell a story of personal experience, we remember how we were, how we believe we are, or how we wish to be. Evaluation in narrative exposes mirrors of multiple senses or tenses of the self: not only those of past, present, and future but also of perfect or imperfect, hypothetical or dream-world selves.

'Evaluation' and 'narrative' are concepts that are multi-layered. As we have outlined, evaluating evaluation in relation to narrative requires an awareness of several points of view. Evaluating evaluation benefits from multi-disciplinary views. At least, that is our evaluation.

7

Evaluation and Organization in Text: The Structuring Role of Evaluative Disjuncts

Geoff Thompson and Jianglin Zhou

People usually talk about coherence as the logical connections that can be made between the various parts of a (written or spoken) text. Specific connections may be signalled by conjunctive items (words such as *and, so, but*), which are one of the categories of cohesion (see Halliday and Hasan 1976; Halliday 1994). The argument underpinning Thompson and Zhou's chapter is that both coherence and cohesion depend on evaluation—what the writer thinks about what he or she is writing— as well as on the logical connections. They argue that what they call 'evaluative coherence' runs alongside the more traditional 'propositional coherence'. They provide evidence that some adverbs which express evaluation (such as *unfortunately, plainly, happily*) perform a function similar to that performed by the traditional category of conjunct. In other words, an adverb such as *unfortunately* does not only comment on the content of the clause of which it is a part, but can also suggest a specific kind of connection between two clauses, thereby establishing a cohesive link.

Like Hoey's chapter (this volume), Thompson and Zhou's chapter draws on the notion of clause relations pioneered by Winter and Hoey (Huddleston *et al.* 1968; Winter 1982; 1994; Hoey 1983). In particular, they present evidence for their argument from a detailed examination of two clause relations: the concessive relation and the hypothetical–real relation. One of the ideas behind the notion of clause relations is that they represent a kind of dialogue, or interaction, between the writer and reader (this can be demonstrated through questions: see the introduction to Hoey's chapter). For example, Winter (in Huddleston *et al.* 1968) argues that a function of a conjunct such as *but* may be to tell the reader that what follows is not what he or she expects to find. In this case, a logical-connection word, *but*, has an interpersonal function. Thompson and Zhou's work complements this, in arguing for a logical-connection function for interpersonal words.

The emphasis upon dialogue is part of a larger concern for the role of the interpersonal and the interactive in monologue (see also Thompson and Thetela 1995).

Like the other chapters in this volume, Thompson and Zhou's argument denies the traditional supposition that evaluation, or the interpersonal, is less important than, and separate from, the main 'informational' work of a text and its organization. A single word, such as *plainly* or *unfortunately* may at the same time tell us what the writer thinks, *and* construct a dialogue between writer and reader, *and* move the argument from one stage to the next. It is thus impossible to separate the interpersonal from the logical.

In systemic linguistics, the ideational, the interpersonal, and the textual are treated as separate metafunctions. Although a clause always realizes all three, different aspects of the clause can be assigned to each (Halliday 1994). Specifically, conjuncts such as *and* and *but* play a role in the textual metafunction, whereas disjuncts or modal adjuncts, such as *unfortunately* and *plainly*, are part of the interpersonal metafunction. This chapter casts doubt upon this distinction. At a very basic level, it suggests that a single word in a clause may have a role in two metafunctions simultaneously. Further, it suggests that whole classes of words—conjuncts and disjuncts—may not be assignable to a single metafunction at all. Most remarkably, Thompson and Zhou suggest that cohesion itself is an interpersonal as well as a textual phenomenon.

*   *   *

Introduction

Much of the extensive literature on textual cohesion (e.g. Halliday and Hasan 1976; Hasan 1984; Hoey 1991*a*) assumes a view of coherence as largely deriving from the logical connections made by readers between units of propositional 'content' in what they read.[1] Cohesion is seen as the explicit textual signalling by the writers of this potential logical coherence, and is primarily realized by repetition and conjunction: in very broad terms, repetition in propositions through the text signals that there is some kind of connection amongst the propositions, while conjunction between the propositions signals the type of connection being set up (Thompson 1996*b*). Repetition may be effected by means of 'grammatical' features such as reference and substitution (Halliday and Hasan 1976; Halliday 1994), or, more pervasively, by lexical repetition (Hoey 1991*b*). Conjunction, which depends largely on co-ordinators and subordinators within the clause complex, can be signalled beyond the sentence by conjuncts such as *however* and by unspecific nouns (Winter 1982—cf. 'labels', Francis 1994), such as *question* and *reason* in:

(7.1)
In reply to that question a golfing colleague of mine offered two reasons. (Example taken from Francis 1994)

---

[1] Since we are looking primarily at written text in this chapter, we refer throughout to writers and readers; but we assume that, in principle though not in every instance of practice, what we say would refer equally to speakers and hearers.

There is no absolute division between these two aspects of cohesion, since on the one hand the relationship between an unspecific noun and its specific lexicalization is in the broadest sense one of repetition, and on the other hand repetition may in itself indicate the type of conjunction (see Winter 1994 on matching relations).

What most of these approaches (and others, such as that outlined in de Beaugrande and Dressler 1981) have in common is that they focus almost exclusively on coherence, and thus cohesion, in propositional terms, with the interpersonal function of the language playing little or no role—see, for example, the very full discussion of conjunction and continuity in Martin (1992*a*: ch. 4). Halliday (1994: 338) mentions that certain types of cohesive resources involve interpersonal rather than ideational meaning, but he does not explore the implications. In general, the important concept of evaluative coherence—the way in which, for example, writers work to convey a consistent personal evaluation of the topic they are dealing with—has received little attention, and there has also been little investigation of the corresponding role of evaluative lexis in creating cohesion (though see Hunston 1989, 1994). What we wish to do in this chapter is to explore one of the ways in which explicit evaluation in a text functions to create texture and structure.

The evaluative items that we are particularly interested in are disjuncts, and we wish to examine their role in signalling conjunction in text. Disjuncts are adverbials such as *unfortunately* and *obviously* which are traditionally seen as expressing the writer's comment on the content or style of the sentence in which they appear. The name 'disjunct' would seem to suggest that these have some kind of connection with (con)junctive items, but that their role is, if anything, to signal an absence of conjunction;[2] and this is certainly the impression that is given by the treatments of disjuncts in, for example, Quirk *et al.* (1985: 612–47). The distinction that they draw between conjuncts (*however, in addition*, etc.) and disjuncts is now well established and corresponds to a broader distinction, based on the propositional view of cohesion outlined above, between text-structuring and writer's comment, which are seen as largely unrelated. The description given in Quirk *et al.* draws the line between the two types of adverbial in the following terms:

Whereas, in the case of disjuncts, we related them to the speaker's 'authority' for (or the speaker's comment on) the accompanying clause, we relate conjuncts to the speaker's comment in one quite specific respect: his assessment of how he views the connection between two linguistic units. (1985: 631–2)

Their approach emphasizes that the scope of disjuncts is simply the sentence in which they appear ('contributing another facet of information to a single integrated unit') while conjuncts function between clauses or other elements ('conjoining independent units'). Halliday (1985/1994) prefers the terms Conjunctive

---

[2] It is possible that, in adopting the term 'disjunct', Quirk *et al.* (1985) were thinking more of the contrast with 'adjunct', and wishing to stress the syntactic detachment of disjuncts from the clause with which they appear. The alternative contrast, with 'conjunct', which is mentioned here is the one that we focus on in this chapter.

Adjuncts and Modal Adjuncts (and includes under the latter items such as *already* which are not disjuncts as defined by Quirk *et al.*); but the line of division is essentially the same. The pervasiveness of the distinction is reflected in, for example, materials for teaching English as a Foreign Language, where conjuncts are frequently taught as a separate topic as part of writing and reading skills, under headings such as 'Signpost words' (see e.g. Williams 1982), whereas disjuncts—if treated at all—appear with other adverbs as part of speaking skills (see e.g. Soars and Soars 1989).

It is true that the apparently sharp distinction is in fact somewhat softened by the way in which the two types of adverbial are described. As the quotation above shows, Quirk *et al.* see them both as expressing the 'speaker's comment', while Halliday emphasizes that both types are 'constructing a context for the clause' (1994: 84). Halliday also mentions that 'Comment Adjuncts' (a sub-set of Modal Adjuncts) are like Conjunctive Adjuncts in that they 'occur at points in the clause which are significant for the textual organisation' (1994: 83). Nevertheless, these shared features are introduced only concessively, as a basis for bringing out the differences: for example, Halliday goes on to say that, unlike Conjunctive Adjuncts, Modal Adjuncts do not have a textual function.

In this chapter, we would like to shift the emphasis away from the differences—without, of course, wishing to deny their existence or importance—and to focus on the similarities. Essentially, we wish to argue that the function of disjuncts can often only be fully understood if they are seen as serving to show how elements of a text are linked, and that their interpersonal function is inextricably combined with a textual, cohesive function. Our basic view of these items is therefore that in many—though by no means all—cases they function as 'conjuncts with attitude' (Zhou 1991).

In order to present the evidence for such a view, we need an approach to the analysis of conjunction which is broader and more discourse-based than traditional approaches; and this is available in clause-relational analysis as elaborated by Winter (e.g. 1982, 1994) and Hoey (e.g. 1983). Winter and Hoey have constantly emphasized the interactive nature of text-structuring as something to be negotiated at each point between reader and writer. Such an emphasis can clearly accommodate the idea that the writer might guide the reader by reference not only to 'external' logical relations between propositions but also to his or her own views on, say, the relevance of one proposition to another.[3] Indeed, one of the main claims that we shall be making, concerning the central role of writer and reader

---

[3] Halliday (1994: 338) also links 'external' conjunction to the ideational metafunction and 'internal' conjunction to the interpersonal. However, he appears to limit internal conjunction to 'relations between the steps in an argument' which are signalled by Conjunctive Adjuncts such as 'firstly'. This is compatible with the broader view of interpersonal conjunction taken here, but he is interested in phenomena which are primarily textual but with an interpersonal function, whereas our emphasis is the opposite. Halliday also does not explore the apparent contradiction of Conjunctive Adjuncts serving an interpersonal function.

expectations in the perception of coherence, is closely based on arguments put forward by Winter as early as 1968 (Huddleston *et al.* 1968: ch. 14). In the discussion that follows, therefore, our analysis of conjunction in the examples will draw chiefly on their approach.[4]

Disjuncts as Cohesive Signals

We begin with relatively straightforward cases where disjuncts contribute fairly directly and unambiguously to cohesion, before moving on to examine less clear-cut cases. For each group, we discuss what features of the meaning of the disjuncts enable them to function cohesively; and this discussion will lead us to an examination of the relationship between interpersonal and textual functions in general.

CONCESSIVE RELATIONS

One group of disjuncts (which fall under 'Mood Adjuncts' in Halliday's categorization) may function to set up a concessive relation between clauses. Here are a few examples, the first within the sentence, and the others between sentences.

(7.2)
And who in the world could possibly make a mistake about a thing like that? *Admittedly* it was painted white, but that made not the slightest difference.
(7.3)
You're exaggerating, dear. *True*, I did at one point do an epitaph and a format for a memorial service. But that's not unusual, it's like making up a will.
(7.4)
Before the war, it was always the working class which bore the brunt [of economic sacrifices]. Since the war the outcome has been quite different ... *Certainly* the middle classes have come off distinctly better under the Tories. Yet a repetition of 1921 or 1931 is unthinkable even now; the national shift to the Left, with all its implications for the balance of power, may be accepted as permanent.
(7.5)
... an orang, particularly when it is young, can stick its legs out at angles that seem, to human eyes, painfully impossible. *Plainly*, they are excellently adapted for the arboreal life. At the same time, their size does seem to be something of a handicap to them.

The concessive relation in these cases has three main characteristics. First, the surface pattern is of a proposition with a disjunct expressing the writer's evaluation of the truth value of the proposition, followed by another proposition which is presented as true but without an explicit evaluation of its truth value. The next characteristic is that the second proposition is presented as not an expected consequence of the first. In Example 7.4, for example, the sentence beginning *Certainly* refers to the advantages enjoyed by the middle classes under the Tories,

---

[4] The examples are all taken from a 20-million word corpus which forms part of the Bank of English at CobuILD, Birmingham; they thus come from a range of different genres.

which might be seen as heralding a return to the conditions of 1921 and 1931 in which the working classes bore the brunt of economic suffering. The following sentence then asserts that this outcome will not happen. From this perspective, as Winter (1994) points out, the concessive relationship can be seen as a combination of logical sequence and matching relations: the second proposition is in a matching relation of incompatibility to an unstated proposition which would, if made explicit, give a possible (expected) logical consequence of the first. Example 7.2 above, in which the speaker is telling how he identified a valuable piece of furniture despite the fact that it was painted white, could be represented as follows with the unstated proposition made explicit:

(7.2a)
It was painted white. *Therefore someone could make a mistake about a thing like that . . .* But that made not the slightest difference: *I did not make a mistake about it.*

The third criterial feature of the relationship is that both propositions are presented as valid, but the second is presented as in some way more valid than the first. This arises partly from the expectation in argumentation that, in cases of incompatibility, the second of two propositions will normally be the one which expresses the writer's own view. In addition, the fact that the first proposition does not have the expected consequence has the effect of restricting the scope of its validity, thereby diminishing its informational 'weight' in relation to the real outcome. One way of capturing the impression given is by saying that the first proposition is conceded, whereas the second is asserted.

Within a hypotactic clause complex, it is possible to signal this kind of relationship with *although*, with the informationally subordinate role of the conceded proposition reflected by its grammatical dependence. In the examples above, on the other hand, the same function is performed between independent clauses by the combination of preparatory disjunct (*certainly*, *admittedly*, etc.) plus completing conjunct/conjunction (*but*, *yet*, etc.). The conjunct/conjunction is, of course, one which can signal concession by itself—for example:

(7.6)
Any reforms that make such cruel charades unnecessary have to be very good laws. *But* will the Lord Chancellor's proposals take the bad taste out of divorce?

This therefore raises the question of whether the disjunct is needed for the relationship to be adequately signalled, and if so, why. In order to arrive at an answer, it is worth noting that in speech, intonation can signal that a proposition is being put forward only concessively, predicting to the hearer that an assertion will follow that the speaker regards as more valid; but in writing there may well be nothing in the first proposition itself, apart from the disjunct, which signals this clearly.

In Example 7.6, the fact that the Lord Chancellor's proposals are going to be evaluated negatively overall has been signalled by the sub-title of the newspaper article from which the extract is taken ('Is the divorce white paper no more than a glossy exercise in cost-cutting?'), and the demands of evaluative coherence lead the reader to expect that any positive evaluation, such as in the first sentence of Example 7.6, will be introduced only concessively. The writer is therefore under less communicative pressure to reinforce the concessive nature of the first sentence with an introductory disjunct such as *certainly* (though it would certainly be possible to do so). Moreover, by not tagging the proposition in the first sentence in advance as a concession, she can give full weight to it (she herself went through one of the 'cruel charades' under the old system and is presenting herself as well aware of the need for reform). In Example 7.5, on the other hand, the main direction of the writer's argument is less obviously flagged in advance.[5] The general context is a discussion of the changes involved in the evolution of the great apes from living in trees to living on the ground. The description of the orang starts two sentences earlier by emphasizing that it is 'the heaviest tree-dweller in existence'. The writer then goes on to talk about its powerful grip and physical flexibility, and the sentence beginning *Plainly* summarizes the point that these characteristics enable it to live in trees. However, this turns out to be a kind of side-step in the argument, since the next part of the text deals at length with the problems for arboreal life caused by its weight. The presence of the disjunct opens up the possibility that their being *excellently adapted* is mentioned as a concession, not the point which the writer wants to develop into the basis of the argument; and this is confirmed when the reader meets *At the same time*, which signals a return to the main line of argument in the following part of the text.

In Example 7.4, the reasons for including the disjunct are slightly different. The main point that the writer, a left-wing politician, is making concerns the steady, and for him now unstoppable, trend towards the brunt of economic sacrifices being borne by the middle class rather than the working class. The apparent change of direction under the Tory government is presented as a temporary blip. The disjunct signals a point that can only be brought in as a minor side-step in an argument whose direction is already well-established. This is also true of Examples 7.2 and 7.3, where the first sentence given in each case indicates the writer's main line of argument ('impossible to make a mistake', 'exaggerating') and the conceded proposition represents a side-step, with the asserted proposition representing a return to the previously established line.

It is important to note that in both Examples 7.4 and 7.5 the coherence of the text would be compromised if the disjunct were removed. In Example 7.5 *Plainly* is perhaps not essential, but it considerably 'softens up' the reader for the switch back to the main argument in the following sentence. Since the conjunctive signal *At the same time* is in some ways a 'weaker' signal of concession than *but* or *yet*, it may be that the combination of the disjunct *plainly* and the conjunct *at the same time* is more necessary.[6] In Example 7.4 it is difficult to see any other way in which

---

[5] The extract is actually from the commentary to a television documentary on the great apes; but since the text is scripted we continue to talk about the 'writer' of the text.

[6] Neither *plainly* nor *at the same time* are unambiguously signals of concession, of course. However, evidence from the corpus suggests that when they are found in sentence-initial position they both

the *Certainly* sentence could be introduced—without the disjunct it would most probably be interpreted as the specific lexicalization of the unspecific *different out-come*, thus giving exactly the opposite reading to the one intended.

The choice between the two options of giving a preparatory signal or not will typically involve a question of informational balance. The writer may wish to signal as the reader encounters the concession that this is merely a concession and not an assertion, thus downgrading the informational weight of the conceded proposition; or he or she may wish to introduce it simply as an unmarked proposition and only retrospectively categorize it as a concession in relation to the following assertion, thus maintaining a more equal balance of weight. There is in fact a cline in the balance of weight between the two propositions (cf. Halliday 1994: 241), which can be seen if we invent possible paraphrases of Example 7.4:

(7.4*a*)
Despite the distinct advantages enjoyed by the middle classes under the Tories, a repetition of 1921 or 1931 is unthinkable.
(7.4*b*)
Although the middle classes have come off distinctly better under the Tories, a repetition of 1921 or 1931 is unthinkable.
(7.4*c*)
Certainly the middle classes have come off distinctly better under the Tories. Yet a repetition of 1921 or 1931 is unthinkable.
(7.4*d*)
The middle classes have come off distinctly better under the Tories. Yet a repetition of 1921 or 1931 is unthinkable.

The two interrelated choices open to the writer relate to the grammatical status of the conceded proposition (from phrase in 7.4*a* to dependent clause in 7.4*b*, to independent sentence in 7.4*c* and 7.4*d*) and to whether or not the clause relation is signalled in advance (as in 7.4*a*, 7.4*b*, and 7.4*c*) or only retrospectively (as in 7.4*d*).[7] It is clear that the disjunct is functioning to mark a separate point on the cline; and it is worth noting that the function of pre-signalling an independent clause or sentence as a concession can only be carried out by a disjunct. The cline represents a

---

appear to be fairly strongly associated with concession: of 11 such examples of *plainly*, 5 introduce a conceded proposition; and of 135 examples of *at the same time*, 94 introduce an assertion following a conceded proposition. The fact that the two occur here in successive sentences seems likely to make the potential semantic component of concession in both 'resonate' (Thompson 1998) and thus strengthen this interpretation.

[7] With Examples 7.4*a* and 7.4*b* it would, of course, be possible for the concession to appear after the assertion. In this case the factor of end-focus (see Quirk *et al.* 1985: 1357) would complicate the picture by adjusting the informational balance towards the concession. Halliday (1994: 235) mentions that 'though', which is normally a hypotactic conjunction, sometimes occurs 'in what seems closer to a paratactic [i.e. non-subordinated] function', and the example he gives has the concession following the assertion: the ordering appears to be the source of this shift towards greater independence for the conceded proposition.

set of textual choices which relate to conjunction; and the disjunct is therefore functioning conjunctively.[8]

One difference between conjuncts and disjuncts is that most conjuncts appear to express only the logical relationship that they signal: for example, *in addition* appears to signal simply '+' (we say 'appears to' because we follow Sinclair 1981, in viewing conjuncts as normally construing interactive meanings as well as textual ones). On the other hand, whatever their conjunctive function, the disjuncts in Examples 7.2 to 7.6 above clearly have an evaluative meaning which goes beyond the signalling of the logical relation of concession. It is therefore necessary to explore what it is about their interpersonal meaning which allows them to perform their textual function.

In many ways, this is most straightforward with *admittedly* (see Example 7.2 above). The disjunct is, of course, related to the verb *admit* which, in itself, encodes concession in the non-technical sense, a reluctant acceptance that something is true. It is possible to concede a point without giving an explicit counter-assertion:

(7.7)

If I became a witness against him, he might also become a witness against me. Admittedly he might already have done so. I felt like a man trying to walk over ice in shoes made of glass.

However, given human nature, it is at least not surprising to find a counter-assertion in this situation: having given in on one point, it is natural to want to re-assert oneself (and in fact of the 89 comparable instances of *admittedly* in the corpus only 18 do not have a following counter-assertion).[9] With *admittedly*, it is fairly clear that the concession–assertion relation is inherently interactive, since what one 'admits' is normally something that has already been asserted or at least implied by someone else. The disjunct is therefore part of the negotiation between writer and reader or, as in Example 7.2, between the character whose thoughts are being reported and an imagined interlocutor. Since the conceded proposition is not in fact the point that the writer wants to make, the need to mention it at all must derive from the writer's assumption that the other person might raise it as an objection and that he or she needs to forestall this. Thus what might be treated as an 'objective' logical connection by using *although* or *nevertheless* ('A and B are

---

[8] It is useful to compare the disjunct–conjunct pairs discussed here with intrasentential conjunction–conjunct pairs such as *if–then* (see the discussion of 'correlatives' in Quirk *et al.* 1985: 644–5). The conjunct in the latter case is seen as reinforcing the logical relationship already signalled by the conjunction, whereas in disjunct–conjunct pairs it is the conjunct which is the key signal of the relationship (a case of pre-inforcement by the disjunct?). Nevertheless, the effect of correlation is equally strong in both cases, and Quirk *et al.*'s comment that 'formal correlation contributes both to stylistic elegance . . . and to textual clarity' also applies to disjunct–conjunct correlation.

[9] These figures leave out 37 instances of *admittedly* used parenthetically—e.g. 'the Duke of Portland (admittedly eccentric if not mad) sacked any housemaid who had the misfortune to meet him in the corridor' or in premodifying position in a nominal group—e.g. 'entirely novel and admittedly incalculable risks'. In such cases the 'concession' is interpolated rather than part of the line of argument, and there is normally no counter-assertion.

both true; *A* is not entirely compatible with B; *A* does not invalidate B') is cast in overtly interpersonal terms by the use of the disjunct ('You may think *A*; *I* agree that *A is* true; for me, *A* does not rule out B'). The means by which the conjunctive relationship is signalled are different, but the result is cohesive in both cases.

We have mentioned that *admittedly* implies that negotiation is going on between the writer and reader. In cases where the interpersonal option for doing concessive conjunction is taken, there is in fact a revealing parallel to be drawn with the way in which turns in dialogue are interpreted as coherent. The following rewrite of Example 7.2, we would argue, reflects the underlying dialogue taking place in the speaker's mind:

(7.2*b*)
'Who in the world could possibly make a mistake about a thing like that?'
'But it was painted white!'
'Yes, but that made not the slightest difference.'

The presence of the disjunct *admittedly is* one of the 'dialogic overtones' (Bakhtin 1986: 93) which signal that the speaker is conducting the argument 'against' the imagined objections of the interlocutor: replacing *admittedly* with *although* has the effect, amongst other things, of muffling or removing this overtone.[10]

(7.2*c*)
Although it was painted white, that made not the slightest difference.

How, though, does this work with the disjuncts which do not evoke interaction in the same overt way? *Certainly*, for example, might appear simply to be a comment on the truth value of the proposition. However, as has frequently been pointed out, we do not normally find it necessary to proclaim explicitly the truth value of a proposition unless that value is in some way in question. As Halliday (1994: 89) puts it: 'you only say you are certain when you are not'—or, in a broader and perhaps more accurate wording, saying explicitly that you believe something to be true admits the possibility of it not being believed to be true by everyone. In the case of a concession, of course, it is the writer who is simultaneously accepting the truth of the proposition and in a way calling it into question in relation to the following dominant assertion. The proposition itself is not dismissed, but the scope of its truth value is questioned by the denial of the consequences which might be expected to follow from it. Therefore the use of the modal disjunct sets up a natural textual environment for the following counter-assertion.

EXPECTANCY RELATIONS

To formulate the function of the disjunct in this way points to one crucial difference between disjuncts and conjuncts, at least in the case of concession: whereas

---

[10] Although this is outside the focus of the present discussion, it is worth noting that the dialogic tone can be introduced by other means. In Example 7.2, for instance, making 'was' contrastively prominent in speech would suggest that the speaker was denying an implied objection even if *admittedly* were not used: 'It *was* painted white, but that made not the slightest difference'.

conjuncts signal the relation being established, disjuncts provide a potential context for the relation without in themselves signalling it (although, in the case of *True*, particularly, the potential is so strong that, of 119 examples that we have examined, all but 5 are followed by a counter-assertion). In Examples 7.2 to 7.5 above the removal of the conjunct would result in the concessive relation being lost, or at least obscured, even if the disjunct remained. However, there are disjuncts signalling other relations apart from concession which function more independently: they can generally be replaced, and in some cases reinforced, by a conjunct, but they can signal the relation with no support from a conjunct and their removal would often result in a sense of incoherence. The most salient of these are the disjuncts which relate to expectations.

(7.8)
All of these sports and many others are dominated by the human urge to aim at something. *Surprisingly,* this aspect of sport is often overlooked when underlying motivations are being discussed.

(7.9)
After 10 years of standardization on IBM PC-compatible micros, there should be a healthy UK market for used models. *Curiously,* there seems to be only one big second-hand PC dealer, Morgan Computer, in London.

In this group, we can include disjuncts such as *unfortunately* which deny the positive expectations set up by the preceding text.

(7.10)
Our intelligence was almost always better than that of the British. *Unfortunately* Washington's judgement sometimes disallowed facts.

(7.11)
We take barrels for granted, and assume there will always be enough of them about for our purposes. *Sadly* there will not be, because there are practically no coopers left in the Western World.

Disjuncts which comment on good news rather than bad, such as *fortunately,* may also be used in the same kind of way. In this case, it is negative expectations set up by the preceding text which are denied.[11]

---

[11] Both bad and good news disjuncts can, of course, be used to signal negative and positive expectations fulfilled (Winter's *and* relation). This is more frequent with positive cases: '*Provision of concrete aircraft shelters, command bunkers, and hardened fuel and weapon storage were seen as essentials. Happily, a NATO-wide programme of such improvements had been brought to an advanced stage by the spring of 1985.*'

In negative cases, the normal use of the disjunct to signal expectation denied has a stronger influence, and the relation of negative expectation fulfilled (often ironic in tone) is usually highlighted by the explicit presence of *and*: '*Other people have the itch to dominate children and unfortunately they can succeed*'.

As Winter (in Huddleston *et al.* 1968: 570) points out, both expectation fulfilled and expectation denied are included under the clause relation of specified expectancy. Thus in either case the disjunct is signalling a clause relation.

(7.12)
I had no illusions about our disparate rock-climbing abilities—what he found easy, I might find bloody desperate! *Happily*, in this case I did not.

Corresponding to these signals of counter-expectation, we have signals of expectation fulfilled:

(7.13)
Einstein's theory had predicted it would, and that went a great way toward establishing the validity of general relativity. *Naturally* astronomers were anxious to make further checks on the theory.

(7.14)
In volume terms business virtually stagnated. *Predictably*, the management blames the recession.

The crucial importance of the writer's view of the reader's expectations in signalling conjunction has, as mentioned above, been identified by Winter (Huddleston *et al.* 1968). He argues that there are three basic ways in which pairs of clauses may be related—three sets of clause relations, each of which may relate pairs of clauses by itself or in combination with one of the others: logical sequence, matching, and expectancy. For him, the central function of *but is* not to signal contrast but more specifically to signal that 'the juxtaposition [of two clauses] conflicts with what is expected', while *and* essentially signals that 'the expectation is fulfilled' (ibid. 570). The fact that *but* and *and* are frequently used both to specify expectancy and to signal one of the other types of clause relation such as comparison has tended to obscure the fact that the expectancy-related function is more central. At each juncture in the text, the writer can opt to indicate whether or not a proposition is expected in the light of what has preceded it. There are cases of what Winter calls 'neutral expectancy', where this option is not taken, but in principle the option is available. The importance of this insight is that, since expectations inherently draw on the interaction between the writer and reader, it places interpersonal, evaluative judgements on a par with more accepted 'external' logical signals as complementary ways of establishing cohesion in text. One obvious way of indicating the expectedness or otherwise of a proposition is by commenting explicitly on it by means of a disjunct.

In the examples which signal counter-expectation (7.8 to 7.12 above), the disjunct could in each case be replaced by *but* or *however*—for example:

(7.8*a*)
All of these sports and many others are dominated by the human urge to aim at something. But this aspect of sport is often overlooked when underlying motivations are being discussed.

The disjunct could also appear with the conjunct—for example:

(7.10*a*)
Our intelligence was almost always better than that of the British. Unfortunately, however, Washington's judgement sometimes disallowed facts.

If both appear, *but*, because of its origins as a normal conjunction within the clause complex, must appear first; but the normal position of *however* in written text is following the disjunct:

(7.15)
Many children receive some kind of sex education in school. *Sadly, however,* it continues to reflect a double standard of morality for men and women.

To replace or complement the disjunct in these ways clearly changes the meaning to some extent. In Example 7.8*a* compared with 7.8, the writer's presence is less strongly felt—in cases like 7.8, the 'conjuncts with attitude' description seems most apt for the disjunct. In Example 7.10*a* compared with 7.10, it could be argued that the two functions—comment and conjunction—are separated out, with the disjunct performing the first and the conjunct the second. However, this does not correspond to our intuitions about the relative weight of the two adverbials: the conjunct appears simply to reinforce the conjunctive link which has already been set up by the disjunct.

We have talked about maintaining the impression of coherence by replacing or reinforcing the disjunct with a conjunct. It is noticeable that what we cannot do in any of these cases is to remove the disjunct without seriously impairing that impression:

(7.9*a*)
After 10 years of standardization on IBM PC-compatible micros, there should be a healthy UK market for used models. There seems to be only one big second-hand PC dealer, Morgan Computer, in London.
(7.10*b*)
Our intelligence was almost always better than that of the British. Washington's judgement sometimes disallowed facts.

In Example 7.9*a*, the intended matching contrast relation (which is a contrast between the Hypothetical proposition in the first sentence and the Real in the second—see Winter 1994) is extremely difficult to discern, not least because *seems* in the second sentence might well be interpreted as a signal of continuing hypotheticality in harmony with *should* in the first. In Example 7.10*b* the removal of the disjunct renders the juxtaposition of the two clauses incoherent, particularly because the repetition on which the denial of expectation is based is not lexically explicit ('our intelligence was better' = 'we knew more *facts*'; 'Washington disallowed *facts*'). The disjunct signals retrospectively that the first sentence has carried an expectation which the second sentence is to be interpreted as denying; without the disjunct there are insufficient cohesive signals for the reader to see the intended relationship. Thus the disjuncts clearly have a cohesive function in themselves, and one which is innately connected with their interpersonal meaning.

In the examples which signal expectation fulfilled (7.13 and 7.14 above), the situation is less clear cut. If the disjunct were omitted, the sentences would still appear reasonably coherent:

(7.14a)
In volume terms business virtually stagnated. The management blames the recession.

However, in a sense this is predictable. The *and* relation is far more common than the *but* relation (as a very rough and ready indication of this, in word frequency calculations on a range of texts *and* consistently appears in a ratio of at least five occurrences for every occurrence of *but*); and in cases where the relation between clauses is not signalled, the one that is most likely to be assumed is non-problematic (i.e. not unexpected) addition. This is, of course, the *and* relation (which is the most likely interpretation of the relation between the two sentences in Example 7.14a). Thus in many cases the use of a conjunct, such as *in addition*, to signal this relation may be seen as reinforcement for the sake of clarity (not least by explicitly ruling out the possibility of the relation being something different). The use of a disjunct such as *predictably* also has much the same reinforcing function but performs it from an interpersonal perspective. In fact, to signal explicitly that a proposition is expected in the light of what has preceded it can be seen as a marked option—that is, conveying something more than simple positive expectancy. The 'something more' is often (as in Example 7.14) irony, with the second proposition being presented as expected but not necessarily welcome or acceptable.

HYPOTHETICAL–REAL PATTERNS

We have mentioned that in Example 7.9 the disjunct is placed at the junction between Hypothetical and Real; and the same is true of Examples 7.11 and 7.12 (with the hypothetical status of the first proposition signalled by *assume* and *might* respectively). In these cases, the Hypothetical–Real pattern is carried by matching relations of contradiction,[12] and, strictly speaking, the disjuncts signal that relation rather than the Hypothetical–Real pattern directly. However, a hypothesis entails the existence of a person hypothesizing—evaluating the possibilities—and hypothetical propositions are thus typically signalled by reference to the beliefs of the audience (as in Example 7.11) and/or the writer (as in Example 7.12). Therefore it is not surprising that disjuncts can also be used to pre-signal explicitly that a proposition is hypothetical:

(7.16)
Ostensibly, he is a walking exemplar of change. When we look more closely, however, we find that he has stayed on the same job.

The status of a proposition as Real can equally be signalled by a disjunct:

---

[12] For the difference between clause relations and discourse patterns, see Hoey (1983). The Hypothetical–Real relation is a discourse structure rather than a clause relation: that is, it provides a larger-scale context within which clause relations such as contradiction or contrast operate. However, it is still based on the relationship between two parts of a text and any signal of its presence contributes to the cohesion of the text.

(7.17)

I allowed Jefferson to think that I favoured his so-called principle. *Actually* I have always preferred a judiciary independent of the other two branches of government.

(7.18)

Boycott's detractors talk as if trouble only began in the dressingroom when the balding bespectacled youth from Fitzwilliam played his first game. *In fact,* Willie Watson left the county for Leicester and his best years back in 1957.

Occasionally, we find pairs of disjuncts working together to signal both Hypothetical and Real:

(7.19)

Ostensibly, I was teaching acting to a group of English professionals; *in fact,* they were teaching me.

This kind of link between interpersonal evaluation and textual cohesion is inherent in the clause-relational approach. By taking a wider view of conjunction than that encouraged by a focus on traditional 'linking words', Winter and Hoey have shown that coherence is not restricted to objective logical connections and that cohesion embraces a broader range of signals than usually allowed for. For them, all conjunction is a matter of negotiation between writer and reader (see e.g. Hoey's use of question and answer in *On the Surface of Discourse* (1983)). Among the relations that they discuss are a number which rely particularly heavily on interpersonal meanings, and Hypothetical–Real is one of those: Winter describes it as 'the basic text structure which we use to report our response to the perceived truth of somebody else's or our own statements' (1994: 63).

ALTERNATIVE RELATIONS

A further area where interpersonal disjuncts appear to serve a cohesive function, though perhaps less clearly so, is when two or more clauses are to be interpreted as alternative possible interpretations of the same event. Unlike the expectancy relation, which falls broadly under the semantics of *but* or *and*, this is essentially an *or* relation.

(7.20)

There are always police sirens going and army jeeps roaring past. *Maybe* they are coming to break up the lecture. *Maybe* they are shooting our friends. We don't know.

(7.21)

Saturday night's rioting in London may have been quite different from earlier riots. *Perhaps* this time it was planned. *Perhaps* it was organized. *Perhaps* the crowd started it. *Perhaps* the police were the innocent victims of the cowardly, vicious and criminal attacks of people who 'went to the demonstration to make a riot' as Neil Kinnock put it yesterday. *Perhaps* this time the violence was mindless and the looting indiscriminate.

In Examples 7.20 and 7.21, the alternatives may or may not be mutually exclusive: the riot in Example 7.21 could have been both 'planned' and 'organized', but it would be odd to describe it as both 'planned' and 'indiscriminate'. Thus the *or* relation that is signalled may tend towards contrast (exclusive) or compatibility (not exclusive). In some cases the contrast tendency seems stronger:

(7.22)
But just as the Renaissance science of expression had tumbled into mannerism, so too did the new abstract expression. *Arguably*, it was even more prone to do so because . . .

Here the writer begins by emphasizing the similarity in the way the two forms of expression developed, but then offers a possible alternative view which highlights the difference; and only one of these views can be correct. This shift between being compatible and mutually exclusive is typical of the *or* relation generally (see Quirk *et al.* 1985: 932–3), and thus the disjuncts in this grouping closely parallel the range of behaviour of conjuncts such as *alternatively* or *instead*.

In order to understand how the disjuncts can function in this way, we have, as with the concessive disjuncts, to link them to their modal meaning. If something 'may happen', the alternative—that it may equally well not happen—is inherent in the meaning (*may* is often informally described as indicating 50% certainty). Therefore, by commenting on the modal status of a proposition as possible, the writer is simultaneously implying that an alternative is available. In some cases, this implication may not be exploited, but in others, such as the examples above, the existence of the alternative is made explicit, and it is the disjunct which indicates that this is how the clauses are to be interpreted.

OTHER CASES

So far, we have examined cases in which it seems indisputable that the disjunct serves some kind of conjunctive function. It must be stressed, however, that we are not (yet) claiming that this will be true of all uses of disjuncts. There are many examples where it is difficult to discern a linking function, and it could be argued that the disjunct behaves more or less in the role traditionally ascribed to it, to convey the writer's comment as a separate, detachable element—'disjuncts' therefore in the sense of not really being an integral part of the clause with which they appear.

(7.23)
Timothy Blauvelt, the college Unitarian chaplain, presided. *Naturally*, Ray Stratton was there, and I also invited Jeremy Nahum.

(7.24)
A male impersonator is almost unheard of today, though in the late Victorian era, when women were still forbidden by custom to wear male dress, they were common on the stage. *Interestingly enough*, women who wear men's clothes usually dress like gentlemen, or even like aristocrats, whereas men who dress in women's clothes seldom look like ladies.

(7.25)
By and large the function of educating public opinion, in all but a handful of western countries, is going by default. *Significantly*, the three countries with the best aid performance also spent most on education about development.

What still remains to be explained in these cases, of course, is why the writer feels the need to include personal comment at precisely this point in the text. Our own basic position is that the apparent lack of a coherence-signalling role for the disjunct may well derive mainly from the fact that an adequate picture of inter-personal coherence has not yet been built up. Studies of conjunction (with the notable exception of the work of Winter and Hoey, and its extension in rhetorical structure theory—see e.g. Mann and Thompson 1988) have largely been constrained by an almost exclusive focus on those relations between clauses which can be signalled by a conjunction or conjunct. Indeed, in the discussion so far we ourselves have to a large extent relied on types of conjunction where we can compare disjuncts with conjuncts signalling the same or similar relations. In cases such as Examples 7.23–7.25 above, however, we would argue that the difficulty in pinning down the conjunctive function of the disjuncts may arise because they are signalling a type of conjunction for which an alternative encoding by means of conjuncts is not available (which makes it difficult to label or explicate the relation in a concise way).

In Example 7.25, for instance, the two sentences are clearly mutually relevant, and the disjunct clearly contributes to the perception of coherence (if it is removed, it is much harder to discern the mutual relevance); but our best attempts at capturing the form of this relevance result in unsatisfactory circumlocutions. The second sentence explicitly picks up the 'handful of western countries' in the first and the idea of 'educating public opinion' about aid, but the reason for mentioning the 'best aid performance' here is unclear. However, the second sentence is contributing to a larger argument, which emerges when more of the original text is included:

(7.25+)
Attitudes like these stem from chauvinistic ignorance of the extent of need in the Third World. Instead of blindly following public opinion, political leaders ought to attempt to change it. Ethnocentric education systems could help by teaching children about the problems of three quarters of the human race. By and large the function of educating public opinion, in all but a handful of western countries, is going by default. Significantly, the three countries with the best aid performance also spent most on education about development.

The larger argument is that satisfactory aid performance goes together with educating public opinion: if people are better informed about aid, they will be more willing to offer it. The place of the sentence beginning *Significantly* in this argument is as a Basis for the Evaluation, combined with the role of Specific in relation to the General in the first three sentences in 7.25+ (see Winter 1994, on multiple clause relations). In itself, *Significantly* does not signal these relations (it is difficult to think of one item which could); what it does appear to indicate is something like: 'The following proposition has a significant bearing on what I have said above in ways which you, the reader, will be able to work out on the basis of other signals (repetition, etc.) in the text'.

One aspect of the links being established is that there is no conjunct which could fulfil the function of signalling the relation. The importance of this is that we are, in effect, claiming that there are types of conjunctive relations which can *only* be signalled by disjuncts. This goes against traditional approaches to the analysis of conjunction, but it fits in with Winter and Hoey's clause-relational approach which begins from the assumption that any clause (in a potentially coherent text) is in a relation of some kind with the preceding clause or clauses. It also fits in with their view of coherence as negotiated between writer and reader at each point—this emerges particularly clearly from the discussion of *Significantly* in Example 7.25.

This still does not amount to a claim that all disjuncts have a conjunctive function. We have identified at least two types of use where they appear not to have. The first occurs particularly in narrative.

(7.26)
The next actor to come on stage in our little amorality play was the good Doktor Rudolph Koenig. One of the managing directors of the Swiss Bank Corporation. *Surprisingly*, he came directly to me.

In such cases, the disjunct can perhaps be described as 'personal' rather than 'interpersonal': that is, it expresses the writer's reaction (surprise) at the time of the event rather than his comment on the proposition at the time of writing. Whereas, for example, *unfortunately* in Example 7.10 above can be paraphrased as 'It is unfortunate that' (where the present tense verb form is possible, even though the events themselves are set in the past), in Example 7.26 the most appropriate paraphrase seems to be 'I was surprised that'. This type of disjunct use is therefore closer to having an ideational function, describing real-world events (which happen to involve feelings) rather than construing interaction with the reader. In terms of our argument, it is clearly significant that it does not have any conjunctive-signalling function, and could be omitted with no effect on the cohesiveness of the passage.

The second type of use arises particularly with some of the disjuncts which Quirk *et al.* (1985: 615) categorize as 'style' disjuncts. In many cases, these do seem to have a genuinely disjunctive function, in that part of their function appears to be to signal a *lack of* a definite logical link.

(7.27)
The SDP began life as a breakaway party of Parliamentarians: all chief and no Indians. When 60,000 activists rushed to join, two-thirds of them with no previous party allegiance, the leadership was wholly unprepared. *Broadly*, the social democrats were the baby boom generation of the postwar years who were students in the sixties.
(7.28)
The children are divided into three age groups: the youngest range from five to seven, the intermediates from eight to ten, and the oldest from eleven to fifteen. *Generally* we have a fairly large sprinkling of children from foreign countries.

In these cases, the implication for the reader seems to be that the sentence introduced by the disjunct is to be interpreted as continuing the same topic as in the preceding sentence(s) but not as being in a specific conjunctive relation with it. Interestingly, removing the disjunct seems to highlight the lack of connection and make the text appear awkward or incoherent: it should perhaps be seen as an open admission of disjunction by the writer which functions to forestall an expected objection from the reader. It may be useful to compare disjuncts of this type with thematic circumstantial adjuncts, whose primary function is to signal a change of frame within the same overall topic (Davies 1997):

(7.29)
The foul led to an ugly 21-man scuffle—an incident which Warrington referee Joe Worrall will NOT be officially reporting. *Afterwards* Fergie blazed: 'Pointon made a stupid challenge. He tried to do the boy harm.'

In Example 7.30, this possible parallelism emerges more clearly because the first sentence is introduced by a circumstantial adjunct which has much the same meaning as the disjunct which introduces the second:

(7.30)
In most cases a legal agreement must be signed before occupation. *Generally* a deposit of one month' s rent is required.

One way of viewing this function of disjuncts is that just as some disjuncts 'interpersonalize' conjunction (see 'Concessive Relations' above), so others interpersonalize framing. This area would obviously need more exhaustive investigation—not least of the relationship between conjunction and framing—before any definite claims could be made, but the hypothesis of interpersonal framing does fit in with the broader picture of coherence-signalling strategies that is emerging.

Conclusion

We have argued in this chapter that coherence in text can only be adequately understood if the concept of propositional coherence is complemented by that of evaluative coherence, and that, amongst other things, this involves recognition of the conjunctive function of disjuncts. It must be emphasized that the present study is intended to be exploratory rather than definitive. For example, we have deliberately restricted ourselves to an examination of disjuncts in initial position. When disjuncts appear in non-initial positions, other factors affecting their function seem to come into play; and we prefer to build up a clearer picture of the cases where comparison with other types of conjunction is more straightforward before extending the analysis to even more complex cases. In addition, the types of conjunction that we have discussed above have, for obvious exemplificatory reasons, been mostly those where the signalling role of the disjuncts seems indisputable; but there are still a large number of less clear-cut examples in our data. As we have argued in 'Other Cases' above, we believe that this is mainly because our present understanding of conjunction needs to be refined.

It may be mentioned in passing that the position we have put forward appears to be not entirely compatible with the hypothesis in Systemic–Functional Grammar that the four metafunctions—interpersonal, experiential, logical and textual—are largely realized by distinct systems (see e.g. Halliday and Hasan 1985: ch. 2; Martin 1992a: ch. 1). In Halliday's (1994) introduction of the three metafunctions operating within the clause, it is clear that the choice of an element as, say, Subject (interpersonal), Actor (experiential), and Theme (textual) involves three choices which can, for the purposes of analysis at least, be separated: that is, the choice of Subject does not in itself determine the choice of Theme or of Actor. This can be seen in an example such as 7.31, where Subject and Actor (*I*) are realized by the same element, but Theme (*Ten quid*) *is* realized by a different one:

(7.31)
Ten quid I spent on that rubbish.

Similarly, textual signals of logical relations are generally discussed in terms of elements such as *so* and *nevertheless* which do not appear in the analyses of experiential and interpersonal functions (see e.g. Halliday 1994: 378). In the view set out here, however, disjuncts do not simply serve two functions—interpersonal and textual: the textual function derives directly from the interpersonal function. To express the opinion that one proposition is, say, surprising in the light of the preceding proposition signals explicit intrusion by the writer into the text; but the interpersonal comment itself expresses the logical relation between the two propositions and thus acts as a cohesive signal. Thus, whereas *I* in Example 7.31 is not Subject *because* it is Actor, disjuncts appear to be cohesive signals because of the interpersonal meaning they express. This calls into question the theoretical basis for viewing the metafunctions as inherently realized by different systems, although the implications are beyond the scope of the present chapter.

Certain important themes have run through the discussion in this chapter. One is the emphasis on seeing texture and structure as created by interactive negotiation between writer and reader, rather than simply as the reflection of objective logical relations between propositions. From this perspective, the role of interpersonal disjuncts in signalling conjunction is understandable—even predictable. As noted in 'Concessive Relations' above, disjuncts contribute to what Bakhtin calls the dialogic overtones of a text: they invoke both the writer's presence and the writer's awareness of the reader. Writers can therefore exploit them to make what is in fact a monologue sound like a dialogue—and thus achieve a more reader-friendly tone.

Closely related to this is the theme of what might be called the relative 'diffuseness' in the signalling role of disjuncts. This has emerged particularly in the discussion in 'Other Cases' above, but it is also there in our analysis of disjuncts in 'Concessive Relations'. There is often disagreement about how to categorize the relations signalled by conjuncts or conjunctions (see e.g. Martin 1992 on the differing sets of analyses proposed by different linguists), but the broad kinds of relations are reasonably well defined, whatever the difficulties in deciding exactly how those relations work in any specific context. Disjuncts, on the other hand—as the analyses above have shown—appear to function cohesively in a less easily definable way. This diffuseness need not be a negative feature in communicative terms. It may be that in fact one of the advantages of disjuncts for the writer is that they can often signal the presence of complex relations which could not be adequately captured by a conjunct. Perhaps, by overtly appealing to the reader, disjuncts invoke negotiation and the reader's co-operation in constructing coherence, whereas conjuncts reflect a more dominant role for the writer in that they guide the reader towards the type of conjunction which the writer has already decided on. If this is so, it suggests the possibility that, within general generic constraints, expert writers may aim at a balance between telling the reader where to go next (by means of conjuncts and other experientially oriented signals) and asking for the reader's co-operation in working out the line of development (by means of disjuncts and other interpersonally oriented signals), in order to produce a text that feels purposeful but not overly directive. Whether or not the 'diffuseness' and co-operation-inducing role of disjuncts turns out to be a line worth pursuing in future research, we feel that their cohesive function cannot be overlooked in a full account of the linguistic resources available for constructing text that will appear coherent to the reader.

8

Beyond Exchange: APPRAISAL Systems in English

J. R. Martin

EDITORS' INTRODUCTION

∗ ∗ ∗

In this chapter Martin examines evaluative lexis expressing the speaker or writer's opinion on, very broadly, the good/bad parameter. His study is set within the systemic functional linguistic tradition; and the account is therefore couched in terms of systems: sets of options which are available to the speaker or writer covering the meanings that can be and are typically expressed in particular contexts, and the linguistic means of expressing them.

The overall system of choices used to describe this area of meaning potential is called APPRAISAL (labels for systems are in capitals). The enormously varied lexical choices within the area are seen as construing (i.e. expressing and simultaneously 'creating') a small range of general categories of reactions. The main category or sub-system is AFFECT, which deals with the expression of emotion (happiness, fear, etc.). Related to this are two more specialized sub-systems: JUDGEMENT, dealing with moral assessments of behaviour (honesty, kindness, etc.), and APPRECIATION, dealing with aesthetic assessments (subtlety, beauty, etc.). Martin links these systems in with other areas of meaning in a number of ways. One of these is through the concept of ENGAGEMENT. This is the system of options for indicating the speaker's degree of commitment to the appraisal being expressed, and is expressed through modality and related systems—thus again underlining the close connection between these different aspects of evaluation.

Another way in which the appraisal systems can be seen to link in is through the technical concept of redundancy: each system 'redounds with' systems in other parts of the lexicogrammar (that is, in oversimple terms, they cover the same semantic area using different linguistic resources). For example, appreciative meanings (*the film was very **sad***) are close in semantic terms to mental processes of affection (*the film **moved** me to tears*)—see Halliday (1994) on transitivity. This leads Martin to postulate an important distinction between inscribed and evoked appraisal. Inscribed appraisal is explicitly expressed in the text (*a **bright** kid, a **vicious** kid*), whereas with evoked appraisal an evaluative response is projected by reference to events or states which are conventionally prized (*a kid who **reads a lot***) or frowned on (*a kid who **tears the wings off butterflies***).

The systemic account of appraisal resources is then used as a basis for an examination of how and why interlocutors engage in appraisal in a number of extracts from spoken and written texts. Martin explores the deployment of the resources as an integral part of the negotiation of meanings that goes on. He demonstrates, for example, the ways in which different contexts are likely to draw on different combinations of options, and examines how speakers can exploit different ranges of appraisal to construct particular personae for themselves. He also emphasizes that the expression of attitude is not, as is often claimed, simply a personal matter—the speaker 'commenting' on the world—but a truly interpersonal matter, in that the basic reason for advancing an opinion is to elicit a response of solidarity from the addressee.

Like Hunston (this volume), Martin is concerned to show both that evaluation is complex in operation, and that it can nevertheless be reduced (in the positive sense, as one reduces a sauce to concentrate the flavour) to a small number of basic sets of options: what appears at first to be an unmanageably diverse group of lexical items turns out to be systematically organized. Crucially, he demonstrates that those sets of options are consistently related to other sets of options in the meaning potential of the language. Viewing appraisal in lexical terms thus does not mean that it is relegated to the fringes, as it can appear to be in traditional accounts of attitudinal vocabulary; instead, it is given full value both as a central aspect of evaluation and as a vital part of the meaning negotiation that is at the heart of all communication.

* * *

Beyond NEGOTIATION

Within systemic functional linguistics (hereafter SFL), excursions into interpersonal discourse semantics have generally been grammatical in their foundation. That is to say, clause rank interpersonal systems such as MOOD and MODALITY have served as points of departure for the development of discourse models (of speech function, exchange structure, and the like; Halliday 1984; Ventola 1987). Martin (1992a: 31–91 and 461–88) documents one such excursion, developed throughout the 1980s in and around the Department of Linguistics at the University of Sydney. This chapter will address the development of a complementary perspective, founded on 'evaluative' lexis, which has been evolving during the 1990s in the metropolitan Sydney region.[1]

Traditionally then, the grammar-based tradition has focused on dialogue as an exchange of goods and services (Example 1)[2] or information (Example 2), which is

---

[1] Of the many people involved, I am especially indebted to Joan Rothery and Peter White for their work developing the framework presented here.

[2] Examples 8.1–8.5; 8.9–8.11; 8.14–8.20 are taken from the play *Educating Rita* by Willy Russell. For reasons of space, most stage directions have been omitted and the text has been shortened in several places. A complete analysis of the full text would be different in detail, though not in essence.

either given or demanded in initiations or responses.[3] Dialogue is analysed as a series of moves, which may in some registers be usefully grouped together into an exchange (Ventola 1987; Eggins and Slade 1997)—generally on the basis of grammatical evidence such as the MOOD of the clause (declarative, imperative, etc.), its person, its ellipticity, its KEY (MOOD in relation to TONE; Halliday 1994), interpersonal adjuncts, vocatives, and the phenomenon of grammatical metaphor (direct and indirect speech acts; Martin 1995a). As Martin 1992a reviews, the discourse variables involved are abstracted from the grammar of MOOD, with MODALITY treated as a resource for negotiating the semantic region between positive and negative polarity (after Halliday, e.g. 1994: 88–92, 354–63).

> (8.1) Exchanging goods and services
> FRANK. Would you—erm—would you like to sit down?
> RITA. No! Can I smoke?
> FRANK. Tobacco?
> RITA. Yeh. Was that a joke? Here—d' y' want one?
> FRANK. Ah—I'd love one.
> RITA. Well, have one.
> FRANK. I—don't smoke—I made a promise not to smoke.
> RITA. Well, I won't tell anyone.
> FRANK. Promise?

> (8.2) Exchanging information
> RITA. What does assonance mean?
> FRANK. What?
> RITA. Don't laugh at me.
> FRANK. No. Erm—assonance. Well, it's a form of rhyme. What's a—what's an example—erm—? Do you know Yeats?
> RITA. The wine lodge?
> FRANK. Yeats, the poet.
> RITA. No.
> FRANK. Oh. Well—there's a Yeats poem, called 'The Wild Swans at Coole'. In it he rhymes the word 'swan' with the word 'stone'. There, you see, an example of assonance.
> RITA. Oh. It means gettin' the rhyme wrong.
> FRANK. I've never really looked at it like that. But yes, yes you could say it means getting the rhyme wrong.

What has tended to be elided in SFL approaches to data of this kind is the semantics of evaluation—how the interlocutors are feeling, the judgements they make, and the value they place on the various phenomena of their experience. In Example 8.3, for example, Rita attempts to share her emotional response to her tutor Frank's room and the view from his window with him.

> (8.3) AFFECT—emotions; reacting to behaviour, text/process, phenomena
> RITA. I *love* this room. I *love* that window. Do you *like* it?
> FRANK. What?

---

[3] For a valuable deconstruction of this perspective, see Thibault (1992, 1995).

RITA. The window.

FRANK. I don't often consider it actually.

In Example 8.4, Frank declares his judgement about the appropriateness of subjecting Rita to his appalling teaching.

(8.4) JUDGEMENT—ethics; evaluating behaviour

FRANK. And the thing is, between you, me and the walls, I'm actually an *appalling* teacher. Most of the time, you see, *it doesn't actually matter—appalling* teaching is *quite in order* for most of my *appalling* students. And the others manage to get by despite me. But you're different.

And in Example 8.5, Rita evaluates a non-canonical text she has been reading, again attempting to share her valuation with Frank:

(8.5) APPRECIATION—aesthetics; evaluating text/process, phenomenon

RITA. Y' know, Rita Mae Brown who wrote *Rubyfruit Jungle?* Haven't y' read it? It's a *fantastic* book.

Clearly dialogue of this kind is about more than a simple exchange of goods and services or information. Read more delicately, emotions, judgements, and values are sites around which negotiation might take place. In fact, as we will see below, one of the fundamental aspects of the way Rita talks at this stage in the play is her predisposition to construct solidarity with Frank by explicitly inviting him to share her evaluations. Frank, for his part, consistently refuses to negotiate solidarity on these terms. Alongside our grammar-founded models of exchange then, we need to elaborate lexically oriented systems which tune into these additional dimensions of repartee.

Modelling APPRAISAL

The term *appraisal* will be used here for the semantic resources used to negotiate emotions, judgements, and valuations, alongside resources for amplifying and engaging with these evaluations. Comparable regions in alternative frameworks include Labov's work on evaluation and intensity in narrative (e.g. 1972, 1984), Biber and Finegan's studies of stance across a range of registers (e.g. 1988, 1989), and Chafe's research into evidentiality (e.g. 1986).[4] The relevant resources all involve grading, which is to say that the meanings involved can be adjusted by degree to reflect the strength of the evaluation (cf. Martin 1992*b*). This paper will focus on three systems—AFFECT, JUDGEMENT and APPRECIATION. AFFECT is the resource deployed for construing emotional responses ('happiness, sadness, fear, loathing', etc.); JUDGEMENT is deployed for construing moral evaluations of behaviour ('ethical, deceptive, brave', etc.); and APPRECIATION construes the

---

[4] The most relevant work in adjacent disciplines is probably that of Harré (e.g. 1987) and Lutz (e.g. 1988).

'aesthetic' quality of semiotic text/processes and natural phenomena ('remarkable, desirable, harmonious, elegant, innovative', etc.).[5]

Some texts foreground one or another of these three systems. AFFECT stands out in Example 8.6, from the sensitive new age guy (snaggy dad) section of an Australian parenting magazine. Affectual meanings suit affectual grammatical frames (e.g. *I delighted in her, She delighted me, I was delighted by her,* Halliday 1994, Matthiessen 1995).

(8.6) AFFECT—emotions; reacting to behaviour, text/process, phenomena
At last, you are in dreamland. My Goddess of Laughter, the Princess-of-all-that-is-Good. Your skin so smooth and soft. The squeals of sheer and utter joy that you unleashed only a few hours ago echo in my mind. I had to come and look at you. It is all I can do not to reach out and kiss you. But my feelings can't afford for you to wake again.
You cried so hard after we put you down. My heart hurt. It was all I could do not to rush to your side. And then you screamed your cry. I had to come to your door. You had no idea, but I was only feet away. Wanting. Wanting to hold you in my arms. You would have settled within seconds—but it would have been for my benefit, not yours. (*Mother and Baby,* June/July 1994 Sydney. The Dad Department.)

JUDGEMENT is foregrounded in Example 8.7 (in the longest nominal group I have ever analysed); the columnist is commenting on the reluctance of Australian politicians to introduce tough gun law legislation prior to the infamous Port Arthur massacre. Judgemental meanings suit grammatical frames commenting on behaviour (e.g. *It was cowardly of them to do that; For them to do that was cowardly; I consider that cowardly*).

(8.7) JUDGEMENT—ethics; evaluating behaviour
For too long—far too long—capricious, cautious, chicken-livered, cowardly, craven, duck-brained, dim-witted, faint-hearted, gutless, gormless, ignorant, indecisive, irresolute, jelly-backed, limp-wristed, namby pamby, negligent, obdurate, opportunist, perfunctory, poltroonish, pusillanimous, shallow, shameless, spineless, squeamish, timid, weak-kneed, vacuous, backsliding, bending, bickering, cheating, compromising, cringing, deal-doing, dillydallying, dithering, equivocating, failing, faking, faltering, fiddling, fidgeting, grovelling, hesitating, kowtowing, lying, obfuscating, obstructing, oscillating, paltering, pandering, posturing, quitting, quivering, resiling, see-sawing, shilly-shallying, slithering, squabbling, swivelling, tergiversating, teetering, tottering, twisting, vacillating, wavering, weaseling, wobbling, yellowing politicians have buckled to the gun lobby. (Mike Carleton, *Sydney Morning Herald,* Saturday 4 May 1996; News Review, p. 361)

---

[5] In terms of the model of interpersonal discourse semantic systems assumed here, APPRAISAL resources are one of three major systems, alongside NEGOTIATION and INVOLVEMENT (as outlined in Martin 1997a). NEGOTIATION is concerned with speech function and exchange structure (Ventola 1987); INVOLVEMENT deals with non-gradable resources for including and excluding interlocutors, as realized through technical and specialized lexis, taboo lexis and swearing, slang (including anti-languages; cf. Halliday 1976), and naming (Poynton 1984). APPRAISAL, NEGOTIATION, and INVOLVEMENT construe the register variable tenor, which is concerned with the ongoing re/construal of relations of power (equal/unequal status) and solidarity (near/distant contact) among interlocutors (cf. Poynton 1985; Martin 1992a).

APPRECIATION is highlighted in Example 8.8, from a food writer's review of what is generally acknowledged as Sydney's best restaurant. Realizations of appreciation are generally realized through attitudinal adjectives modifying objects of value in one or another institutional realm.

(8.8) APPRECIATION—aesthetics; evaluating text/process, phenomena
Summary: Wow. Incredible. Amazing. Fantastic. Marvellous. Tetsuya's is a modest, comfortable restaurant with some of the best cooking in Sydney. This is food for a mature and intelligent civilisation, and it deserves any superlative you can throw at it. A new and highly immodest wine list now completes the experience. TETSUYA's . . . (Eat Out, Terry Durack, *Sydney Morning Herald,* Tuesday 7 May 1996, Good Living, p. 3)

In a general sense, AFFECT, JUDGEMENT, and APPRECIATION all encode feeling. AFFECT can perhaps be taken as the basic system, which is then institutionalized in two major realms of uncommon sense discourse. As JUDGEMENT, AFFECT is recontextualized as an evaluation matrix for behaviour, with a view to controlling what people do. As APPRECIATION, AFFECT is recontextualized as an evaluation matrix for the products of behaviour (and wonders of nature), with a view to valuing what people achieve. In Halliday's terms, judgement institutionalizes feelings as proposals (about behaviour), whereas appreciation institutionalizes feelings as propositions (about things). A crude map of these recontextualizations is offered in Figure 8.1.

Alongside these three evaluative resources, we also need to account for systems which adjust a speaker's commitment to what he or she is saying (ENGAGEMENT). In the following example Frank uses explicitly subjective modality metaphors (Halliday 1994: 358) to hedge his reply (exasperating Rita in the process).

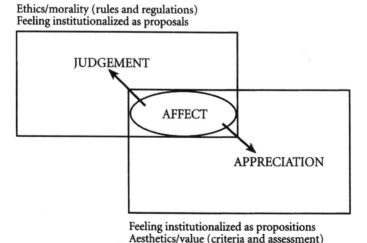

FIGURE 8.1. JUDGEMENT and APPRECIATION as institutionalised AFFECT

(8.9) ENGAGEMENT—resources for construing modal responsibility
RITA. That's a nice picture, isn't it?
FRANK. Erm—yes, *I suppose* it is—nice . . .
RITA. It's very erotic.
FRANK. Actually *I don't think* I've looked at it for about 10 years, but yes, *I suppose* it is.
RITA. There's *no suppose* about it.

APPRAISAL resources also include systems for grading evaluations (AMPLIFICA-TION)—turning up the volume as in the first example, or playing things down as in the second.

(8.10) AMPLIFICATION—resources for upgrading or downgrading
RITA. Y' know when I'm in the hairdresser's—that's where I work—I'll say somethin' like, 'Oh, I'm *really* fucked', y' know, *dead* loud. It *doesn't half* cause a fuss.
(8.11)
FRANK. I've *never really* looked at it like that. But yes, yes *you could say* it means getting the rhyme wrong.

Our concern with appraisal resources grew out of our work on secondary school and workplace literacy, initially out of work on the role of evaluation in narrative (Martin 1996, 1997*b*). Later we turned our attention to appraisal in literary criticism, the issue of objectivity in media, science, and history discourse, the notion of value in creative arts, and the sourcing of responsibility in administrative discourse (for an overview of this research see Christie and Martin 1997). Working within the paradigm of SFL, we wanted a comprehensive map of appraisal resources that we could deploy systematically in discourse analysis, with a view both to understanding the rhetorical effect of evaluative lexis as texts unfold, and to better understanding the interplay of interpersonal meaning and social relations in the model of language and the social we were developing, especially in the area of solidarity (i.e. resources for empathy and affiliation).

AFFECT

Affect is modelled here as a semantic resource for construing emotions. For purposes of text analysis and in line with SFL descriptive principles, we have been developing a global outline of this resource. Our approach has been holistic and culture specific, unlike that of Wierzbicka (e.g. 1986), who tends to concentrate on one emotion at a time across languages and cultures with a view to developing a universal set of semantic primitives. Unlike Lakoff (e.g. Lakoff and Kövecses 1987), we have not yet developed detailed studies of the range of items, including lexical metaphor, which elaborate a range of meanings around any one affect variable.

In building up this outline we covered a range of realizations, comparable in general terms to those covered by Biber and Finegan (1989). In Halliday's (1994) terms, these comprise:

- affect as 'quality'

describing participants	a *happy* boy	Epithet
attributed to participants	the boy was *happy*	Attribute
manner of processes	the boy played *happily*	Circumstance

- affect as 'process'[6]

affective mental	the present *pleased* the boy	Process (effective)
affective behavioural	the boy *smiled*	Process (middle)

- affect as 'comment'

desiderative	*happily*, he had a long nap	Modal Adjunct

By way of classifying affect, we drew on the following factors:

1. Are the feelings popularly construed by the culture as positive (good vibes that are enjoyable to experience) or negative ones (bad vibes that are better avoided)? We are not concerned here with the value that a particular uncommon-sense psychological framework might place on one or another emotion (cf. 'It's probably productive that you're feeling sad because it's a sign that . . . ').

positive affect	the boy was *happy*
negative affect	the boy was *sad*

2. Are the feelings realized as a surge of emotion involving some kind of embodied paralinguistic or extralinguistic manifestation, or more prosodically experienced as a kind of predisposition or ongoing mental state? Grammatically this distinction is constructed as the opposition between behavioural (e.g. *She smiled at him*) versus mental (e.g. *She liked him*) or relational (e.g. *She felt happy with him*) processes.

behavioural surge	the boy *laughed*
mental disposition	the boy *liked* the present/the boy felt *happy*

3. Are the feelings construed as directed at or reacting to some specific external agency (typically conscious) or as a general ongoing mood for which one might pose the question 'Why are you feeling that way?' and get the answer 'I'm not sure'?

reaction to other	the boy *liked* the teacher/the teacher *pleased* the boy
undirected mood	the boy was *happy*

4. How are the feelings graded—towards the lower valued end of a scale of intensity or towards the higher valued end; or somewhere in between? We don't wish at this stage to imply that low, median, and high are discrete values (as with MODALITY—cf. Halliday 1994: 358–9), but expect that most emotions offer lexicalizations that grade along an evenly clined scale.

low	the boy *liked* the present
'median'	the boy *loved* the present
high	the boy *adored* the present

---

[6] Including relational agnates such as *I'm pleased that . . .* , *It's pleasing that . . .*

5. Do the feelings involve intention (rather than reaction), with respect to a stimulus that is irrealis rather than realis (i.e. do the feelings relate to future, as yet unrealized, states rather than present existing ones)?

realis   the boy *liked* the present
irrealis   the boy *wanted* the present

Irrealis affect seems always to be directed at some external agency, and so can be outlined as in Table 8.1 below (setting aside factor 3 above).

TABLE 8.1. *Irrealis* AFFECT

DIS/INCLINATION	SURGE (of behaviour)	DISPOSITION
fear	tremble	wary
	shudder	fearful
	cower	terrorized
desire	suggest	miss
	request	long for
	demand	yearn for

6. The final variable in our typology of affect groups emotions into three major sets having to do with un/happiness, in/security and dis/satisfaction. The framework is based on my general observations of my young sons, when they were in their first stages of socialization (up to about 2 years of age), and in particular on a cycle of demands structuring my elder son's temper tantrums over a period of several months. During these tantrums he would insist on having *baggy* (his blanket), and then when it was proffered and rejected his *bopple* (bottle), and then when this was proffered and rejected *Mummy* or *Daddy* (whichever was not present), and then baggy again, then bopple . . . for up to an hour. If we take these primal screams as primitives, then a framework involving in/security (blanket), dis/satisfaction (bottle) and un/happiness (Mummy/Daddy) can be entertained. The in/security variable covers emotions concerned with ecosocial well-being—anxiety, fear, confidence, and trust; the dis/satisfaction variable covers emotions concerned with telos (the pursuit of goals)—ennui, displeasure, curiosity, respect; the un/happiness variable covers emotions concerned with 'affairs of the heart'—sadness, anger, happiness, and love. Unfortunately we have not been able to develop a more principled basis for classifying emotions in recent years and take little comfort from the array of divergent frameworks available elsewhere in the literature (including the evolving variations in Martin 1992a, 1996 and 1997a)[7].

---

[7] Martin 1992a and 1996 reflect a stage in our work when JUDGEMENT and APPRECIATION had not been distinguished from AFFECT; Martin 1997a doesn't involve the realis/irrealis distinction, squeezing out surprise and desire.

in/security	the boy was *anxious/confident*
dis/satisfaction	the boy was *fed up/absorbed*
un/happiness	the boy was *sad/happy*

TABLE 8.2. *Realis* AFFECT

	SURGE (of behaviour)	DISPOSITION	
UN/HAPPINESS			
unhappiness			
misery	whimper	down	(low)
(mood: 'in me')	cry	sad	(median)
	wail	miserable	(high)
antipathy	rubbish	dislike	
(directed feeling: 'at you')	abuse	hate	
	revile	abhor	
happiness			
cheer	chuckle	cheerful	
	laugh	buoyant	
	rejoice	jubilant	
affection	shake hands	fond	
	hug	loving	
	embrace	adoring	
IN/SECURITY			
insecurity			
disquiet	restless	uneasy	
	twitching	anxious	
	shaking	freaked out	
surprise	start	taken aback	
	cry out	surprised	
	faint	astonished	
security			
confidence	declare	together	
	assert	confident	
	proclaim	assured	
trust	delegate	comfortable with	
	commit	confident in/about	
	entrust	trusting	
DIS/SATISFACTION			
dissatisfaction			
ennui	fidget	bored	
	yawn	fed up	
	tune out	exasperated	
displeasure	caution	cross	
	scold	angry	
	castigate	furious	*cont.*

TABLE 8.2. *cont.*

	SURGE (of behaviour)	DISPOSITION
satisfaction		
interest	attentive	curious
	busy	absorbed
	flat out	engrossed
admiration	pat on the back	satisfied
	compliment	impressed
	reward	proud

As Trekkers (fans of the American TV series *Star Trek*) will no doubt have noted, the framework includes interest (e.g. curiosity) as an emotion in spite of the fact that Spock (a Vulcan/human who has emotions but suppresses them) and Data (an android who has no emotions) often react with 'interest' to a wide range of natural phenomena and human failings. In common-sense terms one might argue that interest is more head than heart; theoretically, however, we are not prepared to invoke a mind/body opposition criterially at this stage of our work (for discussion see Lutz 1986, 1988; Lutz and Abu-Lughod 1990).

By way of illustrating the application of this framework to text analysis, consider Example 8.11. This text is taken from a state-wide Year 10 English exam in New South Wales, Australia and was published by the New South Wales Board of Studies as one of a number of sample answers to a question about why a short story included in the exam paper ended the way it did. Interestingly enough, the text was evaluated as worthless by the examiners, precisely because it was developed as an emotional response to the story. The student in question has misunderstood her teacher's demand for an individual response as a demand for a personal reaction rather than Leavisite interpretation (for further discussion see Rothery and Macken 1991, Rothery 1994).

(8.11) Year 10 Reference test—English
[Examiner's evaluation] This response has attempted to give a personal reaction to the question asked. The student has concentrated on the literary style of the story but has failed to answer the question or show any understanding of the story.
[Exam Answer] The author has intentionally written the ending this way to create the effect that she wanted. I felt eerie and isolated after reading the ending—'like a padlock snapping open' sounded so lonely and made me feel so afraid.
I also felt very empty after reading the passage. It has such a depressing ending that made me feel afraid and scared. The way 'Click' is written by itself in a sentence and in capital letters added to the emptiness I can really imagine the *exact* sound it makes, the way it 'sounded through the room.' 'Sounded through the room' is another example of how the author creates the feeling of isolation so carefully displayed. It sounds hollow and dead and creates fear in your mind.

This is what makes the passage so effective—the way the mood of the characters is portrayed so clearly. I enjoyed this passage immensely the ending was very clear and well written.

A reading of AFFECT in Example 8.11 is provided in 8.11*a* below. Realizations of AFFECT have been placed in small caps throughout the text, followed by features designating the relevant variable from Tables 8.1 and 8.2 in square brackets.

(8.11*a*)
The author has intentionally written the ending this way to create the effect that she wanted. I FELT EERIE [insecurity: disquiet] and ISOLATED [insecurity: disquiet] after reading the ending—'like a padlock snapping open' sounded so LONELY [insecurity: disquiet] and made me FEEL SO AFRAID [disinclination: fear]

I also FELT VERY EMPTY [unhappiness: misery] after reading the passage. It has such a DEPRESSING [unhappiness: misery] ending that made me FEEL AFRAID [disinclination: fear] and SCARED [disinclination: fear]. The way 'Click' is written by itself in a sentence and in capital letters added to the EMPTINESS [unhappiness: misery] I can really imagine the *exact* sound it makes, the way it 'sounded through the room.' 'Sounded through the room' is another example of how the author creates the FEELING OF ISOLATION [insecurity: disquiet] so carefully displayed. It sounds HOLLOW AND DEAD [t-insecurity: disquiet] and creates FEAR [disinclination: fear] in your mind.

This is what makes the passage so effective—the way the mood of the characters is portrayed so clearly. I ENJOYED [happiness: affection] this passage immensely the ending was very clear and well written.

Generally, in Example 8.11, the affectual realizations act prosodically to construe a negative reaction, involving insecurity and unhappiness (as summarized in Table 8.3)—begging the question as to why the writer's final comment reconstrues her reaction as one of having enjoyed the story immensely (for discussion of the English curriculum producing heteroglossic responses of this kind, see Cranny-Francis 1996).

TABLE 8.3. *Summary of* AFFECT *in Example 8.11*

Reaction of reader	AFFECT
EERIE	[insecurity: disquiet]
ISOLATED	[insecurity: disquiet]
LONELY	[insecurity: disquiet]
AFRAID	[disinclination: fear]
EMPTY	[unhappiness: misery]
DEPRESSING	[unhappiness: misery]
AFRAID	[disinclination: fear]
SCARED	[disinclination: fear]
EMPTINESS	[unhappiness: misery]
ISOLATION	[insecurity: disquiet]
HOLLOW AND DEAD	[t-insecurity: disquiet]
FEAR	[disinclination: fear]
ENJOYED	[happiness: affection]

In Table 8.3, the phrase *hollow and dead* was labelled [t-insecurity: disquiet], with 't' standing for token. The point of this coding is that the phrase *hollow and dead* does not directly construe affect, but rather implies an emotional response on the part of the writer—and that the phrase makes an important contribution to the emotional impact of the response. By way of exploring the issue of direct and implied affect, consider Example 8.12. This text is taken from a junior secondary geography classroom, although the geography teacher reads it as an inappropriate incursion of subject English discourse (since the student has reacted to one season's weather instead of explaining climate). To begin, only direct realizations of affect have been considered.

TASK: Explain the climate of Sydney (year 8 Geography) [Teacher's comment: 'You need to write a geography paragraph on temperature and rainfall . . . not an English essay']

(8.12) Explicit evaluation only
Sydney is a beautiful place to visit it has one thing that I DON'T REALLY LIKE [unhappiness: antipathy] that is the weather. It's climate is always different one day it could be rainning and the next day it would be so hot that you would have to have a cold shower. I LIKE [happiness: affection] Sydney's weather when i is NICE [happiness: affection] and Sunny I LIKE [happiness: affection] Summer that is my FAVORITE [happiness: affection] season of the year, because it is mostly Sunny. Although this year in Sydney I't wasn't as sunny as I thought it would be. Because half of Summer it was either rainning or was very windy and very cold.

This reading is a conservative one in the sense that it ignores the emotional impact of ideational meaning that might be read as implicating affect. For example, sunny weather and beautiful places can be associated with happiness, just as wind, rain, and cold weather can be associated with unhappiness. Of course we need to be cautious about reading position when analysing ideational meaning as tokens of affect in this way—it's easy to imagine scenarios in which rain would bring great joy (for farmers at the end of a drought for example). But in the context of the reading position naturalized by Example 8.12, the reading of tokens in Example 8.12*a* is a plausible one.

(8.12*a*) Highlighting ideational 'tokens' of AFFECT
Sydney is a BEAUTIFUL [t-happiness: care] place to visit it has one thing that I DON'T REALLY LIKE that is the weather. IT'S CLIMATE IS ALWAYS DIFFERENT ONE DAY IT COULD BE RAINNING AND THE NEXT DAY IT WOULD BE SO HOT THAT YOU WOULD HAVE TO HAVE A COLD SHOWER [t-unhappiness: antipathy]. I LIKE Sydney's weather when i is NICE and SUNNY [t-happiness: care] I LIKE Summer that is my FAVORITE season of the year, because it is mostly SUNNY [t-happiness: care]. Although this year in Sydney I'T WASN'T AS SUNNY AS I THOUGHT IT WOULD BE [t-unhappiness: antipathy]. Because half of Summer it was EITHER RAINNING OR WAS VERY WINDY AND VERY COLD [t-unhappiness: antipathy].

Note that the analysis of evoked affect in Example 8.12*a* treats units of varying length as implicating affect, whereas inscribed affect in Example 8.12 was associated with specific lexical items and their amplification. This raises an issue as to the appropriate unit of analysis as far as the realization of affect is concerned. Given the prosodic nature of interpersonal realization it is unlikely that this issue can be resolved in constituency terms; for practical coding purposes I have tried to work with the smallest domains that can be associated with a particular affect value. A relatively full reading of affect in Example 8.12 is offered in Example 8.12*b* below, including what we will refer to technically as inscribed and evoked affect.

(8.12*b*) Full reading—inscribed (explicit) and evoked (implicit) AFFECT
Sydney is a BEAUTIFUL [t-happiness: affection] place to visit it has one thing that I DON'T REALLY LIKE [unhappiness: antipathy] that is the weather. IT'S CLIMATE IS ALWAYS DIFFERENT ONE DAY IT COULD BE RAINNING AND THE NEXT DAY IT WOULD BE SO HOT THAT YOU WOULD HAVE TO HAVE A COLD SHOWER [t-unhappiness: antipathy]. I LIKE [happiness: affection] Sydney's weather when i is NICE [happiness: affection] and SUNNY [t-happiness: affection] I LIKE [happiness: affection] Summer that is my FAVORITE [happiness: affection] season of the year, because it is mostly SUNNY [t-happiness: affection]. Although this year in Sydney IT WASN'T AS SUNNY AS I THOUGHT IT WOULD BE [t-unhappiness: antipathy]. Because half of Summer it was EITHER RAINNING OR WAS VERY WINDY AND VERY COLD [t-unhappiness: antipathy].

The analysis suggests that affect (and appraisal systems in general) can be directly construed in text, or implicated through the selection of ideational meanings which redound with affectual meanings. Beyond this, where affectual meaning is evoked, a distinction can be drawn between metaphorical language[8] which in a sense provokes an affectual response (e.g. Springsteen's *At night I wake up with the sheets soaking wet and a freight train running through the middle of my head*) and non-metaphorical language which simply invites a response. As far as reading affect is concerned, inscribed affect is more prescriptive about the reading position naturalized—it is harder to resist or ignore; evoked affect on the other hand is more open—accommodating a wider range of reading positions, including readings that may work against the response otherwise naturalized by the text (for further discussion see Martin 1996).

JUDGEMENT

Unfortunately space does not permit the detail of the very partial exploration of AFFECT undertaken above for other APPRAISAL systems. Our framework for JUDGEMENT is outlined in Table 8.4 (for exemplification see Iedema *et al.* 1994, Martin 1995*b*). As noted above, JUDGEMENT can be thought of as the institutionalization of feeling, in the context of proposals (norms about how people should and shouldn't behave). Like AFFECT, it has a positive and negative dimension—corresponding to positive and negative judgements about behaviour. Media research reported in Iedema *et al.* (1994) has suggested dividing judgements into two major

---

[8] Extended metaphors can perhaps be read as amplifying the relevant affect; for example, the final stanza of Springsteen's 1984 'I'm on Fire'—*Sometimes it's like someone took a knife baby, edgy and dull and cut a six-inch valley through the middle of my soul. At night I wake up with the sheets soaking wet and a freight train running through the middle of my head. Only you can cool my fire. I'm on fire.*

groups, social esteem and social sanction. Judgements of esteem have to do with normality (how unusual someone is), capacity (how capable they are), and tenacity (how resolute they are); judgements of sanction have to do with veracity (how truthful someone is) and propriety (how ethical someone is).[9]

TABLE 8.4. *A framework for analysing* JUDGEMENT *in English*

Social Esteem 'venial'	Positive (admire)	Negative (criticize)
normality (fate) 'is he or she special?'	lucky, fortunate, charmed . . . normal, average, everyday . . . in, fashionable, avant-garde . . .	unfortunate, pitiful, tragic . . . odd, peculiar, eccentric . . . dated, daggy, retrograde . . .
capacity 'is he or she capable?'	powerful, vigorous, robust . . . insightful, clever, gifted . . . balanced, together, sane . . .	mild, weak, wimpy . . . slow, stupid, thick . . . flaky, neurotic, insane . . .
tenacity (resolve) 'is he or she reliable, dependable?'	plucky, brave, heroic . . . dependable . . . tireless, persevering, resolute . . .	rash, cowardly, despondent . . . unreliable, undependable . . . weak, distracted, dissolute . . .

Social Sanction 'mortal'	Positive (praise)	Negative (condemn)
veracity (truth) 'is he or she honest?'	truthful, honest, credible . . . real, authentic, genuine . . . frank, direct . . .	dishonest, deceitful . . . glitzy, bogus, fake . . . deceptive, manipulative . . .
propriety (ethics) 'is he or she beyond reproach?'	good, moral, ethical . . . law-abiding, fair, just . . . sensitive, kind, caring . . .	bad, immoral, evil . . . corrupt, unfair, unjust . . . insensitive, mean, cruel . . .

Social esteem involves admiration and criticism, typically without legal implications; if you have difficulties in this area you may need a therapist. Social sanction on the other hand involves praise, and condemnation, often with legal implications; if you have problems in this area you may need a lawyer. The kind of judgement speakers take up is very sensitive to their institutional position. For example, only journalists with responsibility for writing editorials and other comment have a full range of judgemental resources at their disposal; reporters writ-

[9] At this level of delicacy the types of JUDGEMENT are related to MODALITY (Halliday 1994), in the following proportions—normality is to usuality, as capacity is to ability, as tenacity is to inclination, as veracity is to probability, as propriety is to obligation.

ing hard news that is meant to sound objective have to avoid explicit judgements completely (Iedema *et al.* 1994).

One genre that foregrounds JUDGEMENT is the panegyric—as exemplified in Example 8.13 (Elizabeth Taylor's tribute to Michael Jackson from the notes to his *History* CD). Given Jackson's institutional claim to fame, one might have expected a text focusing on social esteem (capacity and normality), with respect to his extraordinary musical achievements—and certainly these are considered. But even more foregrounded in the text is the question of social sanction (propriety and veracity)—quite understandably as Taylor works to absolve Jackson with respect to the then rampant media attention on the nature of his relationships with young boys.

(8.13)

Michael Jackson *History*: past, present and future. Book 1. Epic 1995.

Michael Jackson is, indeed, an international favorite for all ages, and incredible force of incredible energy. In the art of music, he is a pacesetter for quality of production, in the vanguard for high standards of entertainment.

What makes Michael more unique may be the fact that all of his accomplishments, his rewards, have not altered his sensitivity and concern for the welfare of others, or his intense caring and love for his family and friends, and especially all the children of the world over. He is filled with deep emotions that create an unearthly, special, innocent, childlike, wise man that is Michael Jackson. He is so giving of himself that, at times, he leaves very little to protect that beautiful inner core that is the essence of him. I think Michael appeals to the child in all of us. He has the quality of innocence that we would all like to obtain or have kept.

I think Michael is like litmus paper. He is always trying to learn. He has one of the sharpest wits, he is intelligent, and he is cunning—that is a strange word to use about him, because it implies deviousness and he is one of the least devious people I have ever met in my life.

Michael is highly intelligent, shrewd, intuitive, understanding, sympathetic, and generous to almost a fault of himself. He is honesty personified—painfully honest—and vulnerable to the point of pain. He is also very curious and wants to draw from people who have survived. People who have lasted. He is not really of this planet. If he is eccentric it's because he is larger than life.

What is a genius? What is a living legend? What is a megastar? Michael Jackson—that's all. And just when you think you know him, he gives you more . . .

There is no one that can come near him, no one can dance like that, write the lyrics, or cause the kind of excitement that he does. When I hear the name Michael Jackson, I think of brilliance, of dazzling stars, lasers and deep emotions. I think he is one of the world's biggest and greatest stars, and it just so happens that he is one of the most gifted music makers the world has ever known.

I think he is one of the finest people to hit this planet, and, in my estimation, he is the true King of Pop, Rock and Soul. I love you Michael.

Elizabeth Taylor

The second and third paragraphs of this tribute are analysed for JUDGEMENT in Table 8.5. As the genre dictates, the judgements are overwhelmingly positive. As far as normality is concerned, Jackson is unique, unearthly, and special; as for capacity, he is accomplished, wise, witty, and intelligent; with tenacity, he is always trying to learn—Taylor construes Jackson's social esteem as high indeed.

TABLE 8.5. *JUDGEMENT in Example 8.13*

Inscription/Evocation	JUDGEMENT
unique	+normality
accomplishments	+capacity
sensitivity	+propriety
concern	+propriety
caring	+propriety
love	t-+propriety
filled with deep emotions	t-+propriety
unearthly	+normality
special	+normality
innocent	+propriety
childlike	+propriety
wise	+capacity
so giving	+propriety
beautiful inner core	t-+propriety
appeals to the child . . .	t-+propriety
innocence that we would . . .	+propriety
always trying to learn	t-+tenacity
sharpest wits	+capacity
intelligent	+capacity
cunning	+capacity
deviousness	−veracity
least devious	−veracity

Note. Appraiser: E. Taylor; appraised: M. Jackson. The symbol 't-' denotes a token of evoked JUDGE-MENT; the symbols '+' and '−' denote positive and negative JUDGEMENT.

In the analysis I have placed *cunning* among the positive capacities, which is where Taylor aligns it—alongside wit and intelligence and stripped of negative connotations (. . . *cunning—that is a strange word to use about him, because it implies deviousness and he is one of the least devious people I have ever met in my life*). Taylor's choice of the term, and the way she shapes its meaning to fit her tribute is intriguing. If the positive judgements all around the term weren't enough to colour it as positive, why not edit it out of the text? Why go to the trouble of having to deny that any criticism is intended? I suspect that this part of the text plays itself out as a strategy for dealing with Jackson's veracity in the war of words over the propriety of his dealings with children. It gives Taylor an opportunity to vouch for Jackson's truthfulness without having to explicitly address the fact that it has been challenged. Rather, the challenge comes from Taylor, as a slip of phrase—and 'please don't let my clumsiness tarnish Jackson's image in any way!'

TABLE 8.6. *Social sanction in Example 8.13*

Inscription/Evocation	JUDGEMENT
(implies) deviousness	−veracity
one of the least devious ...	−veracity
sensitivity	+propriety
concern	+propriety
caring	+propriety
love	t-+propriety
filled with deep emotions	t-+propriety
innocent	+propriety
childlike	+propriety
so giving	+propriety
beautiful inner core	t-+propriety
appeals to the child ...	t-+propriety
innocence that we would ...	+propriety
always trying to learn	t-+tenacity

Note: Appraiser: E. Taylor; appraised: M. Jackson. The symbol 't-' denotes a token of evoked JUDGE-MENT; the symbols '+' and '−' denote positive and negative JUDGEMENT.

The analysis of social sanction in Example 8.13 bears on this point (see Table 8.6). Jackson is repeatedly constructed as childlike and innocent, judgements we might at a first glance want to treat as negative capacity. But Taylor does not mean that Jackson is weak and immature. I suspect rather that the childlike innocence is being opposed to something more sinister, again having to do with the propriety of Jackson's sexuality. In this context childlike and innocent means free from sin—and thus innocent of the charges levelled against him and withdrawn. At the time when Taylor would have been writing this text, Jackson was not on trial; nevertheless, the play of judgements in her text construct her panegyric as a rather effective piece of testimony for the defence.

APPRECIATION

The framework for APPRECIATION is outlined in Table 8.7. As noted above, APPRECIATION can be thought of as the institutionalization of feeling, in the context of propositions (norms about how products, performances, and naturally occurring phenomena are valued). Like AFFECT and JUDGEMENT it has a positive and negative dimension—corresponding to positive and negative evaluations of texts and processes (and natural phenomena). The system is organized around three variables—reaction, composition, and valuation.[10] Reaction has to do with the degree to which the text/process in question captures our attention (reaction: impact) and the emotional impact it has on us. Composition has to do with our perceptions of proportionality (composition: balance) and detail (composition: complexity) in a text/process. Valuation has to do with our assessment of the social significance of the text/process.

TABLE 8.7. *A framework for analysing APPRECIATION in English*

	Positive	Negative
Reaction: impact 'did it grab me?'	arresting, captivating, engaging . . . fascinating, exciting, moving . . .	dull, boring, tedious, staid . . . dry, ascetic, uninviting . . .
Reaction: quality 'did I like it?'	lovely, beautiful, splendid . . . appealing, enchanting, welcome . . .	plain, ugly . . . repulsive, revolting . . .
Composition: balance 'did it hang together?'	balanced, harmonious, unified . . . symmetrical, proportional . . .	unbalanced, discordant . . . contorted, distorted . . .
Composition: complexity 'was it hard to follow?'	simple, elegant . . . intricate, rich, detailed, precise . . .	ornamental, extravagant . . . monolithic, simplistic . . .
Valuation 'was it worthwhile?'	challenging, profound, deep . . . innovative, original, unique . . .	shallow, insignificant . . . conservative, reactionary . . .

Of these dimensions, valuation is especially tied up with field, since the criteria for valuing a text/process are for the most part institutionally specific. But beyond this, since both JUDGEMENT and APPRECIATION are in a sense institutionalizations of feeling, all of the dimensions involved will prove sensitive to field. An example

[10] These variables are relatable to the kind of mental processing (Halliday 1994) involved in the appreciation, in the following proportions—reaction is to affection, as composition is to perception, as valuation is to cognition.

TABLE 8.8. *Field-specific* APPRECIATION *(for linguistics)*

linguistics	Positive	Negative
Reaction: impact (noticeability)	timely, long-awaited, engaging, landmark . . .	untimely, unexpected, overdue, surprising, dated . . .
Reaction: quality (likeability)	fascinating, exciting, interesting, stimulating, impressive, admirable . . .	dull, tedious, boring, pedantic, didactic, uninspired . . .
Composition: balance	consistent, balanced, thorough, considered, unified, logical, well argued, well presented . . .	fragmented, loose-ended, disorganized, contradictory, sloppy . . .
Composition: complexity	simple, lucid, elegant, rich, detailed, exhaustive, clear, precise . . .	simplistic, extravagant, complicated, Byzantine, labyrinthine, overly elaborate, narrow, vague, unclear, indulgent, esoteric, eclectic . . .
Valuation (field genesis)	useful, penetrating, illuminating, challenging, significant, deep, profound, satisfying, fruitful . . .	shallow, ad hoc, reductive, unconvincing, unsupported, fanciful, tendentious, bizarre, counterintuitive, perplexing, arcane . . .

of this coupling of ideational and interpersonal meaning is presented for appreciations of research in the field of linguistics in Table 8.8.

Further complicating this issue is the fact that what counts as appraisal depends on the field of discourse. Because of this, ideational meanings that do not use evaluative lexis can be used to evoke appreciation, as with AFFECT and JUDGE-MENT. For example, when Rita mentions Rita Mae Brown's *Rubyfruit Jungle* in Example 8.5 above, it is clearly the case that anyone naively apprenticed into mainstream literary sensibilities will value the book as insignificant, and will therefore judge Rita as ignorant. Mere mention of the book encodes these feelings, without any explicit appraisal having to be construed at all. However, the evocation only works for people who take up the same positioning as Frank with respect to *Rubyfruit Jungle*. The writer of *Educating Rita*, Willy Russell, positions Frank and the play's audience to make these kinds of appraisal.

Every institution is loaded with couplings of this kind, and socialization into a discipline involves both an alignment with the institutional practices involved and an affinity with the attitudes one is expected to have towards those practices. It perhaps should be stressed again here that appraisal analysts do need to declare their reading position[11]—in particular since the evaluation one makes of evocations depends on the institutional position one is reading from. There are many readers, for example, who would have aligned with Rita rather than Frank with respect to a popular culture text like *Rubyfruit Jungle*. Similarly, according to reading position, formal and functional linguists will evaluate terms in the following sets of oppositions in complementary ways—with firm convictions about what the good guys and the bad guys should celebrate:

rule/resource:: cognitive/social:: acquisition/development::
syntagmatic/paradigmatic:: form/function:: langue/parole::
system/process:: psychology&philosophy/sociology&anthropology::
cognitive/social:: theory/description:: intuition/corpus::
knowledge/meaning:: syntax/discourse:: pragmatics/context::
parsimony/extravagance:: cognitive/critical:: technicist/humanist::
truth/social action:: performance/instantiation:: categorical/probabilistic::
contradictory/complementary:: proof/exemplification::
reductive/comprehensive:: arbitrary/natural:: modular/fractal::
syntax&lexicon/lexicogrammar . . .

The following text, from the play *Educating Rita*, foregrounds APPRECIATION with respect to the institution of literary criticism. At this point in the play Rita has learned a canonical discourse for evaluating literary texts and has been favourably impressed by some poetry written by her tutor Frank some years past. Frank is less than impressed by his student's new-found sensibilities.

(8.14) From the play *Educating Rita*—Frankenstein scene
There is a knock at the door.
FRANK. Come in.
RITA *enters.*
FRANK. What the—what the hell are you doing here? I'm not seeing you till next week.
RITA. Are you sober? Are you?
FRANK. If you mean am I still this side of reasonable comprehension, then yes.
RITA. Because I want you to hear this when you're sober. [*She produces his poems.*] These are brilliant. Frank, you've got to start writing again. This is brilliant. They're witty. They're profound. Full of style.
FRANK. Ah . . . tell me again, and again.
RITA. They are, Frank. It isn't only me who thinks so. Me an' Trish sat up last night and read them. She agrees with me. Why did you stop writing? Why did you stop when you can produce work like this? We stayed up most of the night, just talking about it. What did Trish say—? More resonant than—purely contemporary poetry is that you can see in it a direct like through to nineteenth-century traditions of—of like wit an' classical allusion.
FRANK. Er—that's erm—that's marvellous, Rita. How fortunate I didn't let you see it earlier. Just think if I'd let you see it when you first came here.
RITA. I know . . . I wouldn't have understood it, Frank.

[11] Except for Example 8.15 below, where I attempt to read the text from the perspective of the two antagonists, I have analysed texts from the perspective of the mainstream reading position they appear to naturalize (anglo, middle class, mature, male if you will).

FRANK. You would have thrown it across the room and dismissed it as a heap of shit, wouldn't you?

RITA. I know . . . But I couldn't have understood it then, Frank, because I wouldn't have been able to recognize and understand the allusions.

FRANK. Oh I've done a fine job on you, haven't I?

RITA. It's true, Frank. I can see it now.

FRANK. You know, Rita, I think—I think that like you I shall change my name; from now on I shall insist on being known as Mary, Mary Shelley—do you understand that allusion, Rita?

RITA. What?

FRANK. She wrote a little Gothic number called *Frankenstein.*

RITA. So?

FRANK. This—this clever, pyrotechnical pile of self-conscious allusion is worthless, talentless, shit and could be recognized as such by anyone with a shred of common sense. Wit? You'll find more wit in the telephone book, and, probably, more insight. Its one advantage over the telephone directory is that it's easier to rip. It is pretentious, characterless and without style.

RITA. It's not.

FRANK. Oh, I don't expect you to believe me, Rita; you recognize the hallmark of literature now, don't you? Why don't you just go away? I don't think I can bear it any longer.

RITA. Can't bear what, Frank?

FRANK. You, my dear—you . . .

RITA. I'll tell you what you can't bear, Mr Self-Pitying Piss Artist; what you can't bear is that I am educated now. I've got a room full of books. I know what clothes to wear, what wine to buy, what plays to see, what papers and books to read. I can do without you.

FRANK. Is that all you wanted. Have you come all this way for so very, very little?

RITA. Oh it's little to you, isn't it? It's little to you who squanders every opportunity and mocks and takes it for granted.

FRANK. Found a culture have you, Rita? Found a better song to sing have you? No— you've found a different song, that's all—and on your lips it's shrill and hollow and tuneless. Oh, Rita, Rita . . .

RITA. RITA? Rita? Nobody calls me Rita but you. I dropped that pretentious crap as soon as I saw it for what it was. You stupid . . . Nobody calls me Rita.

FRANK. What is it now then? Virginia?

RITA *exits.*

Or Charlotte? Or Jane? Or Emily?

An analysis of the appreciations of Frank's poetry in Example 8.14 is presented in Table 8.9. The analysis is somewhat complicated by the repartee, since Frank and Rita do not agree on the value of his work. Denials of appreciation are shown in the table as -[appreciation], to show one party disagreeing with the other; sarcasm is shown as ?[appreciation], for cases where a positive evaluation is intended as negative (or vice versa). Sarcasm raises the more general problem of humour and appraisal, which we cannot pursue here—how is it that we recognize that someone means the opposite of what they say, or that what they say is intended to be read as funny rather than real? This brings us back to the issue of couplings between ideational meaning and appraisal—at a particular point in the unfolding of a text, for the social subjects involved, at some moment in the evolution of the relevant institution. In these terms, Frank's encouragement to Rita to tell him more about how wonderful his poetry is cannot be taken at face value: it contradicts the rest of the text, Frank's disaffected persona in the play, and the fact that he is not a well-known author. Beyond this, the valuation literally evoked by Frank's *tell me again and again* does not match his affectual pose—which is clearly downcast. Perhaps humour and sarcasm can be further explored along these lines, as involving discordant couplings—either between appraisal selections and what is being appraised, or among the appraisal variables themselves.

TABLE 8.9. *Appreciation of Frank's poetry in Example 8.14*

Inscription/Evocation	**Appraiser**	APPRECIATION
brilliant	Rita	+reaction: quality
brilliant	Rita	+reaction: quality
witty	Rita	+valuation
profound	Rita	+valuation
full of style	Rita	+composition: balance
Ah tell me . . . [witty. . . style]	Frank	?[+valuation/+composition]
They are . . . [witty . . . style]	Rita	-?[+valuation/+composition]
It isn't . . . [witty . . . style]	Rita	+valuation/+composition
She agrees . . . [witty . . . style]	Rita and Trish	+valuation/+composition
resonant	Trish	+valuation
wit	Trish	+valuation
classical allusion	Trish	t-+valuation
a heap of shit	Frank "Rita	−valuation
allusions	Rita	t-+valuation
clever	Frank	−valuation
pyrotechnical	Frank	−composition: complexity
self-conscious allusion	Frank	−valuation
worthless . . .	Frank	−valuation
talentless shit	Frank	−valuation
more wit in telephone . . .	Frank	t-− valuation
more insight [in telephone . . .]	Frank	t-−valuation
one advantage over . . .	Frank	?[+valuation]
easier to rip	Frank	?[+valuation]
pretentious	Frank	−valuation
characterless	Frank	−valuation
without style	Frank	−composition: balance
it's not [pretentious, characterless, without style]	Rita	-[−valuation]
I don't expect . . . [pretentious, characterless, without style]	Frank "Rita	?-[−valuation]

Note: The symbol '"' is used in cases where the speaker attributes appraisal to another person.

By way of summary, a topological perspective (Martin and Matthiessen 1991) on APPRAISAL resources is offered in Figure 8.2. It tries to align types of AFFECT, JUDGEMENT, and APPRECIATION in terms of similarities in meaning across appraisal variables. For example, capacity is aligned with valuation, because of the close relation between judging someone's behaviour as capable and appreciating the text/process arising from the behaviour (e.g. *a skilful cricketer/a skilful innings, a gifted painter/an innovative painting*, etc.). Similarly, reaction is aligned with the relevant types of AFFECT. ENGAGEMENT (modality, projection, mitigation, etc.) and AMPLIFICATION (grading, intensity, etc.) have been included as attendant resources for hedging how committed we are to what we feel and how strongly we feel about it.

Negotiating Solidarity

As noted above, appraisal resources play an important role in negotiating solidarity. In Example 8.11 above, a student writer drew on AFFECT to construct herself as

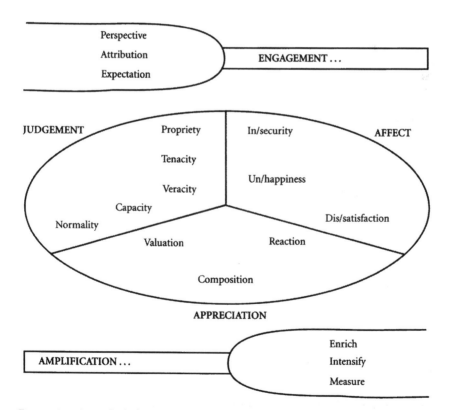

FIGURE 8.2. A topological perspective on APPRAISAL resources

a sensitive reader; but ended up alienating the marker, who was not prepared to align with a sensitivity of that kind. In Example 8.13, a long-time friend drew on JUDGEMENT to reinforce a support group for Michael Jackson, probably with some success since the main audience for her tribute was the legion of fans who bought the *History* CD. In Example 8.14, a mature student drew on APPRECIATION to realign her tutor as a practising poet, only to have him rebuff her readings as naive. The volatility of the inclusions and exclusions engendered by these texts underscores both the bonding and schismatic power of appraisal resources. Just as it is impossible to include without also excluding, so it is impossible to appraise without running the gauntlet of empathy and alienation. As Hunston (1993*a*, 1994) has shown, even academic discourses which elide as far as possible the use of inscribed appraisal are structured to evoke affinity. No text is an island, as far as appraisal and solidarity are concerned.

By way of drawing the discussion together, consider now Example 8.15, from the opening scene of the play *Educating Rita*. In this scene, Rita meets her tutor Frank for the first time. Rita is positioned in this scene through her accent and dress as coming from a regional working class background, Frank as an alcoholic and disaffected academic who is not too keen on shouldering responsibility as Rita's mentor.

(8.15)
FRANK. [*Shouting*] Come in! Come in!
RITA. I'm comin' in, aren't I? It's that stupid bleedin' handle on the door—you wanna get it fixed!
FRANK. Erm—yes, I suppose I always mean to . . .
RITA. Well, that's no good always meanin' to, is it? Y' should get on with it; one of these days you'll be shoutin' 'Come in!' and it'll go on forever because the poor sod on the other side won't be able to get in. An' you won't be able to get out.
FRANK. You are?
RITA. What am I?
FRANK. Pardon?
RITA. What?
FRANK. Now you are?
RITA. I'm a what?
[*Frank looks up and then returns to the papers as Rita goes to hang her coat on the door hooks.*]
RITA. That's a nice picture, isn't it?
FRANK. Erm—yes, I suppose it is,—nice . . .
RITA. It's very erotic.
FRANK. Actually I don't think I've looked at it for about ten years, but, yes, I suppose it is.
RITA. There's no suppose about it. Look at those tits.
[. . .]
FRANK. Would you—erm—would you like to sit down?
RITA. No! Can I smoke?
FRANK. Tobacco?
RITA. Yeh. Was that a joke? Here—d' y' want one?

FRANK. Ah—I'd love one.

RITA. Well, have one.

FRANK. I—don't smoke—I made a promise not to smoke.

RITA. Well, I won't tell anyone.

FRANK. Promise?

RITA. On my oath as an ex Brownie. I hate smokin' on me own. An' everyone seems to have packed up these days. They're all afraid of gettin' cancer. But they're all cowards.

[. . .]

FRANK. Can I offer you a drink?

RITA. What of?

FRANK. Scotch?

[. . .]

RITA. Yeh, all right. [*She takes a copy of* Howards End *from the shelf.*] What's this like?

FRANK. *Howard's End*?

RITA. Yes, it sounds filthy, doesn't it? E. M. Foster.

FRANK. Forster.

RITA. Oh yeh. What's it like?

FRANK. Borrow it. Read it.

RITA. Ta. I'll look after it. If I pack the course in I'll post it to y'.

FRANK. Pack it in? Why should you do that?

RITA. I just might. I might decide it was a soft idea.

FRANK. Mm. Cheers. If—erm—if you're already contemplating 'packing it in', why did you enrol in the first place?

RITA. Because I wanna know.

FRANK. What do you want to know?

RITA. Everything.

FRANK. Everything? That's rather a lot, isn't it? Where would you like to start?

RITA. Well, I'm a student now, aren't I? I'll have to do exams, won't I?

FRANK. Yes, eventually.

RITA. I'll have to learn about it all, won' I? Yeh. It's like y' sit there, don't y', watchin' the ballet or the opera on the telly an'—an' y' call it rubbish cos that's what it looks like? Cos y' don't understand. So y' switch it off an' say, that's fuckin' rubbish.

FRANK. Do you?

RITA. I do. But I don't want to. I wanna see. Y' don't mind me swearin', do y'?

FRANK. Not at all.

RITA. Do you swear?

FRANK. Never stop.

RITA. See, the educated classes know it's only words, don't they? It's only the masses who don't understand. I do it to shock them sometimes. Y' know when I'm in the hair-dressers—that's where I work—I'll say somethin' like 'Oh, I'm really fucked', y' know, dead loud. It doesn't half cause a fuss.

FRANK. Yes—I'm sure . . .

RITA. But it doesn't cause any sort of fuss with educated people, does it? Cos they know it's only words and they don't worry. But these stuck-up idiots I meet, they think they're royalty just cos they don't swear; and I wouldn't mind but it's the aristocracy that swears more than anyone, isn't it? It's all 'Pass me the fackin' grouse' with them, isn't it? But y' can't tell them that round our way. It's not their fault; they can't help it.

But sometimes I hate them. [...] I love this room. I love that window. Do you like it?

FRANK. What?

RITA. The window.

FRANK. I don't often consider it actually. I sometimes get the urge to throw something through it.

RITA. What?

FRANK. A student usually.

RITA. You're bleedin' mad you, aren't you?

FRANK. Probably.

[*Pause.*]

RITA. Aren't you supposed to be interviewin' me?

FRANK. Do I need to?

RITA. I talk too much, don't I? I know I talk a lot. I don't at home. I hardly ever talk when I'm there. But I don't often get the chance to talk to someone like you: to talk at you. D' y' mind?

FRANK. Would you be at all bothered if I did? [*She shakes her head and then turns it into a nod.*] I don't mind.

RITA. What does assonance mean?

FRANK. What? [*He gives a short laugh.*]

RITA. Don't laugh at me.

FRANK. No. Erm—assonance. Well, it's a form of rhyme. What's a—what's an example—erm? Do you know Yeats?

RITA. The wine lodge?

FRANK. Yeats the poet.

RITA. No.

FRANK. Oh. Well—there's a Yeats poem called 'The Wild Swans at Coole'. In it he rhymes the word 'swan' with the word 'stone'. There, you see, an example of assonance.

RITA. Oh. It means gettin' the rhyme wrong.

FRANK. [*looking at her and laughing*] I've never really looked at it like that. But yes, yes you could say it means getting the rhyme wrong.

RITA. Oh.

[...]

FRANK. What's your name?

RITA. Rita.

FRANK. Rita. Mm. It says here Mrs S. White.

RITA. That's 'S' for Susan. It's just me real name. I've changed it to Rita, though. I'm not a Susan any more. I've called meself Rita—y' know, after Rita Mae Brown.

FRANK. Who?

RITA. Y' know, Rita Mae Brown, who wrote *Rubyfruit Jungle*. Haven't y' read it? It's a fantastic book. D' y' wanna lend it?

FRANK. I'd—erm—I'd be very interested.

RITA. All right.

[...]

FRANK. [*looking at her paper*] You're a ladies' hairdresser?

RITA. Yeh.

FRANK. Are you good at it?

[...]

RITA. I am. But they expect too much. They walk in the hairdresser's, an' an hour later they wanna walk out a different person. [. . .] But if you want to change y' have to do it from the inside, don't y'? Know like I'm doin'. Do y' think I'll be able to do it?

FRANK. Well, it really depends on you, on how committed you are. Are you sure that you're absolutely serious about wanting to learn?

RITA. I'm dead serious. Look, I know I take the piss an' that, but I'm dead serious really. I take the piss because I'm not, y' know, confident like, but I wanna be, honest. [. . .] When d' y' actually, y' know, start teaching me?

FRANK. What can I teach you?

RITA. Everything.

FRANK. I'll make a bargain with you. Yes? I'll tell you everything I know—but if I do that you must promise never to come back here . . . You see I never—I didn't actually want to take this course in the first place. I allowed myself to be talked into it. I knew it was wrong. Seeing you only confirms my suspicion. My dear, it's not your fault, just the luck of the draw that you got me; but get me you did. And the thing is, between you, and me, and the walls, I'm actually an appalling teacher. Most of the time, you see, it doesn't actually matter—appalling teaching is quite in order for most of my appalling students. And the others manage to get by despite me. But you're different. You want a lot, and I can't give it. Everything I know—and you must listen to this—is that I know absolutely nothing. I don't like the hours, you know. Strange hours for this Open University thing. They expect us to teach when the pubs are open. I can be a good teacher when I'm in the pub, you know. Four pints of weak Guinness and I can be as witty as Wilde. I'm sorry— there are other tutors—I'll arrange it for you . . . post it on . . .

[*Rita slowly turns and goes towards the door.*]

This scene, of course, is a heteroglossic one, since Rita and Frank read the context of 'first meeting with tutor' in different ways. The ways in which language, in conjunction with dress and various paralinguistic features, construes this difference are multiple (see Cranny-Francis and Martin 1994 for discussion of the film version). Here we will focus on the role played by APPRAISAL. To simplify the discussion irrealis affect will be set aside, since so many of its instances in the scene are used to construct indirect speech acts (i.e. indicative mood for offers and commands—*you should get on with it, do you want to lend it, would you like to sit down*, etc.; see Halliday 1984, Martin 1995a for discussion).

A reading of Frank's appraisal in the scene is offered in Table 8.10. On this reading, Frank draws on this resource on 18 occasions (including 2 instances of laughter). One of these repeats Rita's appraisal of assonance (*getting the rhyme wrong*), and two are in fact asking Rita to express her feelings (*are you good at ladies hairdress[ing], are you . . . serious about wanting to learn*). This means that Frank draws on verbal resources for expressing how he feels on just 13 occasions, 12 of which occur in his final monologue (where he constructs an argument for not taking Rita on as a student). Overall, then, it would appear that Frank is not using appraisal as a resource for constructing solidarity with Rita.

Rita, on the other hand, makes use of appraisal on 35 occasions (as outlined in the reading of the scene offered in Table 8.11)—and these are spread more or less evenly throughout the scene. Unlike Frank, she construes the context as one in

TABLE 8.10. *Frank's appraisal in the opening scene of* Educating Rita

Instantiation	Appraiser	APPRECIATION	JUDGEMENT	AFFECT	Appraised
[laughter]	Frank			cheer	Rita
[laughter]	Frank			cheer	Rita's joke
... getting the rhyme wrong	Frank	composition: balance			assonance ... poet
I'd be very interested	Frank			interest	Rita's offer
are you good at it?	Frank? Rita[1]		capacity: competent		Rita
are you ... serious about	Frank? Rita			engagement	wanting to learn
it was wrong	Frank		propriety: ethical		taking the course
not your fault	Frank	-[propriety]			taking the course
just the luck of the draw	Frank	normality: unlucky			taking the course
an appalling teacher	Frank		capacity: incompetent		Frank
it doesn't matter	Frank		propriety: ethical		appalling teaching
quite in order	Frank		propriety: ethical		appalling teaching
appalling teaching	Frank	reaction: quality	capacity: incompetent		Frank's teaching
appalling students	Frank	reaction: quality	capacity: incompetent		Frank's students
different	Frank	reaction: quality			Rita
don't like	Frank			antipathy	hours
a good teacher	Frank		capacity: competent		Frank
witty	Frank		capacity: accomplished		Frank

[1] In this and the following table an entry such as Frank?Rita in the appraiser column signifies that Frank is asking Rita for her appraisal.

which she'll say how she feels. As indicated above, all appraisal involves the negotiation of solidarity—you can hardly say how you feel without inviting empathy.

TABLE 8.11. *Rita's appraisal in the opening scene of* Educating Rita

Instantiation	**Appraiser**	APPRECIATION	JUDGEMENT	AFFECT	**Appraised**
stupid bleeding handle	Rita			antipathy	handle
no good, **is it?**	Rita		-[capacity: incompetent]		Frank
the poor sod	Rita		normality: unlucky		sod
a nice picture, **isn't it?**	Rita	reaction: quality			picture
very erotic	Rita	valuation: titillating			picture
look at those tits	Rita	reaction: impact			picture
Was that a joke?	Rita?		veracity: bogus		Frank's question
hate	Rita			antipathy	smoking on own
they're afraid	Rita "everyone			apprehension	getting cancer
cowards	Rita		tenacity: cowardice		everyone
sounds filthy, **doesn't it?**	Rita	valuation: titillating			Howard's End
What's it like?	Rita? Frank	reaction			Howard's End
a soft idea	Rita	valuation: unsatisfying	capacity: stupid[1]		doing the course
rubbish	Rita	valuation: worthless			ballet/opera
fuckin' rubbish	Rita	valuation: worthless			ballet/opera
Y' don't mind ...?	Rita? Frank			disquiet	swearing
shock	Rita			disquiet	masses
I'm really fucked	Rita			ennui	Rita
cause a fuss	Rita			disquiet	masses
doesn't cause any sort of fuss, ... **does it?**	Rita			-[disquiet]	educated people

cont.

TABLE 8.11. *cont.*

Instantiation	Appraiser	APPRECIATION	JUDGEMENT	AFFECT	Appraised
stuck-up idiots	Rita		veracity: bogus		masses
(not) their fault	Rita		-[propriety]		masses
hate	Rita			antipathy	masses
love this room	Rita			care	this room
love that window	Rita			care	the window
do you like it?	Rita? Frank			care	the window
bleedin' mad, **aren't y'?**	Rita		capacity: insane		Frank
D' y' mind?	Rita? Frank			disquiet	talking at him
Don't laugh at me	Rita "Frank			-[cheer]	Rita
gettin' the rhyme wrong	Rita	composition: balance	capacity: incompetent		assonance . . . poets
a fantastic book	Rita	reaction: quality			Rubyfruit Jungle
dead serious	Rita			engagement	Rita
take the piss	Rita		veracity: joker		Rita
not, **y' know**, confident	Rita			-[confidence]	Rita
honest	Rita		veracity: honest		Rita

¹ I have double-coded this instance (and *getting the rhyme wrong* below) as realizing both appreciation and judgement, since the appraisal evaluates the idea as soft, implying that its thinker is incompetent.

Where interlocutors are prepared to share your feeling, a kind of bonding occurs; where they are not so prepared, the effect is alienating. And Rita puts a great deal of effort into constructing a relationship with Frank based on shared feeling. Strikingly, in this scene, Rita explicitly invites Frank to share her feelings on a number of occasions (noted in bold face in Table 8.11). These invitations are outlined in Table 8.12 and represent just over a third of Rita's appraisal instantiations. The invitations involve tags, polar questions, and the parenthetical expressions *between you and me* and *you know*.

TABLE 8.12. *Rita's invitations to share feeling in Example 8.15*

RITA. Well, that's *no good*—always meanin' to *is it*?
RITA. That's *a nice picture*, *isn't it*?
RITA. Yeah. *Was that a joke*?
RITA. It sounds *filthy*, *doesn't it*?
RITA. Oh yeh. *What's it like*?
RITA. Y' don't *mind* me swearin', *do y'*?
RITA. It doesn't cause *any sort of fuss* with educated people, *does it*?
RITA. I *love* this room. I *love* that window. *Do you like* it?
RITA. You're *bleeding mad* you, aren't y'?
RITA. . . . to talk at you. *D' y' mind*?
RITA. . . . because I'm not y' know, *confident* like.

Throughout the scene Frank either ignores or actively resists these invitations. For him the context is not one in which he chooses to build a relationship based on shared feeling. Consider for example his resistance to Rita's appraisal of the view from his room:

(8.16) Expanding Example 8.3 above
RITA. I love this room. I love that window. Do you like it?
FRANK. What?
RITA. The window.
FRANK. I don't often consider it actually. I sometimes get an urge to throw something through it.
RITA. What?
FRANK. A student usually.
RITA. You're bleedin' mad you, aren't y'?
FRANK. Probably.

And contrast Rita's direct reply to Frank's question about the quality of her hairdressing:

(8.17)
FRANK. You're a ladies' hairdresser?
RITA. Yeh.
FRANK. Are you good at it?
RITA. I am.

In general terms then, Rita's strategy is to try and build up a relationship with Frank by revealing her emotions, judgements, and appreciations to him and inviting him to react. This is a powerful strategy for building up a relationship, since shared feelings tend to draw people together. Rita uses the meeting to size Frank up; to see what evaluations they might be able to share or not. Subsequently she can draw on what she has learned to develop the relationship. This would appear to be part of an orientation to meaning and the negotiation of relationships that Bernstein (e.g. 1975) refers to as positional (see also Hasan 1990).

For his part, in Rita's terms, Frank reveals very little about himself. Up to his parting monologue where he evaluates his appalling teaching and appalling students, he gives next to no opinions at all. Rather, for Frank, the point of the meeting seems to be to establish himself as a very special kind of individual ('bleeding mad' is Rita's assessment). As a result of this orientation to meaning in this context, when pressed by Rita, Frank appears to hedge and prevaricate:

(8.18) Expanding Example 8.1 above
RITA. Here—d' y' want one?
FRANK. Ah—I'd love one.
RITA. Well, have one.
FRANK. I—don't smoke—I made a promise not to smoke.
RITA. Well, I won't tell anyone.
FRANK. Promise?
RITA. On my oath as an ex Brownie. I hate smokin' on me own. An' everyone seems to
 have packed up these days. They're all afraid of gettin' cancer. But they're all cowards.

Compared with Rita, Frank does not answer directly. Note how directly Rita comes to the point when Frank offers her a seat:

(8.19)
FRANK. Would you like to sit down?
RITA. No!

But the more important point here, as far as gender, class, and social meaning are concerned, is that by avoiding a direct answer Frank creates an opportunity to 'personalize' his response. He sets himself up as someone who'd like a cigarette but doesn't want one, who's promised not to smoke but would like to, and who will smoke as long as someone promises not to tell. Frank is not just someone accepting a cigarette, in other words; rather, he is a naughty boy who just might sneak a fag on the understanding he won't get caught. In constructing this part of his persona, Frank is presenting himself as something special—a little boy in tutor's clothing (cf. above where Frank avoids Rita's query about the view in order to position himself as a raving lunatic, in whose care students are probably far from secure—a wolf in tweed clothing).

The complementarity of Rita and Frank's orientations to meaning is summed up nicely in the following exchange. Rita tries to share feelings about a picture hanging in Frank's room (in bold face below: *a nice picture, very erotic, look at those tits*); Frank personalizes his response (using explicit subjective interpersonal metaphors of modality[12] to create a negotiating space: *I suppose, I don't think, I suppose*) and takes the opportunity to specialize himself as someone who hasn't looked at the picture in ten years:

(8.20) Repeating Example 8.9 above
RITA. That's a ***nice picture***, isn't it?
FRANK. Erm—yes, *I suppose* it is—nice . . .

---

[12] For modality metaphor see Halliday (1994), Martin (1995*a*).

RITA. It's *very erotic.*

FRANK. Actually, *I don't think* I've looked at it for about ten years, but yes, I *suppose* it is.

RITA. There's no suppose about it.

Remarkably, Rita takes the step of commenting directly on and resisting Frank's individuation when she says 'There's no suppose about it.' Rita's challenge to Frank's coding in this exchange is symbolic of her refusal to comply passively with his positionings of her throughout the play. She's an assertive working class woman; and she wants change.

Re/appraisal

In this chapter I have tried to present a brief overview of APPRAISAL resources in English[13] and to illustrate their instantiation across a range of spoken and written texts. In the course of our research, we began with AFFECT, working in the context of secondary school English narratives and responses (Martin 1996; Rothery 1994, Rothery and Stenglin 1994*a, b, c*); JUDGEMENT evolved out of AFFECT in the context of our work on media (Iedema *et al.* 1994), and later history (Coffin 1997); and APPRECIATION evolved last in the context of our work on creative arts. What began as a small project, aimed at developing a better analysis of evaluation in narrative, has grown into a large, unfinished project for which this chapter provides at best an interim report. A virtual Pandora's box of issues awaits research, which demands new kinds of research orientation—towards lexis (alongside grammar), towards corpus (alongside text), towards prosody (alongside particle and wave), towards solidarity (alongside hegemony), towards multi-modal analysis, including paralanguage, body, and image (alongside verbiage), towards heteroglossia (alongside system), towards resistant and tactical readings (alongside compliant ones), and so on: a massive recontextualization of linguistic enterprise—and one perhaps long overdue.

In the course of the *Star Trek Next Generation* episodes 'Unification I and II', Spock and Data are at work together on an encrypted Romulan communication. Engaging Spock in conversation, Data takes an interest in the fact that whereas he, an android with no feelings, has spent his lifetime trying to acquire some so as to become more human, Spock, a Vulcan/human born with emotions, has spent his lifetime suppressing them. It is salutary to note that of all the Enterprise crew, it is only the lexicogrammars of Spock and Data that contemporary linguistics has begun to describe. Perhaps, as this volume heralds for evaluative language, it is time to explore strange new worlds, seeking out new life, where few linguists have gone before.

---

[13] This approach to appraisal was inspired in large part by research into secondary school and workplace literacy conducted by Caroline Coffin, Susan Feez, Sally Humphreys, Rick Iedema, Henrike Korner, David McInnes, David Rose, Joan Rothery, Maree Stenglin, Robert Veel, and Peter White as part of the Disadvantaged Schools Program's Write it Right project; Joan Rothery (APPRECIATION) and Peter White (JUDGEMENT) in particular constructed a great deal of the framework presented here.

9

Evaluation and the Planes of Discourse: Status and Value in Persuasive Texts

Susan Hunston

It will certainly have emerged in this volume that evaluation is a highly complex linguistic function. Most of the other chapters have dealt with the complexity by isolating certain aspects to focus on. In this chapter, Hunston faces it head-on. She sets out to explore the different types of evaluation that are expressed and their relationship to the different things that are evaluated.

In part, her analysis takes the preliminary distinction made in the introduction to this book between entities and propositions as the objects of evaluation, and develops the idea much more rigorously in terms of Sinclair's (1981) planes of discourse. On the *interactive plane* in Sinclair's model, the text reflects (and constructs) the ongoing interaction between writer and reader: the writer signals to the reader what the role of any particular proposition is in the larger meanings being expressed in the text as a whole. If we consider the kind of signalling discussed by Thompson and Zhou (this volume), the use of *Certainly . . . But . . .* to start consecutive sentences indicates to the reader that whatever is said in the first statement should be understood as a concession and that the following statement is an assertion. Evaluation on this plane therefore relates to the function of the proposition in the text: for example, whether it is to be taken as expressing the writer's opinion (not normally open to contradiction by the writer within the same text) or the opinion of someone else (potentially open to be contradicted by the writer). On the second plane, *the autonomous plane*, the text 'says things' about the world—in other words, we are looking at the text in terms of its content rather than of its construction. Evaluation on this plane relates to the expression of the writer's 'angle' on the world: whether a chance meeting is *fortunate* or *unfortunate*, whether a politician is a *statesman* or a *demagogue*, and so on. This is the area where Hunston's chapter overlaps most closely with Martin's (this volume): his concept of appraisal relates primarily to what in Hunston's terms is evaluation on the autonomous plane. The other main distinction on which Hunston's analysis rests is that between *status* and *value*. On the interactive plane, each statement is of a particular type (e.g. a fact or an assessment) and has a source (e.g. averred by the writer, or attributed to someone else): these determine its status. At the same time many of the statements are given a positive or negative value (e.g. that it is supported by evidence, or that it is not true). Hunston explores in depth the ways in which the status of a statement constrains the kind of value that it can be given. On the autonomous plane, the distinction is more fluid, but again the status given to the entities referred to in the text constrains the value that they can subsequently be given (and often simultaneously expresses the value). For example, the word *weed* constructs the existence of (i.e. gives status to) a grouping of plants whose only common feature is that they are not wanted by gardeners, and simultaneously gives the grouping a negative value.

The resulting picture of how evaluation works in text is inevitably, and quite deliberately, complex. Hunston's aim—and the underlying message of this book as a whole—is to show that evaluation in text is difficult to tease out but that the teasing is both necessary and worthwhile.

* * *

Introduction

Certain observable factors concerning evaluation need to be accounted for by any system of analysis. In particular, the complex nature of evaluation must be reflected. Evaluation incorporates various parameters, it is often implicit and relies for its effect on intertextuality, and in many texts it is multilayered. Evaluation plays a key role in the construal of a particular ideology by a text or set of texts. It also plays a key role in discourse organization.

The texts under consideration in this chapter belong to different genres, but might all be characterized as having a persuasive function. They include research papers from the journal *Nature*, articles from the *New Scientist*, political and social comment articles from *The Times* and the *Guardian* newspapers, and book reviews from those newspapers. Persuasive texts have been chosen because, in them, evaluation is important to the purpose of the text. In systemic-functional terms, evaluation construes the field as well as the tenor of persuasive texts.

In a genre such as the experimental research article, where the persuasive nature of the text tends to be hidden behind a veneer of 'objectivity' (Latour and Woolgar 1979; Bazerman 1988), the phenomenon of evaluation is relatively simple, because only certain things (e.g. the experimental method, the authors' results and conclusions, other researchers' results and conclusions) are evaluated and only in certain ways (e.g. as free from bias, fitting a range of data, applicable to a range of situations). This chapter takes a set of concepts devised to account for the evaluation in research articles (Hunston 1989, 1993a, 1994) and applies them to a different set of data, in which the range of things evaluated is far greater, in order to explore further the complexity of evaluation.

The chapter begins by exploring some of the complexity of evaluation, particularly with relation to averral and attribution. It goes on to consider an analysis of evaluation on each of two planes: the interactive and the autonomous. Finally, there is a theoretical discussion of the model of evaluation and an indication of how the two planes contribute to the organization of a text. Throughout the paper, a text-encoder is referred to as the writer and a text-decoder is referred to as the reader, as all the texts considered here are written ones. Spoken texts could be discussed in the same terms, however.

Exploring Complexity in Evaluation

ATTRIBUTION AND AVERRAL

As Sinclair notes (Sinclair 1986; Tadros 1993), the distinction between averral and attribution is a crucial one. If a piece of language—spoken, written, or thought— is attributed, it is presented as deriving from someone other than the writer. If a piece of language is averred, the writer him or herself speaks. The distinction between averral and attribution is important to the study of evaluation, because it can be used to position the reader to attach more or less credence to the various pieces of information (see Martin, this volume, for comment on the 'normal' reading of a text). Here is an example, with the attributed statements in italics.

(9.1)
The history of AIDS took a new twist last week with the disclosure that *a seaman from Manchester appears to have had the disease as far back as 1959.* In the earliest case of AIDS on record, a team of researchers has shown that *stored tissues from the man's body contained genetic material from HIV.* Other scientists said *the work could shed new light on the evolution of the virus and the rate at which it mutates.*

As readers, we are clearly expected to attach a great deal of credence to the validity of the evidence about the Manchester seaman and AIDS. This is achieved by the attribution of some statements to 'respectable' sources: *a team of researchers* and *other scientists.* The statements that are averred are those which are true only if what the scientists say is true: *the history of AIDS took a new twist* and the Manchester seaman is *the earliest case of AIDS on record.* In addition, some of the attribution uses nouns and verbs which indicate writer agreement or factuality: *disclosure, has shown.* The statement by the 'other scientists' is accorded a lower truth value, with the verb *said.* In short, by manipulating attribution and averral, the writer evaluates the story highly, yet evinces a scientific caution and deference to authority which her readers in turn are likely to evaluate highly.

As Sinclair (1986) has noted, in general a writer assumes responsibility for what is averred, but delegates responsibility for what is attributed to the attributee. This is demonstrated in the example above, where the writer takes responsibility for *the history of AIDS took a new twist last week* but transfers responsibility for *the work could shed new light on the evolution of the virus and the rate at which it mutates* to *other scientists.* This distinction between assuming and not assuming responsibility can be modified, however. Averral may be modified to a certain extent by modals or by vague language (Channell 1994) so that the writer accepts responsibility for only a hedged statement. Attribution may be modified, more radically, by the way it is expressed, for example by the choice of attributing verb or noun (Thompson and Ye 1991; Tadros 1993; Hunston 1994; Thompson 1996a). In the example above, the use of *has shown* indicates that the writer evaluates as true and therefore shares responsibility for *stored tissues from the man's body contained genetic material from HIV*. Similarly, *disclosure* indicates that the writer evaluates as true and therefore shares responsibility for the modified proposition *a seaman from Manchester appears to have had the disease as far back as 1959*, although at this point the attributee is not mentioned. As well as certain verbs and nouns (see Thompson 1994 for a full list), the subordinator *as* can be used to similar effect, as in

(9.2)
Paralinguistic features in spoken language . . . may make construal easier, as Olsen suggests, but they may also make the task more complex.

One complicating factor in distinguishing between averral and attribution is that every attribution is also averred. Sinclair (1986) makes this point, showing that attributed utterances are embedded within averred ones. Thus, in the clause complex *a team of researchers has shown that stored tissues from the man's body contained genetic material from HIV*, the proposition expressed by the clause *stored tissues from the man's body contained genetic material from HIV* is attributed, but the proposition expressed by *a team of researchers has shown that . . .* is averred. In fact, the starting-point for saying that every attributed proposition is interpreted and evaluated by the attributor must be to say that every attribution is embedded within an averral.

In the examples given above, attribution takes the form usually described as indirect speech (Thompson 1994). Another kind of attribution involves a non-clausal proposition. Here also, attribution is embedded within averral.

(9.3)
George I regarded [Gibraltar] as an expensive symbol.

In this example, the implied proposition 'Gibraltar is an expensive symbol' is attributed to George I, but there is no implication that the proposition is a verbatim report, rather it is a summary or interpretation of George I's ideas. Responsibility for the truth of that summary as a summary is assumed by the writer, while responsibility for the assessment of Gibraltar is given to George I.

In addition to the types of attribution shown above, I also treat some concessions as a type of attribution, because they are treated by the writer as if they had been uttered by a debating partner. They are, however, an attribution without an attributee: the debating partner is unnamed and silent. Concessions are, by their very nature, evaluated as true (though they predict a counter-argument in the counter-assertion): the writer thereby shares responsibility for the proposition. The signal of concession and attribution in the following example is *may . . . but*.

(9.4)
The Scottish Secretary, Michael Forsyth, may be crude in the way he bangs on about the dangers of a 'tartan tax' and the 'slippery slope' to independence, but in a political vac-uum, he who shouts loudest uses up all the oxygen.

In this example, utterances concerning the dangers of a tartan tax and the slippery slope to independence are attributed to Michael Forsyth and evaluated with the verb *bang on about*. An assessment of those utterances as *crude* is attributed to an unnamed debater by the concession, and evaluated as true. In this one sentence, then, there are several layers of attribution and of evaluation. These can be set out as shown in Table 9.1.

TABLE 9.1. *Analysis of Example 9.4*

What is evaluated	Who evaluates it	How it is evaluated
possible events in Scotland	Michael Forsyth	*dangers of a tartan tax . . . slippery slope to independence*
Michael Forsyth's utterances about tartan tax and independence	the writer	*bangs on about*
Michael Forsyth's utterances about tartan tax and independence	the unnamed debater	*crude*
the unnamed debater's opinion of Michael Forsyth as 'crude'	the writer	evaluated as true by being conceded, but counter-argument predicted

Here is another example which expresses a number of voices, some named, some unnamed:

(9.5)
Sir James may have caused apoplexy in the Tory party with his tirades against Eurodoctrine, but he has not so far moved enough voters for them to register on an opin-ion poll.

Attributed to Sir James are speeches against Europe, which the writer evaluates as *tirades*; attributed to members of the Tory party are reactions to these speeches, which the writer evaluates as *apoplexy*. The fact that Sir James has caused apoplexy is conceded, that is, it is attributed to the unnamed debater, with whom the writer agrees. Once again we can represent the layers of evaluation and attribution in a table (see Table 9.2).

TABLE 9.2. *Analysis of Example 9.5*

What is evaluated	Who evaluates it	How it is evaluated
policies concerned with Europe	Sir James	negatively: Sir James has spoken *against* them
Sir James's speeches	the writer	*tirades*
Sir James's speeches	the Tory party	with anger
the Tory party's reactions to Sir James's speeches	the unnamed debater	*apoplexy*
the unnamed debater's assertion about how the Tory party has reacted to Sir James's speeches	the writer	evaluated as true by being conceded, but counter-argument predicted

It should be pointed out at this stage that the people and groups to whom language is attributed are only part of a larger phenomenon: the ascription of information or opinion in a text to sources, which may be animate or inanimate. Indications of these sources are sometimes referred to as 'evidentials' (Chafe 1986; Barton 1993). The writer, of course, chooses the sources, and may select named people or construct groups (Hunston 1993b). The sources together constitute a constructed culture of knowledge and opinion, which the reader is expected to share and be convinced by.

MORE MULTILAYERING IN EVALUATION

The above discussion of attribution and averral has focused on the multilayering of attribution and thus of evaluation. We shall now take this discussion of multilayering a little further by considering another example, which is the first sentence of the text it comes from:

(9.6a)
Right now a new wave of anti-sect paranoia is sweeping the world.

In this example, the prevalence of something called *anti-sect paranoia* is averred. *Anti-sect paranoia* indicates a reaction to groups of people ('sects'), a reaction attributed to unspecified people. The reaction is evaluated by the writer as unreasonable (*paranoia*). The anti-sect paranoia is further evaluated in a negative way as being widespread (*new wave . . . sweeping the country*). Furthermore, the sentence as a whole constitutes a judgement, or opinion, or claim, on the part of the writer. It stands as a thing that is evaluated in the next sentence, which provides evidence to support the claim:

(9.6*b*)

All ruling bodies, political parties and the media seem unanimous in their suspicion and hostility towards sects and any group of people labelled a 'sect' are automatically viewed with prejudiced eyes.

In other words, certain groupings are evaluated as 'sects' by unnamed people, and this idea is evaluated as 'paranoia', which itself is evaluated as widespread, and this assertion is evaluated as supported by evidence.

As before, we can represent this multilayering in a table (see Table 9.3).

TABLE 9.3. *Analysis of Example 9.6*

What is evaluated	Who evaluates it	How it is evaluated
groups of people	unnamed people	negatively, as *sects*
people's feelings about sects	the writer	as *paranoia*
anti-sect paranoia	the writer	as common: *sweeping the world*
the writer's assertion that paranoia is sweeping the world	the writer	as true, by adding details as evidence

As Thetela (1997) has pointed out, much of the complexity in the study of evaluation derives from the fact that many different things may be evaluated in a single text. Thetela proposes distinguishing world-entities and discourse-entities. In her terms, the first three 'what is evaluated' items in column 1 of Table 9.3 are world-entities, while the last one is a discourse-entity. A similar distinction is made here, and will be discussed below in terms of 'planes of discourse'.

As another example, consider the following paragraph from a book review:

(9.7)

[1] O'Toole's descriptions of Rada classes pin down precisely the Dickensian eccentricity of his teachers. [2] There is the voice-coach Clifford Turner who magically repeats every phrase three times; the ballet-mistress Madame Fletcher ('Fletcher the Stretcher') who, getting O'Toole into the Fifth Position, leaves him doubting the whereabouts of his testicles; and the movement teacher Miss Boalth, who has our hero floating about as a bubble while his fellow student Albert Finney spins by as a leaf. [3] As a bookie's son who, at 21, had already knocked about the world a bit, O'Toole describes the mysteries of his initiation with an ironic amusement.

Several 'world-entities' are evaluated here. These are:

• part of the book being reviewed, that is, *O'Toole's descriptions of Rada classes*, which are evaluated positively in that they *pin down precisely* the character of the teachers with *an ironic amusement*;
• the various Rada teachers, who demonstrate *Dickensian eccentricity*;
• O'Toole as a 21-year-old, who is evaluated positively as experienced and worldly-wise: *a bookie's son who, at 21, had already knocked about the world a bit*.

In addition, sentence 2 corroborates—and so evaluates positively—the claim made in sentence 1, thus a 'discourse-entity' is evaluated.

THE PLANES OF DISCOURSE

In the examples above, then, two kinds of entity are evaluated, which Thetela refers to as 'discourse-entities' and 'world-entities'. In each case, a claim is evaluated by being substantiated. The evaluation of the claim is an evaluation of a discourse act, an evaluation of part of the discourse itself. On the other hand, the other evaluations—of people's ideas and behaviour, of a book—are not evaluations of discourse acts from this discourse (though they do evaluate, intertextually, other discourses).

The distinction between 'evaluating a part of the discourse' and 'evaluating something else' may be seen as corresponding to Sinclair's distinction between interactive and autonomous planes of discourse (Sinclair 1981). This distinction may be thought of in terms of the roles of the writer and reader. At any one time, the writer is an informer, and the reader is informed of the content of the text (the autonomous plane). Simultaneously, the writer is a text-constructor, and the reader is informed of the structure of the text (the interactive plane). According to Sinclair, every sentence in a text operates on each plane simultaneously, although some sentences draw attention to their status on the interactive plane more explicitly than others. Predicting sentences such as *We discuss below three further examples* (Tadros 1994) are examples of these.

Returning to Example 9.6, we can see that if we take sentence 1.1—*Right now a new wave of anti-sect paranoia is sweeping the world*—as a claim (or an assertion, or an averral—the terminology does not matter) which is evaluated in subsequent sentences, we are seeing sentence 1.1 from the point of view of the writer-as-text-constructor. The writer constructs the text by making an assertion and then corroborating it. This is evaluation on the interactive plane. But if we take sentence 1.1 as a comment on certain things other than this discourse, including other discourses, we are seeing it from the point of view of writer-as-informer. This is evaluation on the autonomous plane.

Differentiating between the autonomous and interactive planes of discourse is one of the ways that we can take account of the complexity of evaluation in text. The crucial distinction lies in what is evaluated: a discourse act in the discourse itself (interactive) or something else (autonomous). I shall argue that on the interactive plane, the distinction between one thing-that-is-evaluated and another thing-that-is-evaluated lies in the variable alignments of 'world' and 'statement', or in Sinclair's terms of 'fact' and 'averral' (this terminology will be explained below), whereas on the autonomous plane the distinctions depend on how the world is labelled.

We can now reinterpret the analysis of

Right now a new wave of anti-sect paranoia is sweeping the world.

that was given above, distinguishing between interactive and autonomous planes, as in the revised table shown as Table 9.4.

TABLE 9.4. *Example 9.6: the two planes*

The Autonomous Plane		The Interactive Plane	
What is evaluated	How it is evaluated	What is evaluated	How it is evaluated
groups of people	as *sects*	the writer's assertion that paranoia is sweeping the world	as true
people's feelings about sects	as *paranoia*		
anti-sect paranoia	as common		

Status and Value on the Interactive Plane

THE STATUS OF STATEMENTS

In his article 'Fictional Worlds', Sinclair (1986) argues that interaction proceeds by means of an acceptance by the hearer of a correspondence between 'fact' ('a state of affairs in the real world around us') and 'averral' ('the verbal assertion that something is the case') in the speaker's utterance. Averrals that are understood to be non-fictional in character are open to judgement by the hearer in terms of their correspondence or otherwise with the 'facts' as experienced by the hearer. Averrals that are fictional in character (for example, they occur in a novel) are judged quite differently, for 'verisimilitude' and for aesthetic value rather than truth. In other words, there is a sharp distinction between the way a hearer (or reader) responds to a non-fictional averral and the way he or she responds to a fictional one. It is therefore important that a hearer or reader rightly assesses whether a particular text is fictional or non-fictional. Sinclair terms this fictionality or otherwise the 'status' of a text (Sinclair 1986: 57).

The importance of status, using Sinclair's terminology, is that it determines how a reader responds to any statement within a given text: in essence, to what extent the reader judges that statement in the context of the actual world experienced by the reader. Although I here use the term 'status' in a slightly different way, this important characteristic of status remains: statements of different statuses are responded to differently by the reader, and are judged by the reader according to different criteria.

Unlike Sinclair, I propose to assign the term 'status' not to a whole text, but to each of the clauses in a text. (In fact, 'status' is a feature not only of clauses, but of all propositions in a text, including those which are not expressed as clauses. This is one of the reasons for the complexity of evaluation. For the sake of simplicity, however, I shall discuss status here only in terms of explicit statements, that is, clauses.) We can say that every clause or every statement in a text carries with it a particular status. That is, every statement is understood as having a particular orientation with respect to the world outside the text. In academic writing, writers modify the status of the statements with a high degree of exactness, so that the reader is positioned to accept both the writer's immediate argument and his or her academic credentials. In the example below, the reader is positioned to interpret the first sentence as a given fact but to respond to the second sentence as a more cautious interpretation of that fact in the light of common sense:

(9.8)
Over its evolution, the plant kingdom has accumulated a large repertoire of mechanisms for coping with cold, drought, and CO_2 starvation. Presumably, these mechanisms have weakened the relation between CO_2 and productivity and have reduced the effect of CO_2 fertilization and greenhouse warming on vegetation.

It is important to stress that it does not matter whether or not the reader accepts the positioning offered. The expert reader may indeed reject the truth of the first sentence utterly, accusing the writer of ignorance or of a misrepresentation of the relevant research. This is, in fact, within the range of responses predicted by that sentence, which include 'rejection as wrong' as well as 'acceptance as correct'.

On the other hand, it is also a result of the status accorded the two sentences cited above that the text itself will proceed under the assumption that the reader accepts the statements in them as true. As well as determining the range of responses open to the reader, the status of a statement also limits the range of subsequent statements it is possible for the text to make. For example, as Sinclair (1986: 45–6) points out, a statement which does not modify the alignment of world and statement ('fact' and 'averral' in Sinclair's terms) cannot simply be contradicted by the same averrer:

A speaker cannot say: 'This costs £5, but it doesn't.'

However, a statement which *does* modify this alignment can be contradicted:

'This should cost £5, but it doesn't.'

In the following example from an academic article, the proposition beginning *deciduous angiosperms weather rock more effectively than evergreen gymnosperms* remains open to contradiction by the writer because it is attributed to *the latter authors* with the verb of attribution *argue*, which does not signal writer agreement.

(9.9)
Using data from Likens et al, the latter authors argue that deciduous angiosperms weather rock more effectively than evergreen gymnosperms, thus the advent of the angiosperms during the Cretaceous caused a major increase in rates of weathering.

One of the functions of the choice of report verb, therefore, is either to leave open the option of disagreement with the attributed statement (e.g. *argue*) or to preclude such disagreement (e.g. *point out*). It is not only attribution to others that constrains the subsequent text in this way. In the following example, the writer absolves himself from the necessity of supporting the statement *nonliterate adult speakers are as capable of perceiving disparities between words and meanings as literate speakers* in the subsequent text. Because the status of the statement is an assumption, readers may agree or disagree with it, but the text proceeds as if the reader agrees without the need for further evidence.

(9.10)
I am going to take it for granted as requiring no argument that nonliterate adult speakers are as capable of perceiving disparities between words and meanings as literate speakers.

In summary, then, status on the interactive plane refers to the alignment of statement and world, which determines or at least constrains the reader's reaction to the statement and subsequent further evaluation. Status reifies, that is, it makes each statement into a 'thing' (a hypothesis, assumption, fact, and so on) which is open to further evaluation. The assignment of status is not optional: each statement in a text has a status of some kind.

In order to analyse status in a text, a set of status categories must be proposed. These could be stated in the form of a list: 'averred fact', 'attributed opinion', 'averred hypothesis', and so on, but such a list quickly becomes complicated. We might rephrase the question in terms of what the key differences between categories of status are. The primary differences lie in the type of statement and in the source of each statement. Figure 9.1 is a possible network showing types of statement.

In terms of the type of statement, it is probable that the significance of different parts of the network is dependent on the genre. For academic articles that describe experimental research, for example, it has been argued (Hunston 1989) that a primary contrast lies between statements that create a possible or hypothetical world ('world-creating': assumptions and descriptions of hypothetical events, for example) and those which claim knowledge about the actual world ('world-reflecting': reports of experimental method and results, for example). A further significant difference is between that which is claimed to be true (facts, events, experimental results, for example), and that which is claimed to be possibly true (hypotheses and interpretations, for example). For journalistic persuasive writing, the most significant division seems to be between 'fact' and 'assessment'. That is, a writer either gives information which purports to have truth-value and which can be contradicted only by calling the writer a liar (a 'fact'), or he or she gives an opinion, something which cannot of itself be said to be true or not true (an 'assessment').

I shall now give some examples of the network shown in Figure 9.1.

1. Focusing and Informing

Focusing statements describe the current text itself. They include statements concerning the aims or organization of the text, such as *This point will be discussed*

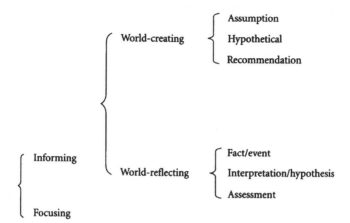

FIGURE 9.1. Statement types

again in Chapter 8 . . . This chapter is divided into two sections . . . Figure 1 shows
. . . Informing statements set up an alignment between the words of the text and
the world.

2. Reflecting the World: Facts, Interpretations, and Assessments

Here is an example of an averred fact:

(9.11)
I belong to a spiritual movement called the Wild Goose Company, some of whose members live at Energy World, a community in rural France.

and an example of an averred assessment:

(9.12)
It does not seem outrageously liberal to allow a group of people to gather together and
experiment with styles of living that differ from those of conventional society.

The essential difference between fact and assessment is that fact makes an assertion that is open to verification, while assessment does not. Thus, the fact that *I
belong to a spiritual movement called the Wild Goose Company* can be verified (by
checking the Wild Goose Company's records, for example) but the assertion that
it [is] not outrageously liberal to allow a group of people to gather together . . . is not:
it is simply an opinion that at any given moment some people will hold and
others will not. In both Example 9.11 and Example 9.12 above the reader is positioned to agree with the proposition. However, the examples do differ in the range
of reactions open to the reader. Because the first example is expressed as something open to objective verification, denial of the truth of the statement is not an
option for the reader, or rather, since all things are possible, denial of the truth
would imply that the writer is a liar or dangerously delusional. The situation is

analogous to that in a research article when the writer makes a statement of result: the reader cannot deny that those results occurred without accusing the writer of fraud. In the case of the assessments, however, the reader is free to disagree with the writer. In the example of assessment above, it might be argued that the writer has misinterpreted certain events. The primary difference between fact and assessment is the implications for the following text. Facts will not be further evaluated for their truth-value. Assessments may be further evaluated (but only positively) for their truth-value: in fact, they are very often supported by evidence given in the subsequent text.

'Facts', of course, may be expressed in ways that make the involvement of the writer's opinion either more or less apparent. In the following, for example, the recounting of events clearly involves a considerable amount of interpretation on the part of the writer:

(9.13)
Energy World was recently invaded by police without warning at seven one morning. Exits were sealed, and all the computer files were commandeered; Mr Barnett's private quarters were ransacked.

It would be open to the reader to accept, for example, that the police entered a house, closed the doors, took away computer files and searched a man's room, without for a moment believing that the police *invaded, sealed, commandeered,* or *ransacked.*

On the other hand, an assessment may be expressed as if it were a fact. Example 9.6*a* is an assessment, because it cannot be said to be verifiable, but it is expressed as if something verifiable were happening.

(9.6*a*)
Right now a new wave of anti-sect paranoia is sweeping the world.

Intermediate between 'fact' and 'assessment' is a category named here 'interpretation' or 'hypothesis'. These are statements that are evaluated by the writer as possibly true. They occur very typically in scientific and other academic discourse, where, as noted above, a sharp distinction is made between what is known and what is open to verification. In the following example, sentence 3 is an attributed hypothesis that arises out of an interpretation of events analogous to an experimental method (hammering a piece of wood) and its result (ash forming miniature mounds):

(9.14)
[1] While building a dog kennel, [Berg] happened to hammer on a piece of plywood which was covered with a thin layer of volcanic ash. [2] The vibration caused the ash to clump together to form miniature mounds. [3] Berg realized that Mima mounds might form in a similar way.

3. Creating the World: Assumptions, Hypotheticals, and Recommendations

As well as reflecting the world, a writer has the choice of making a hypothetical world, which is simply assumed or hypothesized and is not tested in relation to the actual world. In academic discourse, a writer sometimes asserts that something is to be taken as an assumption, that is, assumed for the time being to be true, rather than argued, as in Example 9.10. In this example, the writer in effect creates a world in which nonliterate and literate adults are equivalent, and this world constitutes the background against which the rest of the argument is set. The relation between the created world and the actual world does not need to be argued.

(9.10)

I am going to take it for granted as requiring no argument that nonliterate adult speakers are as capable of perceiving disparities between words and meanings as literate speakers.

Similar world-creation happens when the writer makes a recommendation:

(9.15)

If I was Major I would try to make some such deal with Spain.

The question of truth-value is irrelevant here. The speech act is one of directive (giving advice) rather than assertive (giving information).

Having dealt with the major statement types, we now turn to the other variable in the assignment of status: statement source. Expressing the source of a statement in terms of choices is somewhat problematic. Take, for example, the following three examples, each of which is also quoted elsewhere in this chapter:

(*a*) Higgins maintains that gophers destroy mounds not build them.

(*b*) I have to say I very much doubt it.

(*c*) It [the preceding text] does suggest that their causes have some way to go before they achieve real weight.

Clearly, each of these has a different source: (*a*) is a report of another person's claim, (*b*) is a strong expression of personal opinion, (*c*) is a conclusion drawn from a preceding argument. How are these differences to be expressed in terms of choices? In each of the examples, there is a projecting clause with a verb indicating some kind of verbal process, and a projected clause. Because of that, we could say that they are all attributions, and that the attribution is, respectively, to a named other person, to the self, and to preceding text. Alternatively, we could interpret example (*b*) as a strongly marked averral, with the writer keeping responsibility, and (*a*) as a true attribution, leaving a doubt as to whether (*c*) belongs with (*a*), on the grounds that it appears to attribute, or with (*b*), on the grounds that the attribution is a kind of trick: it is actually the writer, not the preceding text, that 'suggests'. The apparent choices, then, will depend on whether priority is given to the grammatical form of the clause complex, the named source of the statement, or the question of responsibility. I have chosen to give priority to the source. Figure 9.2 shows a network of possible sources.

There follow some examples of the network shown in Figure 9.2.

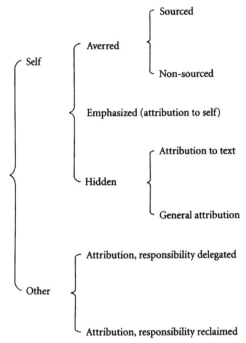

FIGURE 9.2. Statement sources

4. Self and Other

As mentioned above, the distinction between self and other as source has been given priority over the grammatically distinguished averral and attribution.

5. Self as Source: Averral, Emphasized, and Hidden

Within the category 'self' as source, a distinction is made between straightforward averral, which will be discussed further below, and attributions where the source is not another person or text. Where the attribution is to self, this is described as emphasized self as source, as in:

(9.16)
I have to say I very much doubt it.

The writer's self as the source of a statement may be disguised, as it is in cases where attribution is made to the preceding text. In the following example, although a report structure is used, it is the writer who is responsible for the suggestion:

(9.17)
It [the preceding text] does suggest that their causes have some way to go before they achieve real weight.

Alternatively, the writer's own opinion may be attributed to 'people in general'. This again disguises the writer's self as source:

(9.18)
No one is pretending that Gibraltar is either a big issue or even, at this stage, a particularly pressing one.

The function of this is to set up an 'in-group' of like-minded people, to which the reader is positioned as belonging, and thus to construct consensus.

6. Other as Source: Responsibility Delegated or Reclaimed

In prototypical cases of attribution, responsibility is diverted to the attributee. The attributee may be a specific person or group, as in:

(9.19)
In the past century, geologists have proposed many explanations for the mounds' existence. *Some have claimed* that they were built by gophers or that they are the product of selective erosion of the soil. *Others believe* they result from glacial deposition or the accumulation of soil around the roots of plants . . .

(9.20)
George Cox of San Diego State University points out that the mounds in North America overlap the range of the pocket gopher. But *Higgins maintains* that gophers destroy mounds not build them.

It may be to a less specific group, as in:

(9.21)
. . . Major *is said by some* to have secured his famous single currency and social chapter opt-outs at Maastricht only in return for an agreement to support Germany over the recognition of Croatia.

The attribution may even be to a speech act rather than to a person or group:

(9.22)
Myth has it that O'Toole, along with Finney, spearheaded a new breed of fifties working-class actor . . .

though a trace of the people responsible for the speech act may appear in the clause, as in:

(9.23)
The standard *devolutionist* response to this is to say that the arguments for reform have long been made and won . . .

(9.24)
. . . a rumour went round *the neighbourhood* that they were built as repositories for any human corpses left after your average 'cult activity'.

The writer may, however, reclaim responsibility for the statement, as discussed above, by choosing a verb that signals agreement, such as *prove, point out,* or *show,* or by using an 'as . . . ' structure.

7. Sourced and Non-sourced Averral

A statement which is averred, not attributed, may still be expressed as deriving from a source. This source is evidence for the truth of the statement, and is expressed as a prepositional phrase or as an adverbial. The source of an averral may be an entity (in this and the following examples, the source is shown in italics):

(9.25)
Peter O'Toole is a born romantic; that much is clear from *this beguiling second volume of a set of memoirs that looks likely to last to infinity.*

Alternatively, the source may be an implied consensus:

(9.26)
Gibraltar is a small, costly, and *by all accounts* not very prepossessing colony of only 30,000 people.
(9.27)
For *when one thinks back,* all his best performances, on stage and screen, have been as larger-than-life outsiders. T. E. Lawrence, *obviously* . . .
(9.28)
A man who made a pact like that would *certainly* be a man who could trade the Rock for fish.

Some sourced averrals are also concessions and predict a counter-argument. These concessions do not have the strong signals such as *may* or *It is true that* . . . which imply an unnamed attributee, as discussed above. An example of a sourced averral acting as a concession is:

(9.29)
Undoubtedly some track should be kept of religious communities . . .

Non-sourced averrals have no such modification. Here are some examples, the first two represent averred facts, the third is an averred assessment:

(9.30)
On the morning of the white paper's release, I had a briefing from a minister.
(9.31)
Ten years ago we [Britain] still had upwards of 2,000 military personnel on the Rock. Today we have 700.
(9.32)
So far there is little evidence that the issues championed by the two millionaires have done much to capture the public imagination.

There can be indeterminacy between sourced and non-sourced averrals. This is particularly true if the potential source of a statement lies outside the sentence. In the following example, the evidence for the averral *O'Toole is initially poleaxed by the temptations on offer* presumably lies in the book mentioned in the first sentence.

(9.33)
[1] The book also accurately evokes the sexual tensions of fifties student life. [2] O'Toole is initially poleaxed by the temptations on offer . . .

USING STATUS IN ARGUMENT

In both academic and non-academic argument, status is manipulated to give greater credence to the writer's own statements (the proposed claims) than to statements attributed to people whom the writer opposes (the opposed claims) (Hunston 1993c). In many cases there is a simple contrast between a statement that is averred (the proposed claim) and one that is attributed (the opposed claim). However, differences may be quite subtle, particularly in academic articles, where reputations are at stake and writers must argue with circumspection (Myers 1989). In the following example (from Hunston 1993c), the implied statement 'there was a limiting dichroism of +0.06, with saturation of orientation at voltages above 15 kV/cm' is more reliable than 'there was a limiting dichroism of about −0.2 and there was no saturation of the orientation'. This difference is constructed by the contrast between attributing a finding to named individuals carrying out an experiment (*McGhee et al found . . . did not observe*) and expressing a finding as the neutral outcome of an experiment.

(9.34)
McGhee et al. . . . found a limiting dichroism of about −0.2 and did not observe saturation of the orientation at increasing electric field. Our experiments . . . showed a limiting dichroism of +0.06, with saturation of orientation at voltages above 15kV/cm.

Here is an example, similar in that it manipulates both report verb and attributee, from a non-academic article. First, the proposed claim:

(9.35)
. . . what politicians and journalists reluctantly have to concede is that it [the devolution debate] still fails to ignite passion on the doorstep.

and the corresponding opposed claim (subsequently refuted):

(9.36)
The standard devolutionist response to this is to say that the arguments for reform have long been made and won . . .

In both Examples 9.35 and 9.36, there is an attributed assessment (*it still fails to ignite passion on the doorstep* and *the arguments for reform have long been made and won . . .*). However, in the first example (9.35), the verb of attribution is *concede*, which indicates that the averrer shares responsibility for the truth of the statement, indeed that the averrer had the idea first and won the 'politicians and journalists' to his or her point of view (Hunston 1995), whereas the verb of attribution in the second example is *say*, which indicates that responsibility for the statement remains with the attributee ('devolutionists'). In addition, the statement in the second example is described as *standard*, which makes it appear less convincing.

VALUE ON THE INTERACTIVE PLANE

Status reifies statements, making each discourse-entity into a thing that can be given a value. For example, an assessment can be supported by evidence, or by its fit to common sense, both of which evaluate the assessment positively. Alternatively, it can be shown not to fit with the facts, or to be open to criticism in other ways, which evaluates the assessment negatively. An assessment for which the source is self, or for which the writer reclaims responsibility, is more likely to be given positive value than an assessment which is attributed, with responsibility delegated.

It has been argued above that all statements in a text are assigned status. Some of these statements will also assign value to other statements. As an example, consider again the first two sentences in a text that were discussed near the beginning of this paper:

(9.6)
Right now a new wave of anti-sect paranoia is sweeping the world. All ruling bodies, political parties and the media seem unanimous in their suspicion and hostility towards sects and any group of people labelled a 'sect' are automatically viewed with prejudiced eyes.

All the clauses here are averred assessments, but in addition the second sentence gives evidence for the truth of the first. Using Winter's (1982) criteria, the second sentence answers the question 'Is this opinion supported by evidence?' Thus we can say that the second sentence gives value to the first sentence.

The grounds upon which a statement is given value depend on its status. In the following example, sentences 1 and 2 describe something with the status of an attributed theory. That theory is given negative value in sentence 3, on the grounds that it is incomplete and therefore not open to verification:

(9.37)
[1] According to Berg's theory, particles of material are shaken loose from high-amplitude areas and pushed towards the null zones. [2] It is here that they accumulate to form Mima mounds. [3] Unfortunately, Berg does not have a quantitative model of this phenomenon, and cannot predict how much seismic energy would be needed.

In the next example, the first sentence is a recommendation. A recommendation may be given value in terms of what good or bad consequences are likely to follow. These consequences are indicated in sentence 2. Sentence 2 in turn has the status of an averred assessment, evidence for which is given in sentences 3–4. Thus, sentence 2 gives value to sentence 1, and sentences 3 and 4 give value to sentence 2.

(9.38)
[1] Nor should Blair be afraid of the precedent factor. [2] The inevitable argument about withdrawal from Gibraltar could be turned to positive advantage. [3] It would show that Britain is serious about grabbing the remaining post-imperial nettles and facing up maturely to its position as a European nation. [4] If it opened the way to a more constructive approach to a settlement with Argentina over the Falklands, then so much the better.

In each case, the process of giving value on the interactive plane contributes to the organization of the text. If we ignore the status of those sentences which give value, we can express the analysis of each of the above three examples in terms of pairs of clause relations, each pair consisting of status + value: assessment + evidence; theory + criticism; recommendation + justification/assessment + evidence.

ANALYSING A TEXT ON THE INTERACTIVE PLANE

Below is an analysis of the text 'We Need Sects Education' (WNSE: see Appendix) in terms of evaluation on the interactive plane. It is of course possible to analyse status and value on the interactive plane separately, and such analyses can lead to interesting insights (Hunston 1989). Here, however, we shall continue to prioritize value, and indicate the status of those clauses only which are also given value. The status of clauses which give value will not be indicated.

The analysis is given in a table (Table 9.5) consisting of three columns. Two columns show status and value. In the final column of the table, the grounds for the evaluation of value are expressed in a question. The result is an outline of the text showing how the argument is put together.

Status and Value on the Autonomous Plane

The analysis given above treats the text as an artefact whose function is to construct a persuasive argument. It is, therefore, a meta-analysis. As the discussion of complexity in evaluation above has pointed out, however, such an analysis captures only a small part of the evaluation in a text. The purpose of this section of the chapter is to propose an analysis of evaluation on the autonomous plane. As before, we first look at the things that are evaluated, and then at how they are evaluated.

LABELLING THE WORLD: STATUS ON THE AUTONOMOUS PLANE

If we take 'status' to mean the alignment of statement and world, it belongs clearly on the interactional plane only. If, however, we accept that the function of status is to ascribe 'thing-ness' and to constrain how something may be given value, this function, and therefore the term 'status', may be extended to the autonomous plane. People, events, and things that in Thetela's (1997) terms are 'world-entities' belong to categories, and upon these categories depends how each entity is given value.

It is unnecessary to labour the point that the words chosen to describe the world in a text inevitably reflect the ideology of the writer or, more properly, the ideology of the section of society from which the writer comes. Discussion of how people and events are labelled in texts of various kinds is central to the work of critical discourse analysts, for example (e.g. Fairclough 1989; van Leeuwen 1996). To the alert reader, the point immediately becomes apparent when similar or comparable entities are lexicalized in different ways, or when the same entity is lexicalized in different ways by different groups. The reader is positioned to respond to

TABLE 9.5. *WNSE: the interactive plane*

Sentence	Status	Value	Question to establish grounds for value
1.1	averred (non-sourced) assessment		Do you have any evidence for the assessment?
1.1–2.2		1.1 is supported by evidence	
2.1–2	averred (non-sourced) account of events		What is your personal response to the events?
2.3	averred (non-sourced) assessment	2.1–2 is *alarming*	Do you have any evidence for the assessment?
2.4		2.3 is supported by implied evidence: following the logic of the report would lead to the ruling out of alternative medicine etc.	
3.3	implied attributed (responsibility delegated) assessment: the government believes Energy World is coercive		Is there any evidence for the assessment?
4.1–3		not supported by evidence	
5.7	attributed (responsibility delegated) assessment		What is your personal response to the assessment?
5.8		equivalent to Pontius Pilate	
5.6–7	averred (non-sourced) account of events		What are the consequences of these events?
6.1–3		undesirable consequences	
6.1	averred (non-sourced) assessment		Do you have any evidence for the assessment?
6.2–3		supported by evidence	
7.1	averred (non-sourced) recommendation		Is the recommendation reasonable? *cont.*

Sentence	Status	Value	Question to establish grounds for value
7.2–5		recommendation not based on anything *outrageously liberal* or *illogical*	
7.4	averred (sourced) recommendation (concession)		What is the counter-argument to the recommendation?
7.5		*makes good sense* but has unfortunate consequences	
7.6a	averred (sourced) assessment (concession)		What is the counter-argument to the assessment?
7.6b		counter-evidence	

something according to the label it is given (*press briefing* or *propaganda, freedom fighter* or *terrorist*), and the way that the thing is further evaluated in the text depends on what it is. A speech event labelled as *propaganda*, or a person labelled as a *terrorist*, is open to being given negative value, in the same way as an attributed assessment or theory is.

There is, however, a crucial difference between status on the interactive plane and on the autonomous plane. On the interactive plane, because status is associated with the alignment of statement and world, and is in part assigned by reporting structures and other indications of modality, it is typically also associated with the evaluative parameter of certainty. Value, on the other hand, is typically associated with the good–bad parameter. However, status is not the same as certainty, nor value the same as the good–bad parameter. Rather, we might interpret status and value as functions, not parameters, of evaluation. The status function ascribes thing-ness, the value function ascribes quality. These functions transfer to the autonomous plane, but on this plane, status is not necessarily associated with the certainty parameter, nor value necessarily with the good–bad parameter. Because of this, the distinction between status and value is more fluid on this plane. A term such as *propaganda*, for example, evaluates the texts or modes of discourse so labelled as having negative qualities and as such may be interpreted as evaluation of value. It also, however, establishes those texts or modes of discourse as a single entity, labelled in such a way that subsequent evaluations are constrained. *Propaganda* may be evaluated as 'effective' but not as 'true'. Because of this, the term may be interpreted as bestowing 'thing-ness' and therefore as evaluation of status.

We might explore this dilemma by looking again at Table 9.6, where part of Table 9.4, which gave an account of some of the evaluation in Example 9.6*a*, is presented.

TABLE 9.6.   *Example 9.6a: the autonomous plane*

What is evaluated	How it is evaluated
groups of people	as *sects*
people's feelings about sects	as *paranoia*
anti-sect paranoia	as common (and therefore dangerous)

(9.6*a*)
Right now a new wave of anti-sect paranoia is sweeping the world.

A legitimate interpretation would be to take everything in the column 'What is evaluated' as having status, and everything in the column 'How it is evaluated' as giving value. The status is, of course, implied by the value; you cannot call something a *sect* unless it comprises a group of people. The advantage to this analysis is that it demonstrates the interaction between the world of the text and the world outside it. The disadvantages are, first, that a great deal more appears in the analysis than is in the text itself, and secondly, that the noun group that actually appears in the text—*anti-sect paranoia*—appears both as value and as status. It may be that the phrase does indeed have this dual role. For the purposes of aligning evaluation on the autonomous plane with that on the interactive plane, however, I shall ignore the complexities represented by the first two lines of Table 9.4, and shall treat *anti-sect paranoia* as performing the evaluative function termed status, not value.

Sometimes, the status of an entity is the point of the text itself: in the text WNSE, for example, the status of Energy World as a 'sect' or 'spiritual community' is precisely the point at issue in the text. In such cases, the label itself represents a point of ideological tension. There are also, however, many more mundane cases, where the choice of label does not have obvious sociopolitical significance. Even in these cases, however, it remains true that the choice of status label constrains the value that may be given to an entity. In the following example, what is being evaluated is a 'book', specifically a 'memoir', and it is given value as such. If it had been labelled as a 'history', the evaluations of the book as enjoyable but not very serious—*beguiling, sees life through the bottom of a glass lightly, hymn to the vagabond tradition in British acting*—would appear less consistent.

(9.39)
Peter O'Toole is a born romantic: that much is clear from this beguiling second volume of a set of memoirs that looks likely to last to infinity. Covering O'Toole's first year as a Rada student in 1953/4, it sees life through the bottom of a glass lightly, is written in a

word-drunk, Dylan Thomas-saturated prose and is a hymn to the vagabond tradition in British acting whose patron saint is Edmund Kean.

Just as the status of a statement may be lexicalized in a noun phrase (e.g. *this idea, this suggestion*) but may also remain unnominalized, so the status of a thing may remain implicit. In the following example, the writer evaluates 'Gibraltar' as unhelpful to Britain, inconvenient as a possession. This makes sense only if we assume that the status of 'Gibraltar' in this text is not just a place, certainly not a tourist destination, but a political entity, a colony.

(9.40)
And in a small way, Gibraltar is now an active disadvantage to this country's interests rather than an asset.

GIVING THE WORLD VALUE

It has been argued that the status of something constrains the criteria or grounds on which it can be given value. In the review of the memoirs that was referred to above, for example, the book and its writer are given value according to two broad criteria: the clarity and pleasingness of the writing ('style'), and the degree of accuracy and insight with which it tells its story ('content'). Particular aspects of both these criteria may be identified, as Table 9.7 suggests. Any autobiography might be expected to be evaluated similarly.

The criteria for evaluation rely in part on the shared assumptions that form part of the message of any text. As a result, evaluation of value is often expressed in ways that are highly implicit. Solidarity is built between writer and reader precisely by *not* making explicit the evaluative significance of certain parts of the text. As an example, here are two paragraphs from the text WNSE, in which the writer tries to persuade the reader that many unconventional spiritual communities, which might be given the label 'sect', are in fact harmless or even beneficial groups.

(9.41)
[1.1] I belong to a spiritual movement called the Wild Goose Company, some of whose members live at Energy Worlds, a community in rural France. [2] The founder, and my spiritual teacher, is Michael Barnett, who endeavours to teach and share his knowledge with anyone who is interested. [3] Energy World has been placed on the [French] government list [of undesirable groups].
[2.1] Extraordinary though it may seem, I chose to come here of my own accord—because the spiritual call is stronger than that of financial, family, or social stability. [2] The only thing I am coerced into doing is the dishwashing when it is my turn; [3] and I work in the community without financial reward.

The relevance of the second of these two paragraphs can be seen only if one understands it as evaluating the community called Energy World. Yet there are no attributions of the community mentioned in the paragraph, nor are feelings of liking or of positive judgement expressed. What we have in the second paragraph is evidence that counters the unspoken claim that communities coerce their members into living there and taking part in undesirable activities. The second paragraph

TABLE 9.7. *Value in Example 9.39*

Criterion (grounds for giving value)	Example
Style (pace)	*... the book leaves us waiting somewhat impatiently for O'Toole to make his professional debut*
Style	*The book begins with a miasmic prologue set in some mythical playhouse and green room where Kean struts his stuff, where O'Toole's actor-buddies ... tipsily disport themselves in fancy-dress ... this thespian tushery*
Style	*his own writing has a free-floating suppleness and ease*
Style	*... his description ... is enviably good*
Style/Organization	*The book is eccentrically organized and poorly edited*
Style	*... with sardonic wit ...*
Style	*... with ironic amusement ...*
Content (informativeness)	*... it explains a lot about his later career*
Content (depth of interpretation)	*... O'Toole's literary romanticism seems strenuous, self-parodic, actor-laddie stuff*
Content (power of observation/ accuracy of portrayal)	*it becomes a brilliant account of his drama-school training ... Under the romantic, you realise, lies a sharp-eyed observer*
Content (power of observation/ accuracy of portrayal)	*O'Toole's descriptions of Rada classes pin down precisely the Dickensian eccentricity of his teachers.*
Content (power of observation/ accuracy of portrayal	*The book also accurately evokes the sexual tensions of fifties student life.*

succeeds as an evaluation of the community if the reader shares the experience of hearing communities accused in this way. The evaluation thus depends on a shared intertextual experience.

We can clarify how the implicit evaluation works using the terminology of basis, value, and grounds. Given that Energy World belongs to a class of things called 'spiritual communities', one of the bases by which it will be evaluated might be expressed as 'Does it coerce its members?' In other words, one basis for evaluating spiritual communities is the degree of coercion. In this text, the community Energy World is evaluated positively in relation to this basis. In other words, it is given positive value. However, the value is not given as an explicit statement but is implied by the evidence or grounds for evaluation in the second of the two paragraphs quoted above. This can be shown in a table (see Table 9.8).

TABLE 9.8. *Value in Example 9.41*

Thing evaluated	Basis	Value	Grounds
Energy World (a spiritual community)	degree of coercion	positive (no coercion)	writer not coerced to join; only coerced to do washing up

In Example 9.41, only the thing evaluated and the grounds for evaluation actually appear: the basis and the value remain implicit. Any writer has the option, however, of making the basis for evaluation explicit. In the following example, the writer, who wishes to evaluate various campaigns for constitutional reform in the UK, first sets the criterion against which they are to be evaluated, that is, the basis for their evaluation of value. This criterion is the degree to which popular interest is aroused. The basis is formulated first as a question:

(9.42*a*)
Reform is in the air. But does it stir the passions or simply deplete the bank balance?

and then as an attributed statement of need:

(9.42*b*)
Emerson said that all reforms were once private opinion. But he added that if they were to 'solve the problem of the age' they needed to convince the people.

Subsequent attributions of value to the various campaigns depend upon the acceptance of this basis:

(9.42*c*)
So far there is little evidence that [these] issues . . . have done much to capture the public imagination . . . It does suggest that their causes have some way to go before they achieve real weight . . . It still fails to ignite passion on the doorstep.

ANALYSING A TEXT ON BOTH PLANES

It is now possible to present a second analysis of the text WNSE (see Appendix), this time analysing the evaluation on both the autonomous plane and the interactive plane. The analysis is shown in Table 9.9. As can be seen from the table, in a few cases, the autonomous plane and the interactive plane overlap. This is true particularly when events are evaluated (on the autonomous plane) and the account of events is evaluated (on the interactive plane). For example, in paragraph 2 of WNSE, events are described as *alarming*, and this word describes the writer's reaction both to the events themselves (the government has drawn up a list of sects and a report on their activities and is now investigating the groups listed) and to the part of his own text in which these activities are reported. Similarly, in paragraph 5 several activities by the authorities and the media are recounted. The undesirable consequences of these activities are listed in paragraph 6, and this evaluates on both the autonomous and the interactive planes.

The overlap between autonomous and interactive planes could be taken further. Here are the last two sentences in paragraph 5 of WNSE:

(9.43)
The article is prefaced with an editorial which says: 'There is no such thing as an [*sic*] harmless sect.' Pontius Pilate would have heartily agreed.

On the interactive plane, the first sentence has the status of an attributed assessment, with the responsibility delegated. This assessment is, by implication, contradicted in the second sentence, through the association of this idea with Pontius Pilate. This relation between an expression of an idea and its contradiction relates the two sentences on the interactive plane. However, the first sentence, as well as being an attributed assessment in its own right, also refers to an object in the world, an editorial. This editorial is implicitly criticized in the second sentence, again by drawing a parallel with the views of Pontius Pilate. The editorial and the criticism of it constitute evaluation on the autonomous plane. The distinction between the two planes is an extremely fine one, being the difference between a report of a statement (the autonomous plane) and the role of that statement as a constituent of this text (the interactive plane). The second sentence of the pair effectively evaluates on both planes.

Back to theory

STATUS, VALUE, AND THE PARAMETERS OF EVALUATION

We have used the term 'status' to indicate the evaluation that takes place when something, either a statement that forms part of the discourse or a thing in the world, is presented. Status tells us what kind of thing it is that we are talking about. The evaluation of status constrains in general terms the reader's response to the statement or thing, and also constrains in more specific terms how the text itself will further evaluate the statement or thing. The term 'value' has been used to indicate that further evaluation, when the qualities of something are described. The terms of evaluation of value are constrained by the status of the statement or thing.

Status on the interactive plane, that is, the status ascribed to the statements in a text, is largely, though not by definition, concerned with the evaluative parameter of certainty. In other words, the statements differ from each other largely in terms of how certain or uncertain they are. For example, a 'fact' is more certain than an 'assessment', and an averred assessment is treated by the text as more certain than an attributed assessment. In particular, some signals of attribution indicate strongly that a statement is certainly not true. Status on the autonomous plane, however, may evaluate on the good–bad parameter as well as or instead of on the certain–uncertain parameter. For example, *paranoia* is something that is bad, not just something that is not true. The alignment of status with certainty and value with good–bad evaluation, therefore, does not hold up, and status and value must be defined in terms of presenting an entity and ascribing a quality to that entity, rather than in terms of parameters of evaluation.

TABLE 9.9. *Analysis of WNSE*

The Autonomous Plane		The Interactive Plane	
The world is given status	The world is given value	The argument is given status	The argument is given value
Paragraph 1			
ideas: anti-sect paranoia	is widespread	averred (non-sourced) assessment 1.1	supported by evidence 1.2–2.2
ruling bodies, political parties and the media	feel suspicion, hostility, prejudice carry out mislabelling		
Paragraph 2			
action: drew up a list and report	*alarming* 2.3	averred (non-sourced account of events) 2.1–2	*alarming* 2.3
150 groups	attributed: considered to be dangerous		
action: breaking away	attributed: considered to be dangerous	averred (non-sourced) assessment 2.3	supported by implied evidence 2.4
Paragraphs 3–4			
group: community	attributed: placed on hit list	implied attributed (responsibility delegated) assessment 3.3	not supported by evidence 4.1–3
founder, spiritual teacher, Michael Barnett	shares knowledge	averred (non-sourced) account of events 4.1–3	
placement of Energy World on list	is unwarranted		
Paragraph 5			
events: invaded, commandeered, ransacked	have hidden real purpose	averred (non-sourced) account of events 5.1–5	
events: summonses, immigration issues: harassment	have undesirable consequences	averred (non-sourced) account of events 5.6–7	undesirable consequences 6.1–3

cont.

Table 9.9. *cont.*

The Autonomous Plane		The Interactive Plane	
The world is given status	The world is given value	The argument is given status	The argument is given value
leading article	is snide, misleading, contains derogatory comments		
sects	attributed: harmful		
magazine editorial	equivalent to Pontius Pilate	attributed (responsibility delegated) assessment: words of editorial 5.7	equivalent to Pontius Pilate 5.8
Paragraph 6		averred (non sourced) assessment 6.1	supported by evidence 6.2–3
action: built lakes	protect environment		
rumour	implied: contrary to fact		
remarks	implied: unreasonable		
Paragraph 7 ideas: prejudice	takes years to erode	averred (non-sourced) recommendation 7.1	reasonable 7.2–5
group of people gather together	not outrageously liberal		
experiment with different styles of living			
people want this	not illogical		
keeping track of communities	would save lives	averred (sourced) recommendation (concession) 7.4	has unfortunate consequences 7.5
the government report	makes good sense		
ideas: prejudice	leads to discrimination		
master/disciple relationship communal living	is open to abuse	averred (sourced) assessment 7.6*a*	counter evidence 7.6*b*

The Autonomous Plane		The Interactive Plane	
The world is given status	The world is given value	The argument is given status	The argument is given value
master/disciple relationship communal living	has provided inspiration for important steps in understanding the nature of human existence		

THE ROLE OF EVALUATION

Evaluation is important to discourse for two reasons: it plays a vital role in constructing the ideological basis of a text, thereby locating writer and reader in an ideological space; and it plays a vital role in organizing a text (see the introduction to this volume). Evaluation on both the autonomous and the interactive planes take part in both functions.

The ideological space of a discourse is constructed both by the way the world is labelled (evaluation on the autonomous plane) and by the way the argument is constructed (evaluation on the interactive plane). What counts as knowledge or as a valid argument (interactive status) is as important as what the world is seen as made up of (autonomous status).

Evaluation organizes a text by encapsulating what has gone before (Sinclair 1993; Francis 1994). This encapsulation may be on the autonomous or interactive plane. For example, encapsulating noun phrases may assess either world-entities (e.g. *This problem*) or discourse-entities (e.g. *This argument*). Sinclair has argued that some evaluation has a further organizational role in that it acts as the end-point of a discourse unit (Sinclair and Coulthard 1975). This evaluation effectively tells the reader why what has been said is important or significant (Labov 1972). It relates the autonomous to the interactive plane.

Conclusion

In this chapter it has been argued that evaluation is a highly complex phenomenon that can best be handled by making a number of distinctions. The distinction between status and value is one, and the distinction between the interactive and the autonomous plane is another. Status and value operate on the two planes in ways that are comparable but different. A complete analysis of the evaluation in a persuasive text must take account of both planes, and of both status and value.

Appendix: We Need Sects Education (WNSE)

James Bampfield

Paragraph 1

[1] Right now a new wave of anti-sect paranoia is sweeping the world. [2] All ruling bodies, political parties and the media seem unanimous in their suspicion and hostility towards sects and any group of people labelled a 'sect' are automatically viewed with prejudiced eyes.

Paragraph 2

[1] After the dis-Order of the Solar Temple, the French Government drew up a list of more than 150 groups which they considered to be dangerous and a report on the phenomenon. [2] They are now investigating these groups looking for evidence of 'coercion', 'exploitation', and 'mental destabilisation'. [3] More alarming is the attention the report pays to the dangers of 'breaking away from the references normally acknowledged by society'. [4] Does that rule out alternative medicine, education, clothing and toothpaste?

Paragraph 3

[1] I belong to a spiritual movement called the Wild Goose Company, some of whose members live at Energy World, a community in rural France. [2] The founder, and my spiritual teacher, is Michael Barnett, who endeavours to teach and share his knowledge with anyone who is interested. [3] Energy World has been placed on the government list.

Paragraph 4

[1] Extraordinary though it may seem, I chose to come here of my own accord—because the spiritual call is stronger than that of financial, family, or social stability. [2] The only thing I am coerced into doing is the dishwashing when it is my turn; [3] and I work in the community without financial reward.

Paragraph 5

[1] Energy World was recently invaded by police without warning at seven one morning. [2] Exits were sealed, and all the computer files were commandeered. [3] Mr. Barnett's private quarters were ransacked. [4] The pretext was a tax investigation, but there is little doubt as to its real purpose and it has been followed up by various police summonses concerning our small school, as well as immigration issues. [5] Since this harassment started, the local bank has closed the Energy World account and the local insurance company has refused to insure the community. [6] A regional magazine has published a leading article on Energy World which is loaded with snide, misleading, and derogatory comments. [7] The article is prefaced with an editorial which says: 'There is no such thing as an harmless sect'. [8] Pontius Pilate would have heartily agreed.

Paragraph 6

[1] The result is to stoke up public opinion. [2] When Energy World built two sewage-filtering lakes, to protect the environment, a rumour went round the neighbourhood that these were built as repositories for any human corpses left after your average 'cult activity'.

[3]On a visit to the UK I was inundated with remarks about 'free sex' (do ordinary citizens pay for it?) and 'brainwashing'.

Paragraph 7

[1] Prejudice takes years to erode, so what is needed is some kind of political/legal recognition and protection for new religious movements equal to that received by racial minorities and homosexuals. [2] It does not seem outrageously liberal to allow a group of people to gather together and experiment with styles of living that differ from those of conventional society. [3] Nor is it illogical for people to want to do this, given that most come from less-than-perfect societies. [4] Undoubtedly some track should be kept of religious communities—more monitoring of Aum Shinrikyo and the Order of the Solar Temple might have saved lives. [5] Much of the government's report makes good sense, but the well of prejudice in society, and among those who implement the government campaign, is such that any group which is on this list may find itself immediately the subject of discrimination. [6] Of course the master–disciple relationship and communal living are open to abuse, but these very structures—Christ and his disciples, Buddha and his ashram, Plato and his academy—have provided the inspiration for some of the most important steps taken in understanding the nature of human existence.

References

Anderson, L. B. (1986). 'Evidentials, paths of change and mental maps: typologically regular asymmetries', in Chafe and Nichols (1986), 273–312.

Atkinson, P. (1990). *The Ethnographic Imagination: Textual Constructions of Reality.* London: Routledge.

Baker, M., Francis, G., and Tognini-Bognelli, E. (1993). *Text and Technology: In Honour of John Sinclair.* Amsterdam: Benjamins.

Bakhtin, M. M. (1986). *Speech Genres and Other Late Essays* (tr. V. W. McGee). Austin, Tex.: University of Texas Press.

Bamberg, M., and Damrad-Frye, D. (1991). 'On the ability to provide evaluative comments: further explorations of children's narrative competencies'. *Journal of Child Language,* 18: 689–710.

Banks, D. (1994). 'Hedges and how to trim them', in M. Brekke, Ø. Andersen, T. Dahl, and J. Myking (eds.), *Applications and Implications of Current LSP Research.* Bergen: Fagbokforlaget, 587–92.

Barnbrook, G. (1995). 'The language of definition: a COBUILD sublanguage parser'. Unpublished Ph.D. thesis, University of Birmingham.

—— (1995). *Language and Computers: A Practical Introduction to the Computer Analysis of Language.* Edinburgh: Edinburgh University Press.

—— and Sinclair, J. (1995). 'Parsing COBUILD entries', in J. Sinclair, M. Hoelter, and C. Peters (eds.), *The Languages of Definition: The Formalization of Dictionary Definitions for Natural Language Processing.* Studies in Machine Translation and Natural Language Processing Vol. 7. Luxembourg: Office for Official Publications of the European Communities, 13–58.

Barry, A. K. (1991). 'Narrative style and witness testimony'. *Journal of Narrative and Life History,* 1: 281–93.

Bartlett, F. C. (1932). *Remembering.* Cambridge: Cambridge University Press.

Barton, E. (1993). 'Evidentials, argumentation, and epistemological stance'. *College English,* 55: 745–69.

Bauman, R. (1993). 'Disclaimers of performance', in Hill and Irvine (1993), 182–96.

Bazerman, C. (1988). *Shaping Written Knowledge.* Madison: University of Wisconsin Press.

Beach, R., and Anson, C. M. (1992). 'Stance and intertextuality in written discourse'. *Linguistics and Education,* 4: 335–57.

Bell, A. (1991). *The Language of News Media.* Oxford: Blackwell.

Bernstein, B. (1975). *Class, Codes and Control 3: Towards a Theory of Educational Transmissions.* London: Routledge.

Besnier, N. (1993). 'Reported speech and affect on Nukulaelae Atoll', in Hill and Irvine (1993), 161–81.

Biber, D., and Finegan, E. (1988). 'Adverbial stance types in English'. *Discourse Processes,* 11: 1–34.

—— —— (1989). 'Styles of stance in English: lexical and grammatical marking of evidentiality and affect'. *Text,* 9: 93–124.

——Johansson, S., Leech, G., Conrad, S., and Finegan, E. (1999). *The Longman Grammar of Spoken and Written English*. London: Longman.

Bolívar, A. C. (1986). 'Interaction through written text: a discourse analysis of newspaper editorials'. Unpublished Ph.D. thesis, University of Birmingham.

Botha, R. P. (1973). *The Justification of Linguistic Hypotheses*. The Hague: Mouton.

Boxer, D., and Pickering, L. (1995). 'Problems in the presentation of speech acts in ELT materials: the case of complaints'. *English Language Teaching Journal,* 49: 44–58.

Briggs, C. L. (ed.) (1996). *Disorderly Discourse: Narrative, Conflict, and Inequality*. New York: Oxford University Press.

Brown, G. (1995). 'Endpiece'. *BAAL Summer Newsletter*. Clevedon: British Association for Applied Linguistics.

Brown, P., and Levinson, S. (1987). *Politeness: Some Universals in Language Use*. Cambridge: Cambridge University Press.

Brown, R., and Gilman, A. (1960). 'The pronouns of power and solidarity', in T. Sebeok (ed.), *Style in Language*. Cambridge, Mass.: MIT Press, 253–76.

Brumble, H. D. (1990). *American Indian Autobiography*. Berkeley: University of California Press.

Bruner, J. (1985). *Actual Minds, Possible Worlds*. Cambridge, Mass.: Harvard University Press.

Butler, C. (1990). 'Qualifications in science: modal meanings in scientific texts', in Nash (1990), 137–70.

Bybee, J., and Fleischman, S. (1995). *Modality in Grammar and Discourse*. Amsterdam: John Benjamins.

Caldas-Coulthard, C. R., and Coulthard, M. (1996). *Texts and Practices: Readings in Critical Discourse Analysis*. London: Routledge.

Carrithers, M. (1992). *Why Humans have Cultures: Explaining Anthropology and Social Diversity*. Oxford: Oxford University Press.

Carter, R. (1987). *Vocabulary: Applied Linguistic Perspectives*. London: Allen & Unwin.

——and Nash, W. (1990). *Seeing through Language*. Oxford: Blackwell.

——and Simpson, P. (1982). 'The sociolinguistic analysis of narrative'. *Belfast Working Papers in Linguistics*, 6: 123–52.

Chafe, W. L. (1986). 'Evidentiality in English conversation and academic writing', in Chafe and Nichols (1986), 261–72.

——and Nichols, J. (eds.) (1986). *Evidentiality: The Linguistic Coding of Epistemology*. Norwood, NJ: Ablex.

Channell, J. (1994). *Vague Language*. Oxford: Oxford University Press.

——(forthcoming). 'Cultural and pragmatic aspects of vocabulary learning', in R. Carter and A. Sanchez (eds.), *Lengua Inglesa y Vocabulario*. Universitat de València: Serie Linguistica Applicada.

Chomsky, N. (1957). *Syntactic Structures*. Janua Linguarum, Series Minor No. 4. The Hague: Mouton.

——(1964a). 'Formal discussion: the development of grammar in child language', in U. Bellugi and R. Brown (eds.), *The Acquisition of Language*. Monographs of the Society for Research in Child Development 29.1. Indiana: Purdue University.

——(1964b). 'Current issues in linguistic theory', in Fodor and Katz (1964).

——(1965). *Aspects of the Theory of Syntax*. Cambridge, Mass.: The MIT Press.

——(1966). 'Linguistic theory', in R. G. Mead (ed.), *Language Teaching: Broader Contexts*. Reports of Northeast Conference on the Teaching of Foreign Languages, 1965. Reprinted in J. P. B. Allen and P. van Buren (1971). *Chomsky: Selected Readings*. Oxford: Oxford University Press, 152–9.

Christie, F., and Martin, J. R. (eds.) (1997). *Genre and Institutions: Social Processes in the Workplace and School*. London: Cassell.

Coates, J. (1996). *Women Talk*. Oxford: Blackwell.

Coffin, C. (1997). 'Constructing and giving value to the past: an investigation into secondary school history', in Christie and Martin (1997), 196–230.

Collins COBUILD English Dictionary (1995). London: HarperCollins.

Cortazzi, M. (1991). *Primary Teaching, how it is: A Narrative Account*. London: David Fulton.

—— (1993). *Narrative Analysis*. London: The Falmer Press.

Coulthard, M. (1986). *Talking about Text: Studies Presented to David Brazil on his Retirement*. Discourse Analysis Monographs No. 13. University of Birmingham: English Language Research.

—— (ed.) (1994). *Advances in Written Text Analysis*. London: Routledge.

Cranny-Francis, A. (1996). 'Technology and/or weapon: the disciplines of reading in the Secondary English classroom', in Hasan and Williams (1996).

—— and Martin, J. R. (1994). 'In/visible education: class, gender and pedagogy in *Educating Rita* and *Dead Poets Society*'. *Interpretations: Journal of the English Teachers' Association of Western Australia*, 27: 28–57.

Crompton, P. (1997). 'Hedging in academic writing: some theoretical problems'. *English for Specific Purposes*, 16: 271–87.

Cruse, D. A. (1986). *Lexical Semantics*. Cambridge: Cambridge University Press.

Cunningham, P., and Gardner, P. (eds.) (1997). 'Past lives and present concerns: rethinking professional histories of teaching'. Special issue of *Cambridge Journal of Education*, 27, 3.

Davies, F. (1997). 'Marked theme as a heuristic for analyzing text type, text and genre', in J. Pique and D. J. Viera (eds.), *Applied Languages: Theory and Practice in ESP*. Valencia: University of Valencia Press.

de Beaugrande, R., and Dressler, W. (1981). *Introduction to Text Linguistics*. London: Longman.

Dik, S .C. (1968). 'Referential identity'. *Lingua*, 21: 70–97.

Eggins, S., and Slade, D. (1997). *Analysing Casual Conversation*. London: Cassell.

Fairclough, N. (1989). *Language and Power*. London: Longman.

—— (1992). *Discourse and Social Change*. Cambridge: Polity Press.

—— (1993). 'Critical discourse analysis and the marketization of public discourse: the universities'. *Discourse and Society*, 4: 133–68.

—— (1995). *Critical Discourse Analysis*. London: Longman.

Fillmore, C. J., Kay, P., and O'Connor, M. C. (1988). 'Regularity and idiomaticity in grammatical constructions'. *Language*, 64: 501–38.

Firth, J. R. (1935). 'The technique of semantics'. *Transactions of the Philological Society*: 36–72.

Fludernik, M. (1991). 'The historical present tense yet again: tense switching and narrative dynamics in oral and quasi-oral storytelling'. *Text*, 11: 365–97.

Fodor, J. A., and Katz J. J. (eds.) (1964). *The Structure of Language: Readings in the Philosophy of Language*. Englewood Cliffs, NJ: Prentice-Hall.

Fontanelle, T. (1995). 'Turning a bilingual dictionary into a lexical-semantic database'. Ph.D. thesis, University of Liège.

Fowler. R. G. (1990). *Language in the News: Discourse and Ideology in the Press.* London: Routledge.

Francis, G. (1986). *Anaphoric Nouns.* Discourse Analysis Monographs No. 11. University of Birmingham: English Language Research.

—— (1993). 'A corpus-driven approach to grammar: principles, methods and examples', in Baker *et al.* (1993), 137–56.

—— (1994). 'Labelling discourse: an aspect of nominal-group lexical cohesion', in Coulthard (1994), 83–101.

—— Hunston, S., and Manning, E. (1996). *Collins* COBUILD *Grammar Patterns 1: Verbs.* London: HarperCollins.

—— —— —— (1998). *Collins* COBUILD *Grammar Patterns 2: Nouns and Adjectives.* London: HarperCollins.

Gardner, H. (1997). *Leading Minds: An Anatomy of Leadership.* London: Harper Collins.

Gazdar, G. (1979). *Pragmatics: Implicature, Presupposition and Logical Form.* New York: Academic Press.

Gee, J. (1989). 'Two styles of narrative construction and their linguistic and educational implications'. *Discourse Processes,* 12: 287–307.

Georgakopoulou, A., and Goutsos, D. (1997). *Discourse Analysis: An Introduction.* Edinburgh: Edinburgh University Press.

Gross, M. (1993). 'Local grammars and their representation by finite automata', in Hoey (1993), 26–38.

Gudmundsdottir, S. (ed.) (1997). 'Narrative perspectives on research on teaching and teacher education', theme issue of *Teaching and Teacher Education,* 13, 1.

Gunnarsson, B. L., Linell, P., and Nordberg, B. (eds.) (1997). *The Construction of Professional Discourse.* London: Longman.

Halliday, M. A. K. (1976). 'Anti-languages'. *American Anthropologist,* 78, 3: 570–84. Reprinted in Halliday (1978), 164–82.

—— (1978). *Language as Social Semiotic: The Social Interpretation of Language and Meaning.* London: Edward Arnold.

—— (1982). 'The de-automatization of grammar: from Priestley's "An Inspector Calls"', in J. M. Anderson (ed.), *Language Form and Linguistic Variation: Papers dedicated to Angus MacIntosh.* Amsterdam: Benjamins, 129–59.

—— (1984). 'Language as code and language as behaviour: a systemic functional interpretation of the nature and ontogenesis of dialogue', in R. Fawcett, M. A. K. Halliday, S. M. Lamb, and A. Makkai (eds.), *The Semiotics of Language and Culture: Vol. 1: Language as Social Semiotic.* London: Pinter, 3–35.

—— (1994). *An Introduction to Functional Grammar,* 2nd edn. London: Edward Arnold; 1st edn. 1985.

—— and Hasan, R. (1976). *Cohesion in English.* London: Longman.

—— —— (1985). *Language, Context, and Text: Aspects of Language in a Social-Semiotic Perspective.* Geelong, Vic.: Deakin University Press. Republished 1989. Oxford: Oxford University Press.

Hanks, P. (1987). 'Definitions and explanations', in J. M. Sinclair (ed.), *Looking Up: An Account of the* COBUILD *Project in Lexical Computing.* London: HarperCollins, 116–36.

Harré, R. (ed.) (1987). *The Social Construction of Emotions.* Oxford: Blackwell.

—— and Gillett, G. (1994). *The Discursive Mind.* London: Sage.

Harris, Z. S. (1952). 'Discourse analysis'. *Language*, 28: 1–30. Reprinted in Fodor and Katz (1964).

——(1968). *Mathematical Structures of Language*. New York: John Wiley & Sons.

Hasan, R. (1984). 'Coherence and cohesive harmony', in J. Flood (ed.), *Understanding Reading Comprehension: Cognition, Language and the Structure of Prose*. Newark, Dell.: International Reading Association, 181–219.

——(1990). 'Semantic variation and sociolinguistics'. *Australian Journal of Linguistics*, 9: 221–76.

——and Williams, G. (eds.) (1996). *Literacy in Society*. London: Longman.

Haviland, J. B. (1991). ' "Sure, sure": evidence and affect'. *Text*, 9: 27–68.

He, A. W. (1993). 'Exploring modality in institutional interactions: cases from academic counselling encounters'. *Text*, 13: 503–28.

Hicks, D. (1990). 'Narrative skills and genre knowledge: ways of telling in the primary school grades'. *Applied Psycholinguistics*, 11: 83–104.

Hill, J. H., and Irvine, J. T. (eds.) (1993). *Responsibility and Evidence in Oral Discourse*. Cambridge: Cambridge University Press.

Hodge, R., and Kress, G. (1993). *Language as Ideology*. 2nd edn. London: Routledge.

Hoey, M. (1979). *Signalling in Discourse*. Discourse Analysis Monographs No. 6. University of Birmingham: English Language Research.

——(1983). *On the Surface of Discourse*. London: Allen and Unwin.

——(1991a). 'Another perspective on coherence and cohesive harmony', in E. Ventola (ed.), *Functional and Systemic Linguistics: Approaches and Uses*. Berlin: Mouton de Gruyter, 385–414.

——(1991b). *Patterns of Lexis in Text*. Oxford: Oxford University Press.

——(ed.) (1993). *Data, Description, Discourse: Papers on the English Language in Honour of John McH. Sinclair*. London: HarperCollins.

——(1994). 'Signalling in discourse: a functional analysis of a common discourse pattern in written and spoken English', in Coulthard (1994), 26–45.

Holly, M. L., and MacLure, M. (eds.) (1990). 'Biography and Life History in Education'. Special issue of *Cambridge Journal of Education*, 20, 3.

Holmes, J. (1984). 'Hedging your bets and sitting on the fence: some evidence for hedges as support structures'. *Te Reo*, 27: 47–62.

——(1988). 'Doubt and certainty in ESL textbooks'. *Applied Linguistics*, 9: 20–44.

Horvath, B., and Eggins, S. (1995). 'Opinion texts in conversation', in P. Fries and M. Gregory (eds.), *Discourse in Society: Systemic Functional Perspectives*. Norwood, NJ: Ablex (Advances in Discourse Processes L: Meaning and Choices in Language—Studies for Michael Halliday), 29–46.

Huddleston, R., Hudson, R. A., Winter, E., and Henrici, A. (1968). *Sentence and Clause in Scientific English*. (OSTI Research Report) London: University College London Department of General Linguistics.

Hunston, S. (1985). 'Text in world and world in text: goals and models of scientific writing'. *Nottingham Linguistic Circular*, 14: 25–40.

——(1989). 'Evaluation in experimental research articles'. Unpublished Ph.D. thesis, University of Birmingham.

——(1993a). 'Evaluation and ideology in scientific discourse', in M. Ghadessy (ed.), *Register Analysis: Theory and Practice*. London: Pinter, 57–73.

——(1993b). 'Projecting a sub-culture: the construction of shared worlds by projecting clauses in two registers', in D. Graddol, L. Thompson, and M. Byram (eds.), *Language and Culture*. Clevedon: BAAL/Multilingual Matters, 98–112.

——(1993c). 'Professional Conflict: Disagreement in Academic Discourse', in Baker *et al.* (1993), 115–34.

——(1994). 'Evaluation and organization in a sample of written academic discourse', in Coulthard (1994), 191–218.

——(1995). 'A corpus study of some English verbs of attribution'. *Functions of Language*, 2: 133–58.

——and Francis, G. (1998). 'Verbs observed: a corpus-driven pedagogic grammar of English'. *Applied Linguistics*, 19: 45–72.

Hyland, K. (1994). 'Hedging in academic writing and EAP textbooks'. *English for Specific Purposes*, 13: 239–56.

——(1996). 'Talking to the academy: forms of hedging in scientific research articles'. *Written Communication*, 13: 251–81.

——(1998). *Hedging in Scientific Research Articles*. Amsterdam: Benjamins.

Hymes, D. (1996). *Ethnography, Linguistics, Narrative Inequality: Towards an Understanding of Voice*. London: Taylor and Francis.

Iedema, R. (forthcoming). *The Language of Administration*. Sydney: Metropolitan East Region's Disadvantaged Schools Program.

——Feez, S., and White, P. (1994). *Media Literacy* (Write it Right Literacy in Industry Project: Stage Two). Sydney: Metropolitan East Region's Disadvantaged Schools Program.

Irvine, J. (1982). 'Language and affect: some cross-cultural issues', in H. Byrnes (ed.), *Contemporary Perceptions of Language: Interdisciplinary Dimensions*. Washington: Georgetown University Press, 31–47.

——(1990). 'Registering affect: heteroglossia in the linguistic expression of emotion', in Lutz and Abu-Lughod (1990), 126–61.

Jefferson, G. (1978). 'Sequential aspects of storytelling in conversation', in Schenkein (1978), 219–248.

Jin, L. (1992). 'Academic Cultural Expectations and Second Language Use: Chinese postgraduate students in the UK—A Cultural Synergy Model'. Unpublished Ph.D. thesis, University of Leicester.

Johnstone, B. (1987). ' "He says . . . so I said": verb tense alternation and narrative depictions of authority in American English'. *Linguistics*, 25: 33–52.

Jordan, M. P. (1984). *Rhetoric of Everyday English Texts*. London: Allen & Unwin.

——(1998). 'The power of negation in English: text, context and relevance'. *Journal of Pragmatics*, 29: 705–52.

Kernan, K. T. (1977). 'Semantic and expressive elaboration in children's narratives', in S. Ervin-Tripp (ed.), *Child Discourse*. New York: Academic Press, 91–102.

Kress, G. (1991). 'Critical discourse analysis'. *ARAL*, 11: 84–99.

Labov, W. (1972). *Language in the Inner City*. Philadelphia: University of Pennsylvania.

——(1982). 'Speech actions and reactions in personal narrative', in D. Tannen (ed.), *Analysing Discourse: Text and Talk*. Washington: Georgetown University Press, 219–47.

——(1984). 'Intensity', in D. Schiffrin (ed.), *Meaning, Form, and Use in Context: Linguistic Applications*. Washington: Georgetown University Press, 43–70.

——Cohen, P., Robins, C., and Lewis, J. (1968). *A Study of the Non-Standard English of Negro and Puerto-Rican Speakers in New York City*. ii. Washington: Office of Education, US Dept. of Health, Education, and Welfare.

Labov, W., and Fanshel, D. (1977). *Therapeutic Discourse: Psychotherapy as Conversation*. New York: Academic Press.

—— and Waletsky, J. (1967). 'Narrative analysis: oral versions of personal experience', in J. Helm (ed.), *Essays on the Verbal and Visual Arts*. Seattle: American Ethnological Society, 12–44.

Lakoff, G. (1972). 'Hedges: a study in meaning criteria and the logic of fuzzy concepts', in *Chicago Linguistic Society Papers*. Chicago: Chicago Linguistic Society.

—— (1987). *Women, Fire and Dangerous Things: What Categories Reveal about the Mind*. Chicago: University of Chicago Press.

—— and Johnson, M. (1980). *Metaphors We Live By*. Chicago: University of Chicago Press.

—— and Kövecses, Z. (1987). 'The cognitive model of anger inherent in American English', in D. Holland and N. Quinn (eds.), *Cultural Models in Language and Thought*. Cambridge: Cambridge University Press, 195–221.

Latour, B., and Woolgar, S. (1979). *Laboratory Life: The Social Construction of Scientific Facts*. Beverley Hills, Calif.: Sage.

Leech, G. (1974). *Semantics*. Harmondsworth: Penguin Books.

Lehrberger, J. (1986). 'Sublanguage analysis', in R. Grishman and R. Lettredge (eds.), *Analyzing Language in Restricted Domains*. Hillsdale, NJ: Lawrence Erlbaum Associates, 19–38.

Lemke, J. L. (1992). 'Interpersonal meaning in discourse: value orientations', in M. Davies and L. Ravelli (eds.), *Advances in Systemic Linguistics: Recent Theory and Practice*. London: Pinter, 82–194.

Levinson, S. (1983). *Pragmatics*. Cambridge: Cambridge University Press.

Linde, C. (1993). *Life Stories: The Creation of Coherence*. Oxford: Oxford University Press.

—— (1997). 'Evaluation as linguistic structure and social practice', in Gunnarsson *et al.* (1997), 151–72.

Longacre, R. (1976). *An Anatomy of Speech Notions*. Lisse: Peter de Ridder.

Louw, B. (1993). 'Irony in the text or insincerity in the writer? The diagnostic potential of semantic prosodies', in Baker *et al.* (1993), 157–76.

Ludwig, A. M. (1997). *How do we Know Who we Are? A Biography of the Self*. New York: Oxford University Press.

Lutz, C. A. (1986). 'Emotion, thought and estrangement: emotion as a cultural category'. *Cultural Anthropology*, 1: 405–36.

—— (1988). *Unnatural Emotions: Everyday Sentiments on a Micronesian Atoll and their Challenge to Western Theory*. Chicago: University of Chicago Press.

—— and Abu-Lughod, L. (1990). *Language and the Politics of Emotion*. Cambridge: Cambridge University Press.

Lyons, J. (1977). *Semantics*. Cambridge: Cambridge University Press.

McCabe, A., and Peterson, C. (eds.) (1991). *Developing Narrative Structure*. Hillsdale, NJ: Lawrence Erlbaum Associates.

McCarthy, M. (1990). *Vocabulary*. Oxford: Oxford University Press.

Maclean, M. (1988). *Narrative as Performance: A Baudelarian Experiment*. London: Routledge.

Mann, W. C., and Thompson, S. A. (1988). 'Rhetorical structure theory: toward a functional theory of text organization'. *Text*, 8: 243–81.

Martin, J. R. (1992a). *English Text: System and Structure*. Amsterdam: Benjamins.

—— (1992*b*). 'Macroproposals: meaning by degree', in W. C. Mann and S. A. Thompson (eds.), *Discourse Description: Diverse Analyses of a Fund Raising Text.* Amsterdam: Benjamins, 359–95.

—— (1993). 'Life as a noun', in M. A. K. Halliday and J. R. Martin, *Writing Science: Literacy and Discursive Power.* London: Falmer, 221–67.

—— (1995*a*). 'Interpersonal meaning, persuasion and public discourse: packing semiotic punch'. *Australian Journal of Linguistics*, 15: 33–67.

—— (1995*b*). 'Reading positions/positioning readers: JUDGEMENT in English'. *Prospect: A Journal of Australian TESOL*, 10: 27–37.

—— (1996). 'Evaluating disruption: symbolising theme in junior secondary narrative', in Hasan and Williams (1996), 124–71.

—— (1997*a*). 'Analysing genre: functional parameters', in Christie and Martin (1997), 3–39.

—— (1997*b*). 'Register and genre: modelling social context in functional linguistics—narrative genres', in E. R. Pedro (ed.), *Proceedings of First International Conference on Discourse Analysis.* Lisbon: Colibri/Portuguese Linguistics Association, 305–44.

—— and Matthiessen, C. M. I. M. (1991). 'Systemic typology and topology', in F. Christie (ed.), *Literacy in Social Processes: Papers from the Inaugural Australian Systemic Linguistics Conference, held at Deakin University, January 1990.* Darwin: Centre for Studies in Language in Education, Northern Territory University, 345–83.

Masuku, N. (1996). 'A lexicogrammatical approach to the analysis of rhetorical goals in professional academic writing in the social sciences'. Unpublished Ph.D. thesis, University of Birmingham.

Matthiessen, C. M. I. M. (1995). *Lexicogrammatical Cartography: English Systems.* Tokyo: International Language Sciences Publishers.

Meinhof, U., and Richardson, K. (eds.) (1994). *Text, Discourse and Context.* London: Longman.

Mishler, E. G. (1986). *Research Interviewing: Context and Narrative.* Cambridge, Mass.: Harvard University Press.

—— (1997). 'The interactional construction of narratives in medical and life history interviews', in Gunnarsson *et al.* (1997), 223–44.

Moore, T., and Carling, C. (1988). *The Limitations of Language.* Basingstoke: Macmillan Press.

Myers, G. (1989). 'The pragmatics of politeness in scientific articles'. *Applied Linguistics*, 10: 1–35.

—— (1990). *Writing Biology: Texts in the Social Construction of Scientific Knowledge.* Wisconsin: University of Wisconsin Press.

Nash, W. (ed.) (1990). *The Writing Scholar: Studies in Academic Discourse.* London: Sage.

O'Barr, W. M., and Conley, J. M. (1996). 'Ideological dissonance in the American legal system', in Briggs (1996), 114–34.

Ochs, E. (ed.) (1989). 'The Pragmatics of Affect'. Special issue of *Text*, 9, 3.

—— and Schiefflen, B. (1989). 'Language has a heart'. *Text*, 9: 7–25.

—— Smith, R. C., and Taylor, C. E. (1996). 'Detective stories at dinnertime: problem solving through co-narration', in Briggs (1996), 95–113.

Okely, J., and Callaway, H. (eds.) (1992). *Anthropology and Autobiography.* London: Routledge.

Ortony, A., Clore, G. L., and Collins, A. (1988). *The Cognitive Structure of Emotions.* Cambridge: Cambridge University Press.

Palmer, F. R. (1986). *Mood and Modality*. Cambridge: Cambridge University Press.

Pearson, J. (1998). *Terms in Context*. Amsterdam: Benjamins.

Perkins, M. R. (1983). *Modal Expressions in English*. Norwood, NJ: Ablex.

Peterson, C., and McCabe, A. (1983). *Developmental Psycholinguistics: Three Ways of Looking at a Child's Narrative*. New York: Plenum Press.

Polanyi, L. (1989). *Telling the American Story: A Structural and Cultural Analysis of Conversational Storytelling*. Cambridge, Mass.: The MIT Press.

Polkinghorne, D. E. (1995). 'Narrative configuration in qualitative analysis', in J. A. Hatch and R. Wisniewski (eds.), *Life History and Narrative*. London: The Falmer Press, 5–23.

Powell, M. J. (1992). 'Semantic/pragmatic regularities in informal lexis: British speakers in spontaneous conversational settings'. *Text*, 12: 19–58.

Poynton, C. (1984). 'Names as vocatives: forms and functions'. *Nottingham Linguistic Circular*, 13: 1–34.

—— (1985). *Language and Gender: Making the Difference*. Geelong, Vic.: Deakin University Press. Republished 1989. Oxford: Oxford University Press.

—— (1990*a*). 'Address and the semiotics of social relations: a systemic-functional account of address forms and practices in Australian English'. Unpublished Ph.D. Thesis, Department of Linguistics, University of Sydney.

—— (1990*b*). 'The privileging of representation and the marginalising of the interpersonal: a metaphor (and more) for contemporary gender relations', in T. Threadgold and A. Cranny-Francis (eds.), *Feminine/Masculine and Representation*. Sydney: Allen & Unwin, 231–55.

—— (1993). 'Grammar, language and the social: poststructuralism and systemic functional linguistics'. *Social Semiotics*, 3: 1–22.

—— (1996). 'Amplification as a grammatical prosody: attitudinal modification in the nominal group', in M. Berry, C. Butler, and R. Fawcett (eds.) *Meaning and Form: Systemic Functional Interpretations*. Norwood, NJ: Ablex, 211–27.

Pratt, M. L. (1977). *Towards a Speech Act Theory of Literary Discourse*. Bloomington, Ind.: Indiana University Press.

Prince, E. F., Frader, J., and Bosk, C. (1982). 'On hedging in physician–physician discourse', in R. J. di Pietro (ed.), *Linguistics and the Professions*. Norwood NJ: Ablex.

Quirk, R., Greenbaum, S., Leech, G., and Svartvik, J. (1985). *A Comprehensive Grammar of the English Language*. London: Longman.

Riessman, C. K. (1993). *Narrative Analysis*. Newbury Park: Sage.

Rizomilioti, V. (in preparation). 'Modality in academic discourse'. Ph.D. thesis, University of Birmingham.

Rothery, J. (1990). 'Story writing in primary school: Assessing narrative type genres'. Unpublished Ph.D. Thesis, Department of Linguistics, University of Sydney.

—— (1994). *Exploring Literacy in School English* (Write it Right Resources for Literacy and Learning). Sydney: Metropolitan East Disadvantaged Schools Program.

—— and Macken, M. (1991). *Developing Critical Literacy: An Analysis of the Writing Task in a Year 10 Reference Test*. Sydney: Sydney Metropolitan East Region Disadvantaged Schools Program.

—— and Stenglin, M. (1994*a*). *Spine-Chilling Stories: A Unit of Work for Junior Secondary English* (Write it Right Resources for Literacy and Learning). Sydney: Metropolitan East Disadvantaged Schools Program.

——and Stenglin, M. (1994*b*). *Exploring Narrative in Video: A Unit of Work for Junior Secondary English* (Write it Right Resources for Literacy and Learning). Sydney: Metropolitan East Disadvantaged Schools Program.

——and Stenglin, M. (1994*c*). *Writing a Book Review: A Unit of work for Junior Secondary English* (Write it Right Resources for Literacy and Learning). Sydney: Metropolitan East Disadvantaged Schools Program.

Ryave, A. (1978). 'On the achievement of a series of stories', in Schenkein (1978), 113–32.

Sacks, H. (1972). 'On the analysability of stories by children', in J. Gumperz and D. Hymes (eds.), *Directions in Sociolinguistics*. New York: Holt, Rinehart & Winston, 325–45.

——(1974). 'An analysis of the course of a joke's telling in conversation', in R. Bauman and J. Sherzer (eds.) *Explorations in the Ethnography of Speaking*. Cambridge: Cambridge University Press, 337–53.

Sampson, G. (1992). 'Probabilistic parsing', in Svartvik (1992), 429–47.

Schegloff, E. (1978). 'On some questions and ambiguities in conversation', in W. V. Dressler (ed.), *Current Trends in Textlinguistics*. Berlin: Walter de Gruyter, 80–101.

Schenkein, J. (ed.) (1978). *Studies in the Organization of Conversation*. New York: Academic Press.

Schiffrin, D. (1981). 'Tense variation in narrative'. *Language*, 57, 1: 45–62.

Shaul, D. L., Albert, R., Golston, C., and Satory, R. (1987). 'The Hopi Coyote story as narrative'. *Journal of Pragmatics*, 11: 3–25.

Simpson, P. (1990). 'Modality in literary-critical discourse', in Nash (1990), 63–117.

——(1993). *Language, Ideology and Point of View*. London: Routledge.

Sinclair, J. M. (1981). 'Planes of discourse', in S. N. A. Rizvi (ed.), *The Two-Fold Voice: Essays in Honour of Ramesh Mohan*. Salzburg: University of Salzburg, 70–89.

——(1986). 'Fictional worlds', in Coulthard (1986), 43–60.

——(1987). 'Mirror for a text'. MS. University of Birmingham.

——(1991). *Corpus Concordance Collocation*. Oxford: Oxford University Press.

——(1993). 'Written discourse structure', in J. M. Sinclair, M. Hoey, and G. Fox (eds.), *Techniques of Description: Spoken and Written Discourse: A Festschrift for Malcolm Coulthard*. London: Routledge, 6–31.

——(1995). 'The empty lexicon'. *International Journal of Corpus Linguistics*, 1: 99–120.

——and Coulthard, M. (1975). *Towards an Analysis of Discourse: The English used by Teachers and Pupils*. Oxford: Oxford University Press.

Soars, J., and Soars, L. (1989). *Headway Advanced*. Oxford: Oxford University Press.

Stuart, K. (1996). 'A systemic linguistic analysis of point of view in narrative discourse'. Unpublished Ph.D. thesis, University of Liverpool.

Stubbs, M. (1986). 'A matter of prolonged fieldwork: towards a modal grammar of English'. *Applied Linguistics*, 7, 1: 1–25.

——(1996). *Text and Corpus Analysis: Computer-Assisted Studies of Language and Culture*. Oxford: Blackwell.

——(1997). 'Whorf's children: critical comments on critical discourse analysis', in A. Ryan and A. Wray (eds.), *Evolving Models of Language: Papers from the Annual Meeting of the British Association for Applied Linguistics, University of Wales, Swansea, September 1996*. Clevedon: Multilingual Matters/BAAL, 100–16.

——(forthcoming). *Words and Phrases: Corpus Studies of Lexical Semantics*. Oxford: Blackwell.

Svartvik, J. (ed.) (1992). *Directions in Corpus Linguistics*. Berlin: Mouton de Gruyter.

Swales, J. (1990). *Genre Analysis*. Cambridge: Cambridge University Press.

Tadros, A. (1993). 'The pragmatics of text averral and attribution in academic texts', in Hoey (1993), 98–114.

—— (1994). 'Predictive categories in expository text', in Coulthard (1994), 69–82.

Tannen, D. (1980). 'A comparative analysis of oral narrative strategies: Athenian Greek and American English', in W. L. Chafe (ed.), *The Pear Stories: Cognitive, Cultural and Linguistic Aspects of Narrative Production*. Norwood, NJ: Ablex, 51–87.

Taylor, G. (1986). 'The development of style in children's fictional narrative', in A. Wilkinson (ed.), *The Writing of Writing*. Milton Keynes: Open University Press, 215–33.

Tench, P. (1996). *The Intonation Systems of English*. London: Cassell.

Thetela, P. (1997). 'Evaluation in academic research articles'. Unpublished Ph.D. thesis, University of Liverpool.

Thibault, P. (1992). 'Grammar, ethics and understanding: functionalist reason and clause as exchange'. *Social Semiotics*, 2: 135–75.

—— (1995). 'Mood and the ecosocial dynamics of semiotic exchange', in R. Hasan and P. Fries (eds.), *Subject and Topic: A Discourse Functional Perspective*. Amsterdam: Benjamins, 51–90.

Thomas, D. (ed.) (1995). *Teachers' Stories*. Buckingham: Open University Press.

Thompson, G. (1994). *Guide to Reporting*. London: HarperCollins.

—— (1996a). 'Voices in the text: discourse perspectives on language reports'. *Applied Linguistics*, 17: 501–30.

—— (1996b). *Introducing Functional Grammar*. London: Arnold.

—— (1998). 'Resonance in text', in A. Sanchez and R. Carter (eds.), *Linguistic Choice across Genres: Variation in Spoken and Written Language*. Amsterdam: Benjamins, 29–46.

—— and Thetela, P. (1995). 'The sound of one hand clapping: the management of interaction in written discourse', *Text*, 15: 103–27.

—— and Ye, Y. Y. (1991). 'Evaluation in the reporting verbs used in academic papers'. *Applied Linguistics*, 12: 365–82.

Toolan, M. (1996). *Total Speech: An Integrational Linguistic Approach in Language*. Durham, NC and London: Duke University Press.

Ullman, S. (1962). *Semantics: An Introduction to the Science of Meaning*. Oxford: Blackwell.

van Dijk, T. A. (1987). *Communicating Racism: Ethnic Prejudice in Thought and Talk*. London: Sage.

—— (1988). *News as Discourse*. Hillsdale, NJ: Lawrence Erlbaum Associates.

—— (1993). *Elite Discourse and Racism*. Newbury Park: Sage.

van Leeuwen, T. (1996). 'The representation of social actors', in C.-R. Caldas-Coulthard and M. Coulthard (eds.), *Texts and Practices: Readings in Critical Discourse Analysis*. London: Routledge, 32–70.

Ventola, E. (1987). *The Structure of Social Interaction: A Systemic Approach to the Semiotics of Service Encounters*. London: Pinter.

Watson, K. A. (1972). 'The rhetoric of narrative structure: A sociolinguistic analysis of stories told by part-Hawaiian children'. Unpublished Ph.D. thesis, University of Hawaii.

Wierzbicka, A. (1986). 'Human emotions: universal or culture-specific?' *American Anthropologist*, 88: 584–94.

—— (1990a). 'The semantics of emotions: "fear" and its relatives in English'. *Australian Journal of Linguistics*, 10: 359–75.

—— (ed.) (1990*b*). *Australian Journal of Linguistics*, 10, 2 (Special Issue on the Semantics of Emotions).

Wilkinson, J. (1986). 'Describing children's writing: text evaluation and teaching strategies', in J. Harris and J. Wilkinson (eds.), *Reading Children's Writing: A Linguistic View*. London: Allen & Unwin, 11–31.

Williams, R. (1982). *Panorama: An Advanced Course of English for Study and Examinations*. London: Longman.

Winter, E.O. (1977). 'A clause-relational approach to English texts: a study of some predictive lexical items in written discourse'. *Instructional Science*, 6: 1–92.

—— (1979). 'Replacement as a fundamental function of the sentence in context'. *Forum Linguisticum*, 4: 95–133.

—— (1982). *Towards a Contextual Grammar of English: The Clause and its Place in the Definition of Sentence*. London: Allen & Unwin.

—— (1994). 'Clause relations as information structure: two basic text structures in English', in Coulthard (1994), 46–68.

Wolfson, N. (1976). 'Speech events and natural speech: some implications for sociolinguistic methodology'. *Language in Society*, 5: 189–209.

—— (1978). 'A feature of performed narrative: the conversational historical present'. *Language in Society*, 7, 2: 15–37.

—— (1982). *The Conversational Historical Present in American English Narrative*. Dordrecht: Floris.

Yang, L. Y. (1991). *100 Chinese Idioms and their Stories* (trans. from Chinese). Beijing: Foreign Language Translation Publishing House of China and The Commercial Press, Hong Kong.

Zhang, X., and Sang, Y. (1986). *Chinese Profiles*. Beijing: Panda.

Zhou, J. L. (1991). 'The functions of disjuncts in the organisation of written English discourse'. Unpublished MA dissertation, University of Liverpool.

Zwicky, A. M., Salus, P. H., Binnick R. I., and Vanek A. L. (eds.) (1971/1992). *Studies out in Left Field*. Amsterdam: Benjamins.

Index

Made in the USA
Middletown, DE
17 August 2017